It's another great book from CGP...

GCSE Core Science is all about **understanding how science works**.
And not only that — understanding it well enough to be able to **question**
what you hear on TV and read in the papers.

But don't panic. This book includes all the **science facts** you need to learn,
and shows you how they work in the real world. It even includes
a **free** Online Edition you can read on your computer or tablet.

How to get your free Online Edition

Just go to **cgpbooks.co.uk/extras** and enter this code...

1209 5087 6696 2132

By the way, this code only works for one person. If somebody else has used
this book before you, they might have already claimed the Online Edition.

CGP — still the best! ☺

Our sole aim here at CGP is to produce the highest
quality books — carefully written, immaculately presented
and dangerously close to being funny.

Then we work our socks off to get them
out to you — at the cheapest possible prices.

Contents

Published by CGP

From original material by Richard Parsons.

Editors:
Ellen Bowness, Charlotte Burrows, Katherine Craig, Ben Fletcher, Helena Hayes,
Felicity Inkpen, Rosie McCurrie, Edmund Robinson, Jane Sawers, Karen Wells, Sarah Williams.

Contributors:
Mike Bossart, Paddy Gannon, Gemma Hallam, Adrian Schmit.

ISBN: 978 1 84146 703 0

With thanks to Sarah Blackwood, Ellen Bowness, Philip Dobson, Chris Elliss, Sue Hocking,
Martin Payne, Ian Starkey and Llinos Wood for the proofreading.
With thanks to Jan Greenway, Laura Jakubowski and Laura Stoney for the copyright research.

Graph to show trend in atmospheric CO_2 concentration and global temperature on page 62
based on data by EPICA Community Members 2004 and Siegenthaler et al 2005.

www.cgpbooks.co.uk

Printed by Elanders Ltd, Newcastle upon Tyne.
Clipart from Corel®

The Exams

As someone probably quite important once said, 'know your enemy', which for you means 'know how you're going to be <u>examined</u>'. This stuff is as dull as dishwater, but you really need to <u>know what you're in for</u>...

Make Sure You Know Which Exam Route You're Doing

1) You'll have to do exams that test your <u>knowledge of Biology</u>, <u>Chemistry</u> and <u>Physics</u> — there's no getting out of it folks.

2) Unfortunately for you, for these exams you <u>also</u> need to know about <u>How Science Works</u>. Fear not though — I've made a <u>whole section</u> about it to help you — see pages 2-11. Make sure you understand it <u>all</u> before the exams.

3) You also have to do a <u>Controlled Assessment</u> (also known as an 'ISA' — catchy...) — it's a bit like a <u>coursework exam</u>. See page 12 for loads more on what it involves.

4) There are <u>two different ways</u> your course can be examined:

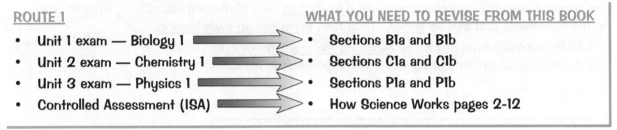

ROUTE 1   WHAT YOU NEED TO REVISE FROM THIS BOOK

- Unit 1 exam — Biology 1   →   • Sections B1a and B1b
- Unit 2 exam — Chemistry 1   →   • Sections C1a and C1b
- Unit 3 exam — Physics 1   →   • Sections P1a and P1b
- Controlled Assessment (ISA) →   • How Science Works pages 2-12

OR

ROUTE 2   WHAT YOU NEED TO REVISE FROM THIS BOOK

- Unit 5 exam — 1st half of Biology 1, →   • Sections B1a, C1a and P1a
  1st half of Chemistry 1,
  1st half of Physics 1

- Unit 6 exam — 2nd half of Biology 1, →   • Sections B1b, C1b and P1b
  2nd half of Chemistry 1,
  2nd half of Physics 1

- Controlled Assessment (ISA) →   • How Science Works pages 2-12

5) If you don't know which route you're doing ASK YOUR TEACHER, so you revise the RIGHT STUFF for the RIGHT EXAM. E.g. if you've got your Unit 1 exam on Monday just look at the Biology sections — don't worry about Physics for now.

Top Tips for Terrific Marks in the Exam

1) For some of the <u>longer answer questions</u> (i.e. ones worth <u>a lot of marks</u>) you'll be marked on your <u>spelling</u>, <u>punctuation</u> and <u>grammar</u>. So double-check any technical science spellings at the end. Your answer also needs to be <u>well structured</u>, so spend a minute figuring out what you're going to say before you start writing.

2) For questions where you have to <u>calculate</u> something, double-check your answer. Write down all your <u>working out</u> and don't forget to include the <u>units</u> either.

3) The examiners expect you to be able to <u>use your knowledge</u> to answer questions about <u>unfamiliar things</u> (how rude, I know), e.g. use your knowledge of wave refraction to answer questions about glasses lenses. Don't panic — you should be able to <u>work it out</u> using <u>what you've learnt about the topic</u>.

Exam routes — thankfully less complicated than bus routes...

Revising for exams is about as exciting as <u>watching paint dry</u>, but it's the only way you'll get <u>good marks</u>. If you know there are a few topics you're a bit hazy on, then spend a little more time revising those. And make sure you know <u>what you're revising for each exam</u> — you'll feel a right idiot if you revise the wrong stuff.

The Scientific Process

You need to know a few things about how the world of science works. First up is the <u>scientific process</u> — how a scientist's <u>mad idea</u> turns into a <u>widely accepted theory</u>.

Scientists Come Up with *Hypotheses* — Then *Test* Them

About 100 years ago, scientists hypothesised that atoms looked like this.

1) Scientists try to <u>explain</u> things. Everything.
2) They start by <u>observing</u> something they don't understand — it could be anything, e.g. planets in the sky, a person suffering from an illness, what matter is made of... anything.
3) Then, they come up with a <u>hypothesis</u> — a <u>possible explanation</u> for what they've observed.
4) The next step is to <u>test</u> whether the hypothesis might be <u>right or not</u> — this involves <u>gathering evidence</u> (i.e. <u>data</u> from <u>investigations</u>).
5) The scientist uses the hypothesis to make a <u>prediction</u> — a statement based on the hypothesis that can be <u>tested</u>. They then <u>carry out an investigation</u>.
6) If data from experiments or studies <u>backs up the prediction</u>, you're one step closer to figuring out if the hypothesis is true.

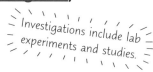

Investigations include lab experiments and studies.

Other Scientists Will *Test* the Hypothesis Too

1) <u>Other</u> scientists will use the hypothesis to make their <u>own predictions</u>, and carry out their <u>own experiments</u> or studies.
2) They'll also try to <u>reproduce</u> the original investigations to check the results.
3) And if <u>all the experiments</u> in the world back up the hypothesis, then scientists start to think it's <u>true</u>.
4) However, if a scientist somewhere in the world does an experiment that <u>doesn't</u> fit with the hypothesis (and other scientists can <u>reproduce</u> these results), then the hypothesis is in trouble.
5) When this happens, scientists have to come up with a new hypothesis (maybe a <u>modification</u> of the old hypothesis, or maybe a completely <u>new</u> one).

After more evidence was gathered, scientists changed their hypothesis to this.

If *Evidence* Supports a Hypothesis, It's *Accepted* — *for Now*

1) If pretty much every scientist in the world believes a hypothesis to be true because experiments back it up, then it usually goes in the <u>textbooks</u> for students to learn.
2) Accepted hypotheses are often referred to as <u>theories</u>.

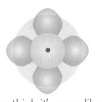

Now we think it's more like this.

3) Our <u>currently accepted</u> theories are the ones that have survived this 'trial by evidence' — they've been tested many, many times over the years and survived (while the less good ones have been ditched).
4) However... they never, <u>never</u> become hard and fast, totally indisputable <u>fact</u>. You can never know... it'd only take <u>one</u> odd, totally inexplicable result, and the hypothesising and testing would start all over again.

You expect me to believe that — then show me the evidence...

If scientists think something is true, they need to produce evidence to convince others — it's all part of <u>testing a hypothesis</u>. One hypothesis might survive these tests, while others won't — it's how things progress. And along the way some hypotheses will be disproved — i.e. shown not to be true.

Your Data's Got To be Good

Evidence is the key to science — but not all evidence is equally good.
The way evidence is gathered can have a big effect on how trustworthy it is...

Lab Experiments and Studies Are Better Than Rumour

See page 6 for more about fair tests and variables.

1) Results from experiments in laboratories are great. A lab is the easiest place to control variables so that they're all kept constant (except for the one you're investigating). This makes it easier to carry out a FAIR TEST.

2) For things that you can't investigate in the lab (e.g. climate) you conduct scientific studies. As many of the variables as possible are controlled, to make it a fair test.

3) Old wives' tales, rumours, hearsay, "what someone said", and so on, should be taken with a pinch of salt. Without any evidence they're NOT scientific — they're just opinions.

The Bigger the Sample Size the Better

1) Data based on small samples isn't as good as data based on large samples. A sample should be representative of the whole population (i.e. it should share as many of the various characteristics in the population as possible) — a small sample can't do that as well.

2) The bigger the sample size the better, but scientists have to be realistic when choosing how big. For example, if you were studying how lifestyle affects people's weight it'd be great to study everyone in the UK (a huge sample), but it'd take ages and cost a bomb. Studying a thousand people is more realistic.

Evidence Needs to be Reliable (Repeatable and Reproducible)

Evidence is only reliable if it can be repeated (during an experiment) AND other scientists can reproduce it too (in other experiments). If it's not reliable, you can't believe it.

> RELIABLE means that the data can be repeated, and reproduced by others.

EXAMPLE: In 1989, two scientists claimed that they'd produced 'cold fusion' (the energy source of the Sun — but without the big temperatures). It was huge news — if true, it would have meant free energy for the world... forever. However, other scientists just couldn't reproduce the results — so the results weren't reliable. And until they are, 'cold fusion' isn't going to be accepted as fact.

Evidence Also Needs to Be Valid

> VALID means that the data is reliable AND answers the original question.

EXAMPLE: DO POWER LINES CAUSE CANCER?
Some studies have found that children who live near overhead power lines are more likely to develop cancer. What they'd actually found was a correlation (relationship) between the variables "presence of power lines" and "incidence of cancer" — they found that as one changed, so did the other. But this evidence is not enough to say that the power lines cause cancer, as other explanations might be possible. For example, power lines are often near busy roads, so the areas tested could contain different levels of pollution from traffic. So these studies don't show a definite link and so don't answer the original question.

RRRR — Remember, Reliable means Repeatable and Reproducible...

By now you should have realised how important trustworthy evidence is (even more important than a good supply of spot cream). Unfortunately, you need to know loads more about fair tests and experiments — see pages 6-11.

Bias and Issues Created by Science

It isn't all hunky-dory in the world of science — there are some problems...

Scientific Evidence can be Presented in a Biased Way

1) People who want to make a point can sometimes present data in a biased way, e.g. they overemphasise a relationship in the data. (Sometimes without knowing they're doing it.)

2) And there are all sorts of reasons why people might want to do this — for example...

- They want to keep the organisation or company that's funding the research happy. (If the results aren't what they'd like they might not give them any more money to fund further research.)
- Governments might want to persuade voters, other governments, journalists, etc.
- Companies might want to 'big up' their products. Or make impressive safety claims.
- Environmental campaigners might want to persuade people to behave differently.

Things can Affect How Seriously Evidence is Taken

1) If an investigation is done by a team of highly-regarded scientists it's sometimes taken more seriously than evidence from less well known scientists.

2) But having experience, authority or a fancy qualification doesn't necessarily mean the evidence is good — the only way to tell is to look at the evidence scientifically (e.g. is it reliable, valid, etc.).

3) Also, some evidence might be ignored if it could create political problems, or emphasised if it helps a particular cause.

EXAMPLE: Some governments were pretty slow to accept the fact that human activities are causing global warming, despite all the evidence. This is because accepting it means they've got to do something about it, which costs money and could hurt their economy. This could lose them a lot of votes.

Scientific Developments are Great, but they can Raise Issues

Scientific knowledge is increased by doing experiments. And this knowledge leads to scientific developments, e.g. new technologies or new advice. These developments can create issues though. For example:

Economic issues: Society can't always afford to do things scientists recommend (e.g. investing heavily in alternative energy sources) without cutting back elsewhere.

Social issues: Decisions based on scientific evidence affect people — e.g. should fossil fuels be taxed more highly (to invest in alternative energy)? Should alcohol be banned (to prevent health problems)? Would the effect on people's lifestyles be acceptable...

Environmental issues: Genetically modified crops may help us produce more food — but some people think they could cause environmental problems (see page 41).

Ethical issues: There are a lot of things that scientific developments have made possible, but should we do them? E.g. clone humans, develop better nuclear weapons.

Trust me — I've got a BSc, PhD, PC, TV and a DVD...

We all tend to swoon at people in authority, but you have to ignore that fact and look at the evidence (just because someone has got a whacking great list of letters after their name doesn't mean the evidence is good). Spotting biased evidence isn't the easiest thing in the world — ask yourself 'Does the scientist (or the person writing about it) stand to gain something (or lose something)?' If they do, it's possible that it could be biased.

Science Has Limits

Science can give us amazing things — cures for diseases, space travel, heated toilet seats...
But science has its limitations — there are questions that it just can't answer.

Some Questions Are Unanswered by Science — So Far

1) We don't understand everything. And we never will. We'll find out more, for sure — as more hypotheses are suggested, and more experiments are done. But there'll always be stuff we don't know.

   EXAMPLES:
   - Today we don't know as much as we'd like about the impacts of global warming.
     How much will sea level rise? And to what extent will weather patterns change?
   - We also don't know anywhere near as much as we'd like about the Universe.
     Are there other life forms out there? And what is the Universe made of?

2) These are complicated questions. At the moment scientists don't all agree on the answers because there isn't enough reliable and valid evidence.

3) But eventually, we probably will be able to answer these questions once and for all...
   All we need is more evidence.

4) But by then there'll be loads of new questions to answer.

Other Questions Are Unanswerable by Science

1) Then there's the other type... questions that all the experiments in the world won't help us answer — the "Should we be doing this at all?" type questions. There are always two sides...

2) Take embryo screening (which allows you to choose an embryo with particular characteristics).
   It's possible to do it — but does that mean we should?

3) Different people have different opinions.

   For example...
   - Some people say it's good... couples whose existing child needs a bone marrow transplant, but who can't find a donor, will be able to have another child selected for its matching bone marrow. This would save the life of their first child — and if they want another child anyway... where's the harm?
   - Other people say it's bad... they say it could have serious effects on the new child. In the above example, the new child might feel unwanted — thinking they were only brought into the world to help someone else. And would they have the right to refuse to donate their bone marrow (as anyone else would)?

   THE GAZETTE
   BONE MARROW BABY'S BROTHER SAVED

   THE POST
   BONE MARROW BABY BORN: WHAT RIGHTS DOES HE HAVE?

4) The question of whether something is morally or ethically right or wrong can't be answered by more experiments — there is no "right" or "wrong" answer.

5) The best we can do is get a consensus from society — a judgement that most people are more or less happy to live by. Science can provide more information to help people make this judgement, and the judgement might change over time. But in the end it's up to people and their conscience.

Chips or rice? — totally unanswerable by science...

Right — get this straight in your head — science can't tell you whether you should or shouldn't do something. That kind of thing is up to you and society to decide. There are tons of questions that science might be able to answer in the future — like how much sea level might rise due to global warming, what the Universe is made of and whatever happened to those pink stripy socks with Santa on that I used to have.

Designing Investigations

Dig out your lab coat and dust down your badly-scratched safety goggles... it's investigation time.
You need to know a shed load about <u>investigations</u> for your <u>controlled assessment</u> and <u>all your exams</u>.
Investigations include <u>experiments</u> and <u>studies</u>. The next six pages take you from start to finish. Enjoy.

Investigations Produce Evidence to Support or Disprove a Hypothesis

1) Scientists <u>observe</u> things and come up with <u>hypotheses</u> to explain them (see page 2).

2) To figure out whether a hypothesis might be correct or not you need to do an <u>investigation</u> to <u>gather some evidence</u>.

3) The first step is to use the hypothesis to come up with a <u>prediction</u> — a statement about what you <u>think will happen</u> that you can <u>test</u>.

4) For example, if your <u>hypothesis</u> is:

> "Spots are caused by picking your nose too much."

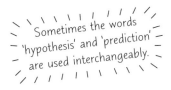
Sometimes the words 'hypothesis' and 'prediction' are used interchangeably.

Then your <u>prediction</u> might be:

> "People who pick their nose more often will have more spots."

5) Investigations are used to see if there are <u>patterns</u> or <u>relationships between two variables</u>. For example, to see if there's a pattern or relationship between the variables 'having spots' and 'nose picking'.

6) The investigation has to be a <u>FAIR TEST</u> to make sure the evidence is <u>reliable</u> and <u>valid</u>...

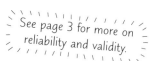
See page 3 for more on reliability and validity.

To Make an Investigation a Fair Test You Have to Control the Variables

1) In a lab experiment you usually <u>change one variable</u> and <u>measure</u> how it affects the <u>other variable</u>.

> **EXAMPLE:** you might change <u>only</u> the temperature of an enzyme-controlled reaction and measure how it affects the rate of reaction.

2) To make it a fair test <u>everything else</u> that could affect the results should <u>stay the same</u> (otherwise you can't tell if the thing you're changing is causing the results or not — the data won't be reliable or valid).

> **EXAMPLE continued:** you need to keep the pH the same, otherwise you won't know if any change in the rate of reaction is caused by the change in temperature, or the change in pH.

3) The variable you CHANGE is called the INDEPENDENT variable.

4) The variable you MEASURE is called the DEPENDENT variable.

5) The variables that you KEEP THE SAME are called CONTROL variables.

> **EXAMPLE continued:**
> Independent variable = temperature
> Dependent variable = rate of reaction
> Control variables = pH, volume of reactants, concentration of reactants etc.

Designing Investigations

Trial Runs help Figure out the Range and Interval of Variable Values

1) It's a good idea to do a <u>trial run</u> first
— a <u>quick version</u> of your experiment.

2) Trial runs are used to figure out the <u>range</u> of variable values used in the proper experiment (the upper and lower limit). If you <u>don't</u> get a <u>change</u> in the dependent variable at the upper values in the trial run, you might <u>narrow</u> the range in the proper experiment. But if you still get a <u>big change</u> at the upper values you might <u>increase</u> the range.

> **EXAMPLE continued:**
> - You might do a trial run with a range of 10-50 °C. If there was no reaction at the upper end (e.g. 40-50 °C), you might narrow the range to 10-40 °C for the proper experiment.
> - If using 1 °C intervals doesn't give you much change in the rate of reaction each time you might decide to use 5 °C intervals, e.g. 10, 15, 20, 25, 30, 35...

3) And trial runs can be used to figure out the <u>interval</u> (gaps) between the values too. The intervals can't be too small (otherwise the experiment would take ages), or too big (otherwise you might miss something).

4) Trial runs can also help you figure out <u>how many times</u> the experiment has to be <u>repeated</u> to get reliable results. E.g. if you repeat it three times and the <u>results</u> are all <u>similar</u>, then three repeats is enough.

It Can Be Hard to Control the Variables in a Study

It's important that a study is a <u>fair test</u>, just like a lab experiment. It's a lot trickier to control the variables in a study than it is in a lab experiment though (see previous page). Sometimes you can't control them all, but you can use a <u>control group</u> to help. This is a group of whatever you're studying (people, plants, lemmings, etc.) that's kept under the <u>same conditions</u> as the group in the experiment, but doesn't have anything done to it.

EXAMPLE: If you're studying the effect of pesticides on crop growth, pesticide is applied to one field but not to another field (the control field). Both fields are planted with the same crop, and are in the same area (so they get the same weather conditions). The control field is there to try and account for variables like the weather, which don't stay the same all the time, but could affect the results.

Investigations Can be Hazardous

1) A <u>hazard</u> is something that can <u>potentially cause harm</u>. Hazards include:

Hmm... Where did my bacteria sample go?

> - <u>Microorganisms</u>, e.g. some bacteria can make you ill.
> - <u>Chemicals</u>, e.g. sulfuric acid can burn your skin and alcohols catch fire easily.
> - <u>Fire</u>, e.g. an unattended Bunsen burner is a fire hazard.
> - <u>Electricity</u>, e.g. faulty electrical equipment could give you a shock.

2) Scientists need to <u>manage the risk</u> of hazards by doing things to reduce them. For example:

> - If you're working with <u>sulfuric acid</u>, always wear gloves and safety goggles. This will reduce the risk of the acid coming into contact with your skin and eyes.
> - If you're using a <u>Bunsen burner</u>, stand it on a heat proof mat. This will reduce the risk of starting a fire.

> You can find out about potential hazards by looking in textbooks, doing some internet research, or asking your teacher.

You won't get a trial run at the exam, so get learnin'...

All this info needs to be firmly lodged in your memory. Learn the <u>names</u> of the different <u>variables</u> — if you remember that the variable you cha<u>N</u>ge is called the i<u>N</u>dependent variable, you can figure out the other ones.

Collecting Data

After designing an investigation that's so beautiful people will marvel at it for years to come, you'll need to get your hands mucky and <u>collect some data</u>.

Your Data Should be as <u>Reliable, Accurate</u> and <u>Precise</u> as Possible

1) To <u>improve</u> reliability you need to <u>repeat</u> the readings and calculate the <u>mean</u> (average). You need to repeat each reading at least <u>three times</u>.

2) To make sure your results are reliable you can cross check them by taking a <u>second set of readings</u> with <u>another instrument</u> (or a <u>different observer</u>).

3) Checking your results match with <u>secondary sources</u>, e.g. other studies, also increases the reliability of your data.

4) Your data also needs to be ACCURATE. Really accurate results are those that are <u>really close</u> to the <u>true answer</u>.

5) Your data also needs to be PRECISE. Precise results are ones where the data is <u>all really close</u> to the <u>mean</u> (i.e. not spread out).

Repeat	Data set 1	Data set 2
1	12	11
2	14	17
3	13	14
Mean	13	14

Data set 1 is more precise than data set 2.

Your <u>Equipment</u> has to be <u>Right for the Job</u>

1) The measuring equipment you use has to be <u>sensitive enough</u> to measure the changes you're looking for. For example, if you need to measure changes of 1 ml you need to use a measuring cylinder that can measure in 1 ml steps — it'd be no good trying with one that only measures 10 ml steps.

2) The <u>smallest change</u> a measuring instrument can <u>detect</u> is called its RESOLUTION. E.g. some mass balances have a resolution of 1 g, some have a resolution of 0.1 g, and some are even more sensitive.

3) Also, equipment needs to be <u>calibrated</u> so that your data is <u>more accurate</u>. E.g. mass balances need to be set to zero before you start weighing things.

Errors can Pop Up if You're Not Careful

1) The results of your experiment will always <u>vary a bit</u> because of <u>random errors</u> — tiny differences caused by things like <u>human errors</u> in <u>measuring</u>.

2) You can <u>reduce</u> their effect by taking many readings and calculating the <u>mean</u>.

3) If the <u>same error</u> is made every time, it's called a SYSTEMATIC ERROR. For example, if you measured from the very end of your ruler instead of from the 0 cm mark every time, all your measurements would be a bit small.

Repeating the experiment in the exact same way and calculating an average won't correct a systematic error.

4) Just to make things more complicated, if a systematic error is caused by using <u>equipment</u> that <u>isn't zeroed properly</u> it's called a ZERO ERROR. For example, if a mass balance always reads 1 gram before you put anything on it, all your measurements will be 1 gram too heavy.

5) You can <u>compensate</u> for some systematic errors if you know about them though, e.g. if your mass balance always reads 1 gram before you put anything on it you can subtract 1 gram from all your results.

6) Sometimes you get a result that <u>doesn't seem to fit in</u> with the rest at all.

7) These results are called ANOMALOUS RESULTS.

8) You should investigate them and try to <u>work out what happened</u>. If you can work out what happened (e.g. you measured something totally wrong) you can <u>ignore</u> them when processing your results.

Park	Number of pigeons	Number of crazy tramps
A	28	1
B	42	2
C	1127	0

Zero error — sounds like a Bruce Willis film...

Weirdly, data can be really <u>precise</u> but <u>not very accurate</u>, e.g. a fancy piece of lab equipment might give results that are precise, but if it's not calibrated properly those results won't be accurate.

Processing and Presenting Data

After you've collected your data you'll have <u>oodles of info</u> that you have to <u>make some kind of sense of</u>. You need to <u>process</u> and <u>present</u> it so you can look for <u>patterns</u> and <u>relationships</u> in it.

Data Needs to be Organised

1) Tables are dead useful for <u>organising data</u>.

2) When you draw a table <u>use a ruler</u>, make sure <u>each column</u> has a <u>heading</u> (including the <u>units</u>) and keep it neat and tidy.

3) Annoyingly, tables are about as useful as a chocolate teapot for showing <u>patterns</u> or <u>relationships</u> in data. You need to use some kind of graph for that.

You Might Have to Process Your Data

1) When you've done repeats of an experiment you should always calculate the <u>mean</u> (average). To do this <u>ADD TOGETHER</u> all the data values and <u>DIVIDE</u> by the total number of values in the sample.

2) You might also need to calculate the <u>range</u> (how spread out the data is). To do this find the <u>LARGEST</u> number and <u>SUBTRACT</u> the <u>SMALLEST</u> number from it.

Ignore anomalous results when calculating these.

EXAMPLE

Test tube	Repeat 1 (g)	Repeat 2 (g)	Repeat 3 (g)	Mean (g)	Range (g)
A	28	37	32	(28 + 37 + 32) ÷ 3 = 32.3	37 − 28 = 9
B	47	51	60	(47 + 51 + 60) ÷ 3 = 52.7	60 − 47 = 13
C	68	72	70	(68 + 72 + 70) ÷ 3 = 70.0	72 − 68 = 4

If Your Data Comes in Categories, Present It in a Bar Chart

1) If the independent variable is <u>categoric</u> (comes in distinct categories, e.g. blood types, metals) you should use a <u>bar chart</u> to display the data.

2) You also use them if the independent variable is <u>discrete</u> (the data can be counted in chunks, where there's no in-between value, e.g. number of people is discrete because you can't have half a person).

3) There are some <u>golden rules</u> you need to follow for <u>drawing</u> bar charts:

If you've got more than one set of data <u>include a key</u>.

Draw it nice and <u>big</u> (covering at least half of the graph paper).

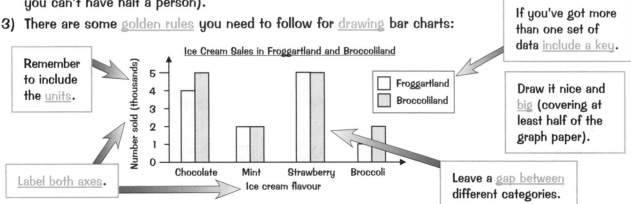

Remember to include the <u>units</u>.

<u>Label both axes</u>.

Leave a <u>gap between</u> different categories.

Discrete variables love bar charts — although they'd never tell anyone that...

The stuff on this page might all seem a bit basic, but it's <u>easy marks</u> in the exams (which you'll kick yourself if you don't get). Examiners are a bit picky when it comes to bar charts — if you don't draw them properly they won't be happy. Also, <u>double check</u> any mean or range <u>calculations</u> you do, just to be sure they're correct.

Presenting Data

Scientists just love presenting data as line graphs (weirdos)...

If Your Data is Continuous, Plot a Line Graph

1) If the independent variable is continuous (numerical data that can have any value within a range, e.g. length, volume, temperature) you should use a line graph to display the data.

2) Here are the rules for drawing line graphs:

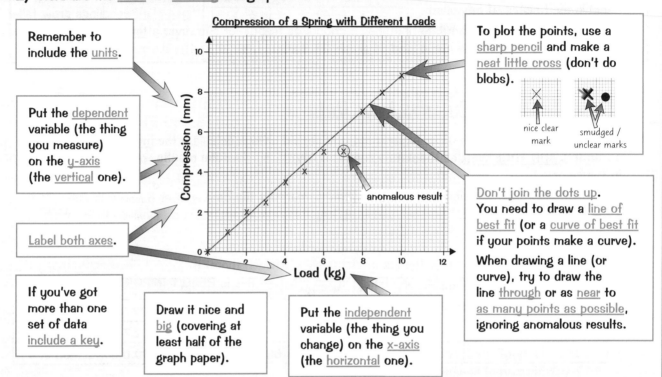

Remember to include the units.

Put the dependent variable (the thing you measure) on the y-axis (the vertical one).

Label both axes.

If you've got more than one set of data include a key.

Draw it nice and big (covering at least half of the graph paper).

Put the independent variable (the thing you change) on the x-axis (the horizontal one).

To plot the points, use a sharp pencil and make a neat little cross (don't do blobs).

nice clear mark

smudged / unclear marks

Don't join the dots up. You need to draw a line of best fit (or a curve of best fit if your points make a curve).

When drawing a line (or curve), try to draw the line through or as near to as many points as possible, ignoring anomalous results.

Compression of a Spring with Different Loads

anomalous result

3) Line graphs are used to show the relationship between two variables (just like other graphs).

4) Data can show three different types of correlation (relationship):

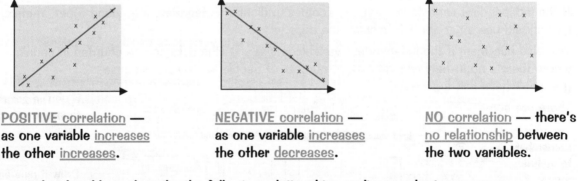

POSITIVE correlation — as one variable increases the other increases.

NEGATIVE correlation — as one variable increases the other decreases.

NO correlation — there's no relationship between the two variables.

5) You need to be able to describe the following relationships on line graphs too:

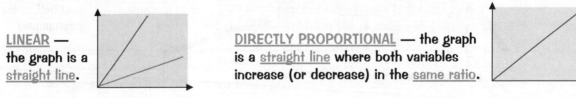

LINEAR — the graph is a straight line.

DIRECTLY PROPORTIONAL — the graph is a straight line where both variables increase (or decrease) in the same ratio.

There's a positive correlation between revision and boredom...

...but there's also a positive correlation between revision and getting a better mark in the exam. Cover the page and write down the eight things you need to remember when drawing graphs. No sneaky peeking either — I saw you.

Drawing Conclusions

Congratulations — you've made it to the final step of a gruelling investigation — drawing conclusions.

You Can Only Conclude What the Data Shows and NO MORE

1) Drawing conclusions might seem pretty straightforward — you just look at your data and say what pattern or relationship you see between the dependent and independent variables.

EXAMPLE: The table on the right shows the heights of pea plant seedlings grown for three weeks with different fertilisers.

Fertiliser	Mean growth / mm
A	13.5
B	19.5
No fertiliser	5.5

CONCLUSION: Fertiliser B makes pea plant seedlings grow taller over a three week period than fertiliser A.

2) But you've got to be really careful that your conclusion matches the data you've got and doesn't go any further.

EXAMPLE continued: You CAN'T conclude that fertiliser B makes any other type of plant grow taller than fertiliser A — the results could be totally different.

3) You also need to be able to use your results to justify your conclusion (i.e. back up your conclusion with some specific data).

EXAMPLE continued: Over the three week period, fertiliser B made the pea plants grow 6 mm more on average than fertiliser A.

Correlation DOES NOT mean Cause

1) If two things are correlated (i.e. there's a relationship between them) it doesn't necessarily mean that a change in one variable is causing the change in the other — this is REALLY IMPORTANT, DON'T FORGET IT.

2) There are three possible reasons for a correlation:

1 CHANCE

1) Even though it might seem a bit weird, it's possible that two things show a correlation in a study purely because of chance.

2) For example, one study might find a correlation between people's hair colour and how good they are at frisbee. But other scientists don't get a correlation when they investigate it — the results of the first study are just a fluke.

2 LINKED BY A 3rd VARIABLE

1) A lot of the time it may look as if a change in one variable is causing a change in the other, but it isn't — a third variable links the two things.

2) For example, there's a correlation between water temperature and shark attacks. This obviously isn't because warmer water makes sharks crazy. Instead, they're linked by a third variable — the number of people swimming (more people swim when the water's hotter, and with more people in the water you get more shark attacks).

3 CAUSE

1) Sometimes a change in one variable does cause a change in the other.

2) For example, there's a correlation between smoking and lung cancer. This is because chemicals in tobacco smoke cause lung cancer.

3) You can only conclude that a correlation is due to cause when you've controlled all the variables that could, just could, be affecting the result. (For the smoking example above this would include things like age and exposure to other things that cause cancer).

I conclude that this page is a bit dull...

...although, just because I find it dull doesn't mean that I can conclude it's dull (you might think it's the most interesting thing since that kid got his head stuck in the railings near school). In the exams you could be given a conclusion and asked whether some data supports it — so make sure you understand how far conclusions can go.

Controlled Assessment (ISA)

Controlled Assessment involves <u>doing an experiment</u> for a topic you've been given and <u>answering two question papers on it</u> under exam conditions. Sounds thrilling.

There are Two Sections in the Controlled Assessment

① Planning

Before you sit down to do the Section 1 question paper you'll be given a <u>hypothesis/prediction</u>. You'll then need to <u>research</u> the topic that's been set and <u>two</u> different methods to test the hypothesis. In your research, you should use a variety of <u>different sources</u> (e.g. the internet, textbooks etc.). You'll need to be able to <u>outline both methods</u> and say which one is <u>best</u> (and why it's the best one) and describe your preferred method in <u>detail</u>. You're allowed to write <u>notes</u> about your two methods on <u>one side of A4</u> and have them with you for both question papers. You could be asked things like:

1) What variables you're going to <u>control</u> (and <u>how</u> you're going to control them).
2) What <u>measurements</u> you're going to take.
3) What <u>range</u> and <u>interval</u> of values you will use for the <u>independent variable</u>.
4) How you'd figure out the range and interval using a <u>trial run</u> (sometimes called a 'preliminary investigation' in the question papers). See page 7 for more.
5) How many times you're going to <u>repeat</u> the experiment — a minimum of <u>three</u> is a good idea.
6) What <u>equipment</u> you're going to use (and <u>why</u> that equipment is <u>right for the job</u>).
7) <u>How to carry out</u> the experiment, i.e. what you do first, what you do second...
8) What <u>hazards</u> are involved in doing the experiment, and <u>how to reduce them</u>.
9) What <u>table</u> you'll draw to put your results in. See p. 9 for how to draw one that examiners will love.

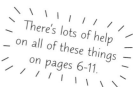

There's lots of help on all of these things on pages 6-11.

When you've done the planning and completed the first question paper you'll actually <u>do the experiment</u>. Then you'll have to <u>present your data</u>. Make sure you use the <u>right type of graph</u>, and you <u>draw it properly</u> — see pages 9-10 for help. After that it's onto the Section 2 question paper...

② Drawing Conclusions and Evaluating

For the Section 2 question paper you have to do these things for <u>your experiment</u>:

1) <u>Analyse</u> and <u>draw conclusions</u> from your results. For this you need to <u>describe the relationship</u> between the variables in <u>detail</u> — see the previous page for how to do this. E.g. 'I found that there is a relationship between picking your nose and having spots. The more often you pick your nose the more spots you'll have. For example, my results showed...'.

2) Say whether your results <u>back up the hypothesis/prediction</u>, and give reasons <u>why</u> or <u>why not</u>. E.g. 'My results did not back up the prediction. The prediction was that picking your nose more has no effect on the number of spots you have. But I found the opposite to be true in my investigation'.

3) <u>Evaluate</u> your experiment. For this you need to <u>suggest ways you could improve your experiment</u>.
   - Comment on your <u>equipment</u> and <u>method</u>, e.g. could you have used more <u>accurate</u> equipment?
   - Make sure you <u>explain how</u> the improvements would give you <u>better data</u> next time.
   - <u>Refer to your results</u>. E.g. 'My data wasn't accurate enough because the mass balance I used only measured in 1 g steps. I could use a more sensitive one next time (e.g. a mass balance that measures in 0.5 g steps) to get more accurate data'.

You'll also be <u>given some secondary data</u> (data collected by other people) from experiments on the same topic and asked to <u>analyse it</u>. This just involves doing what you did for your data with the secondary data, e.g. draw conclusions from it.

If that's controlled assessment, I'd hate to see uncontrolled assessment...

That might be an Everest-sized list of stuff, but it's <u>all important</u>. No need to panic at the sight of it though — as long as you've <u>learnt everything</u> on the previous few pages, you should be fine.

Diet and Metabolic Rate

The first thing on the GCSE AQA A Core Science menu is... well... food. Obviously.
It's where you get your energy from, to do all sorts of things like talking, partying and maybe a bit of revision.

A Balanced Diet Does a Lot to Keep You Healthy

1) For good health, your diet must provide the energy you need (but not more) — see the next page.

2) But that's not all. Because the different food groups have different uses in the body, you need to have the right balance of foods as well.
   So you need:

   ...enough carbohydrates to release energy,

   ...enough fats to keep warm and release energy,

   ...enough protein for growth, cell repair and cell replacement,

   ...enough fibre to keep everything moving smoothly through your digestive system,

   ...and tiny amounts of various vitamins and mineral ions to keep your skin, bones, blood and everything else generally healthy.

People's Energy Needs Vary Because of Who They Are...

1) You need energy to fuel the chemical reactions in the body that keep you alive.
   These reactions are called your metabolism, and the speed at which they occur is your metabolic rate.

2) There are slight variations in the resting metabolic rate of different people.
   For example, muscle needs more energy than fatty tissue, which means (all other things being equal) people with a higher proportion of muscle to fat in their bodies will have a higher metabolic rate.

3) However, physically bigger people are likely to have a higher metabolic rate than smaller people — the bigger you are, the more energy your body needs to be supplied with (because you have more cells).

4) Men tend to have a slightly higher rate than women — they're slightly bigger and have a larger proportion of muscle. Other genetic factors may also have some effect.

5) And regular exercise can boost your resting metabolic rate because it builds muscle.

...and Because of What They Do

Activity	kJ/min
Sleeping	4.5
Watching TV	7
Cycling (5 mph)	21
Jogging (5 mph)	40
Climbing stairs	77
Swimming	35
Rowing	58
Slow walking	14

1) When you exercise, you obviously need more energy — so your metabolic rate goes up during exercise and stays high for some time after you finish (particularly if the exercise is strenuous).

2) So people who have more active jobs need more energy on a daily basis — builders require more energy per day than office workers, for instance. The table shows the average kilojoules burned per minute when doing different activities.

3) This means your activity level affects the amount of energy your diet should contain. If you do little exercise, you're going to need less energy, so less fat and carbohydrate in your diet, than if you're constantly on the go.

Diet tip — the harder you revise the more calories you burn...

So basically, eating healthily involves eating the right amount of food and the right type of food. You've also got to eat enough food to match your energy needs... or do enough exercise to match your eating habits. Well, what are you waiting for — time to burn off those calories by revising all of this page.

Factors Affecting Health

Being healthy doesn't just mean you look great in your swimwear — it means being free of any diseases too.

Your Health is Affected by Having an Unbalanced Diet...

1) People whose diet is badly out of balance are said to be malnourished.
2) Malnourished people can be fat or thin, or unhealthy in other ways:

Malnourishment is different from starvation, which is not getting enough food of any sort.

Eating too much can lead to obesity...

1) Excess carbohydrate or fat in the diet can lead to obesity.
2) Obesity is a common disorder in developed countries — it's defined as being 20% (or more) over maximum recommended body mass.
3) Hormonal problems can lead to obesity, though the usual cause is a bad diet, overeating and a lack of exercise.
4) Health problems that can arise as a result of obesity include: arthritis (inflammation of the joints), type 2 diabetes (inability to control blood sugar level), high blood pressure and heart disease. It's also a risk factor for some kinds of cancer.

...and other health problems

1) Too much saturated fat in your diet can increase your blood cholesterol level (see below).
2) Eating too much salt can cause high blood pressure and heart problems.

Eating too little can also cause problems

1) Some people suffer from lack of food, particularly in developing countries.
2) The effects of malnutrition vary depending on what foods are missing from the diet. But problems commonly include slow growth (in children), fatigue, poor resistance to infection, and irregular periods in women.
3) Deficiency diseases are caused by a lack of vitamins or minerals. For example, a lack of vitamin C can cause scurvy, a deficiency disease that causes problems with the skin, joints and gums.

...Not Getting Enough Exercise...

1) Exercise is important as well as diet — people who exercise regularly are usually healthier than those who don't.
2) Exercise increases the amount of energy used by the body and decreases the amount stored as fat. It also builds muscle so it helps to boost your metabolic rate (see page 13). So people who exercise are less likely to suffer from health problems such as obesity.
3) However, sometimes people can be fit but not healthy — e.g. you can be physically fit and slim, but malnourished at the same time because your diet isn't balanced.

...and Inherited Factors

1) It's not just about what you eat and how much exercise you do — your health can depend on inherited factors too.
2) Some people may inherit factors that affect their metabolic rate, e.g. some inherited factors cause an underactive thyroid gland, which can lower the metabolic rate and cause obesity.
3) Other people may inherit factors that affect their blood cholesterol level. Cholesterol is a fatty substance that's essential for good health — it's found in every cell in the body. Some inherited factors increase blood cholesterol level, which increases the risk of heart disease.

Obesity is an increasingly weighty issue nowadays...

Your health can really suffer if you regularly eat too much, too little, or miss out on a vital nutrient. Exercise is important as well as diet — regular exercise helps to keep you fit. But remember, being fit isn't the same as being healthy — if your diet isn't balanced then you can still be malnourished, even if you do tons of exercise.

Evaluating Food, Lifestyle and Diet

Sometimes you've got to be a bit <u>savvy</u> when working out which is the healthiest food product to eat, or if a <u>claim</u> about a particular slimming diet is actually <u>true</u>.

You Need to be Able to Evaluate Information on Food and Lifestyle

1) In the exam, you may get asked to <u>evaluate information</u> about how <u>food</u> affects health — panic ye not, just take a look at the food label example below:

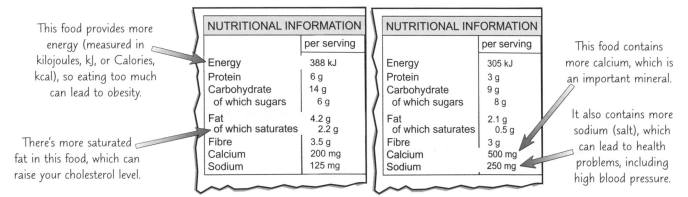

This food provides more energy (measured in kilojoules, kJ, or Calories, kcal), so eating too much can lead to obesity.

NUTRITIONAL INFORMATION	
	per serving
Energy	388 kJ
Protein	6 g
Carbohydrate	14 g
of which sugars	6 g
Fat	4.2 g
of which saturates	2.2 g
Fibre	3.5 g
Calcium	200 mg
Sodium	125 mg

NUTRITIONAL INFORMATION	
	per serving
Energy	305 kJ
Protein	3 g
Carbohydrate	9 g
of which sugars	8 g
Fat	2.1 g
of which saturates	0.5 g
Fibre	3 g
Calcium	500 mg
Sodium	250 mg

This food contains more calcium, which is an important mineral.

It also contains more sodium (salt), which can lead to health problems, including high blood pressure.

There's more saturated fat in this food, which can raise your cholesterol level.

2) You might also get asked to evaluate information about how <u>lifestyle</u> affects health. Your lifestyle includes <u>what you eat</u> and <u>what you do</u>. E.g. a person who eats too much fat or carbohydrate and doesn't do much exercise will increase their risk of <u>obesity</u>. Remember, you'll need to use your <u>knowledge</u> of how diet and exercise affect health to answer exam questions — make sure all the facts on the previous two pages are well lodged in your memory.

Watch Out for Slimming Claims that Aren't Scientifically Proven

1) There are loads of <u>slimming products</u> (e.g. diet pills, slimming milkshakes) and <u>slimming programmes</u> (e.g. the Atkins Diet™) around — and they all claim they'll help you <u>lose weight</u>. But how do you know they work...

2) It's a good idea to <u>look out</u> for <u>these things</u>:

> • Is the report a scientific study, published in a reputable journal?
> • Was it written by a qualified person (not connected with the people selling it)?
> • Was the sample of people asked/tested large enough to give reliable results?
> • Have there been other studies which found similar results?

A "yes" to one or more of these is a good sign.

E.g. a common way to promote a new <u>diet</u> is to say, "Celebrity A has lost x pounds using it". But effectiveness in <u>one person</u> doesn't mean much. Only a <u>large survey</u> can tell if a diet is more or less effective than just <u>eating less</u> and <u>exercising more</u> — and these aren't done often.

3) Really, all you need to do to lose weight is to <u>take in less energy</u> than you <u>use</u>. So diets and slimming products will only work if you...

> • eat <u>less fat or carbohydrate</u> (so that you take in less energy), or
> • do <u>more exercise</u> (so that you use more energy).

4) Some claims may be <u>true</u> but a little <u>misleading</u>. E.g. <u>low-fat bars</u> might be low in fat, but eating them without changing the rest of your diet doesn't necessarily mean you'll lose weight — you could still be taking in <u>too much energy</u>.

"Brad Pitt says it's great" is NOT scientific proof...

Learn what to look out for before you put too much faith in what you read. Then buy my book — 100% of the people I surveyed (i.e. both of them) said it had no negative affect <u>whatsoever</u> on their overall wellbeing!

Fighting Disease

Microorganisms that enter the body and cause disease are called pathogens.
Pathogens cause infectious diseases — diseases that can easily spread.

There Are Two Main Types of Pathogen: Bacteria and Viruses

1. Bacteria Are Very Small Living Cells

1) Bacteria are very small cells (about 1/100th the size of your body cells), which can reproduce rapidly inside your body.

2) They make you feel ill by doing two things: a) damaging your cells, b) producing toxins (poisons).

2. Viruses Are Not Cells — They're Much Smaller

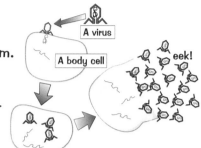

1) Viruses are not cells. They're tiny, about 1/100th the size of a bacterium.

2) They replicate themselves by invading your cells and using the cells' machinery to produce many copies of themselves. The cell will usually then burst, releasing all the new viruses.

3) This cell damage is what makes you feel ill.

Your Body Has a Pretty Sophisticated Defence System

1) Your skin, plus hairs and mucus in your respiratory tract (breathing pipework), stop a lot of nasties getting inside your body.

2) And to try and prevent microorganisms getting into the body through cuts, small fragments of cells (called platelets) help blood clot quickly to seal wounds. If the blood contains low numbers of platelets then it will clot more slowly.

3) But if something does make it through, your immune system kicks in. The most important part is the white blood cells. They travel around in your blood and crawl into every part of you, constantly patrolling for microbes. When they come across an invading microbe they have three lines of attack.

1. Consuming Them
White blood cells can engulf foreign cells and digest them.

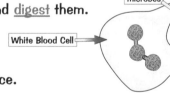

2. Producing Antibodies

1) Every invading cell has unique molecules (called antigens) on its surface.

2) When your white blood cells come across a foreign antigen (i.e. one they don't recognise), they will start to produce proteins called antibodies to lock onto and kill the invading cells. The antibodies produced are specific to that type of antigen — they won't lock on to any others.

3) Antibodies are then produced rapidly and carried around the body to kill all similar bacteria or viruses.

4) If the person is infected with the same pathogen again the white blood cells will rapidly produce the antibodies to kill it — the person is naturally immune to that pathogen and won't get ill.

3. Producing Antitoxins
These counteract toxins produced by the invading bacteria.

Fight disease — blow your nose with boxing gloves...

If you have a low level of white blood cells, you'll be more susceptible to infections. E.g. HIV/AIDS attacks a person's white blood cells and weakens their immune system, making it easier for other pathogens to invade.

Fighting Disease — Vaccination

Vaccinations have changed the way we fight disease. We don't always have to deal with the problem once it's happened — we can prevent it happening in the first place.

Vaccination — Protects from Future Infections

1) When you're infected with a new microorganism, it takes your white blood cells a few days to learn how to deal with it. But by that time, you can be pretty ill.

2) Vaccinations involve injecting small amounts of dead or inactive microorganisms. These carry antigens, which cause your body to produce antibodies to attack them — even though the microorganism is harmless (since it's dead or inactive). For example, the MMR vaccine contains weakened versions of the viruses that cause measles, mumps and rubella (German measles) all in one vaccine.

3) But if live microorganisms of the same type appear after that, the white blood cells can rapidly mass-produce antibodies to kill off the pathogen. Cool.

4) Some vaccinations "wear off" over time. So booster injections may need to be given to increase levels of antibodies again.

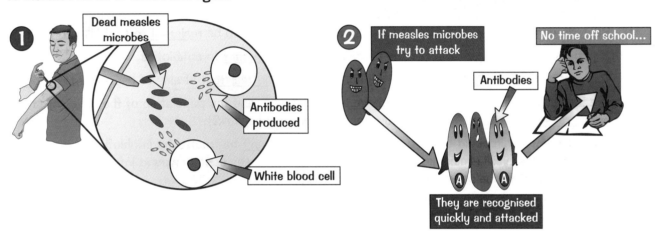

There are Pros and Cons of Vaccination

PROS

1) Vaccines have helped control lots of infectious diseases that were once common in the UK (e.g. polio, measles, whooping cough, rubella, mumps, tetanus...). Smallpox no longer occurs at all, and polio infections have fallen by 99%.

2) Big outbreaks of disease — called epidemics — can be prevented if a large percentage of the population is vaccinated. That way, even the people who aren't vaccinated are unlikely to catch the disease because there are fewer people able to pass it on. But if a significant number of people aren't vaccinated, the disease can spread quickly through them and lots of people will be ill at the same time.

CONS

1) Vaccines don't always work — sometimes they don't give you immunity.

2) You can sometimes have a bad reaction to a vaccine (e.g. swelling, or maybe something more serious like a fever or seizures). But bad reactions are very rare.

Prevention is better than cure...

Deciding whether to have a vaccination means balancing risks — the risk of catching the disease if you don't have a vaccine, against the risk of having a bad reaction if you do. As always, you need to look at the evidence. For example, if you get measles (the disease), there's about a 1 in 15 chance that you'll get complications (e.g. pneumonia) — and about 1 in 500 people who get measles actually die. However, the number of people who have a problem with the vaccine is more like 1 in 1 000 000.

Fighting Disease — Drugs

...a biscuit, nurse? Thanks very much. Sorry, couldn't face that last page — I'm squeamish about needles.*

Some Drugs Just Relieve Symptoms — Others Cure the Problem

1) Painkillers (e.g. aspirin) are drugs that relieve pain (no, really). However, they don't actually tackle the cause of the disease, they just help to reduce the symptoms.

2) Other drugs do a similar kind of thing — reduce the symptoms without tackling the underlying cause. For example, lots of "cold remedies" don't actually cure colds.

3) Antibiotics (e.g. penicillin) work differently — they actually kill (or prevent the growth of) the bacteria causing the problem without killing your own body cells. Different antibiotics kill different types of bacteria, so it's important to be treated with the right one.

4) But antibiotics don't destroy viruses (e.g. flu or cold viruses). Viruses reproduce using your own body cells, which makes it very difficult to develop drugs that destroy just the virus without killing the body's cells.

Bacteria Can Become Resistant to Antibiotics

1) Bacteria can mutate — sometimes the mutations cause them to be resistant to (not killed by) an antibiotic.

2) If you have an infection, some of the bacteria might be resistant to antibiotics.

3) This means that when you treat the infection, only the non-resistant strains of bacteria will be killed.

4) The individual resistant bacteria will survive and reproduce, and the population of the resistant strain will increase. This is an example of natural selection (see page 42).

5) This resistant strain could cause a serious infection that can't be treated by antibiotics. E.g. MRSA (methicillin-resistant *Staphylococcus aureus*) causes serious wound infectious and is resistant to the powerful antibiotic methicillin.

6) To slow down the rate of development of resistant strains, it's important for doctors to avoid over-prescribing antibiotics. So you won't get them for a sore throat, only for something more serious.

You can Investigate Antibiotics by Growing Microorganisms in the Lab

You can test the action of antibiotics or disinfectants by growing cultures of microorganisms:

1) Microorganisms are grown (cultured) in a "culture medium". This is usually agar jelly containing the carbohydrates, minerals, proteins and vitamins they need to grow.

2) Hot agar jelly is poured into shallow round plastic dishes called Petri dishes.

3) When the jelly's cooled and set, inoculating loops (wire loops) are used to transfer microorganisms to the culture medium. The microorganisms then multiply.

4) Paper discs are soaked in different types of antibiotics and placed on the jelly. Antibiotic-resistant bacteria will continue to grow around them but non-resistant strains will die.

colonies of microorganisms

agar jelly

5) The Petri dishes, culture medium and inoculating loops must be sterilised before use, e.g. the inoculating loops are passed through a flame. If equipment isn't sterilised, unwanted microorganisms in the culture medium will grow and affect the result.

inoculating loop

6) The Petri dish must also have a lid to stop any microorganisms in the air contaminating the culture. The lid should be taped on.

7) In the lab at school, cultures of microorganisms are kept at about 25 °C because harmful pathogens aren't likely to grow at this temperature.

8) In industrial conditions, cultures are incubated at higher temperatures so that they can grow a lot faster.

Agar — my favourite jelly flavour after raspberry...

Microorganisms might be the perfect pets. You don't have to walk them, they won't get lonely and they hardly cost anything to feed. But whatever you do, do not feed them after midnight.

*That's my excuse, you'll have to think of your own.

Fighting Disease — Past and Future

The treatment of disease has changed somewhat over the last 200 years or so.

Semmelweis Cut Deaths by Using Antiseptics

1) While Ignaz Semmelweis was working in Vienna General Hospital in the 1840s, he saw that women were dying in huge numbers after childbirth from a disease called puerperal fever.

2) He believed that doctors were spreading the disease on their unwashed hands. By telling doctors entering his ward to wash their hands in an antiseptic solution, he cut the death rate from 12% to 2%.

3) The antiseptic solution killed bacteria on doctors' hands, though Semmelweis didn't know this (the existence of bacteria and their part in causing disease wasn't discovered for another 20 years). So Semmelweis couldn't prove why his idea worked, and his methods were dropped when he left the hospital (allowing death rates to rise once again — d'oh).

4) Nowadays we know that basic hygiene is essential in controlling disease (though recent reports have found that a lack of it in some modern hospitals has helped the disease MRSA spread).

Antibiotic Resistance is Becoming More Common

Remember, antibiotics kill bacteria (see page 18).

1) For the last few decades, we've been able to deal with bacterial infections pretty easily using antibiotics. The death rate from infectious bacterial diseases (e.g. pneumonia) has fallen dramatically.

2) But bacteria evolve antibiotic resistance, e.g MRSA bacteria are already resistant to certain antibiotics. And overuse of antibiotics has made this problem worse — by increasing the likelihood of people being infected by antibiotic-resistant strains (see page 18).

3) People who become infected with these bacteria can't easily get rid of them (because antibiotics don't work) and may pass on the infection to others.

4) So antibiotic resistance is a big problem and it's encouraged drug companies to work on developing new antibiotics that are effective against these resistant strains.

5) Meanwhile, bacteria that are resistant to most known antibiotics ('superbugs') are becoming more common.

We Face New and Scary Dangers All the Time

BACTERIA

1) As you know, bacteria can mutate to produce new strains (see page 18).
2) A new strain could be antibiotic-resistant, so current treatments would no longer clear an infection.
3) Or a new strain could be one that we've not encountered before, so no-one would be immune to it.
4) This means a new strain of bacteria could spread rapidly in a population of people and could even cause an epidemic — a big outbreak of disease.

VIRUSES

1) Viruses also tend to mutate often. This makes it hard to develop vaccines against them because the changes to their DNA can lead to them having different antigens.
2) There'd be a real problem if a virus evolved so that it was both deadly and very infectious. (Flu viruses, for example, evolve quickly so this is quite possible.)
3) If this happened, precautions could be taken to stop the virus spreading in the first place (though this is hard nowadays — millions of people travel by plane every day). And vaccines and antiviral drugs could be developed (though these take time to mass produce).
4) But in the worst-case scenario, a flu pandemic could kill billions of people all over the world.

A pandemic is when a disease spreads all over the world.

Aaargh, a giant earwig! Run from the attack of the superbug...

The reality of superbugs is possibly even scarier than giant earwigs. Actually, nothing's more scary than giant earwigs, but microorganisms that are resistant to all our drugs are a worrying thought. It'll be like going back in time to before antibiotics were invented. So far new drugs have kept us one step ahead, but some people think it's only a matter of time until the options run out.

The Nervous System

The nervous system allows you to react to what goes on around you — you'd find life tough without it.

Sense Organs Detect Stimuli

A stimulus is a change in your environment which you may need to react to (e.g. a grizzly bear looking hungrily at you). You need to be constantly monitoring what's going on so you can respond if you need to.

1) You have five different sense organs — eyes, ears, nose, tongue and skin.

2) They all contain different receptors. Receptors are groups of cells which are sensitive to a stimulus. They change stimulus energy (e.g. light energy) into electrical impulses.

3) A stimulus can be light, sound, touch, pressure, pain, chemical, or a change in position or temperature.

Sense organs and Receptors
Don't get them mixed up:

The eye is a sense organ — it contains light receptors.

The ear is a sense organ — it contains sound receptors.

The Five Sense Organs and the receptors that each contains:

1) Eyes — Light receptors — sensitive to light. These cells have a nucleus, cytoplasm and cell membrane (just like most animal cells).

2) Ears — Sound receptors — sensitive to sound. Also, "balance" receptors — sensitive to changes in position.

3) Nose — Smell receptors — sensitive to chemical stimuli.

4) Tongue — Taste receptors — sensitive to bitter, salt, sweet and sour, plus the taste of savoury things like monosodium glutamate (MSG) — chemical stimuli.

5) Skin — Sensitive to touch, pressure, pain and temperature change.

Sensory Neurones

The nerve cells that carry signals as electrical impulses from the receptors in the sense organs to the central nervous system.

Relay Neurones

The nerve cells that carry signals from sensory neurones to motor neurones.

Motor Neurones

The nerve cells that carry signals from the central nervous system to the effector muscles or glands.

The Central Nervous System Coordinates a Response

1) The central nervous system (CNS) is where all the information from the sense organs is sent, and where reflexes and actions are coordinated. The central nervous system consists of the brain and spinal cord only.

2) Neurones (nerve cells) transmit the information (as electrical impulses) very quickly to and from the CNS.

3) "Instructions" from the CNS are sent to the effectors (muscles and glands), which respond accordingly.

Effectors

Muscles and glands are known as effectors — they respond in different ways. Muscles contract in response to a nervous impulse, whereas glands secrete hormones.

Your tongue's evolved for Chinese meals — sweet, sour, MSG...

Listen up... the thing with GCSE Science is that it's not just a test of what you know — it's also a test of how well you can apply what you know. For instance, you might have to take what you know about a human and apply it to a horse (easy... sound receptors in its ears, light receptors in its eyes, etc.), or to a snake (so if you're told that certain types of snakes have heat receptors in nostril-like pits on their head, you should be able to work out what type of stimulus those pits are sensitive to). Thinking in an exam... gosh.

Synapses and Reflexes

Neurones transmit information <u>very quickly</u> to and from the brain, and your brain <u>quickly decides</u> how to respond to a stimulus. But <u>reflexes</u> are even quicker...

Synapses Connect Neurones

1) The <u>connection</u> between <u>two neurones</u> is called a <u>synapse</u>.

2) The nerve signal is transferred by <u>chemicals</u> which <u>diffuse</u> (move) across the gap.

3) These chemicals then set off a <u>new electrical signal</u> in the <u>next</u> neurone.

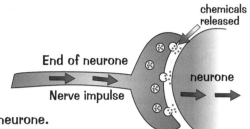

End of neurone

Nerve impulse

chemicals released

neurone

Reflexes Help Prevent Injury

1) <u>Reflexes</u> are <u>automatic</u> responses to certain stimuli — they can reduce the chances of being injured.

2) For example, if someone shines a <u>bright light</u> in your eyes, your <u>pupils</u> automatically get smaller so that less light gets into the eye — this stops it getting <u>damaged</u>.

3) Or if you get a shock, your body releases the <u>hormone</u> adrenaline automatically — it doesn't wait for you to <u>decide</u> that you're shocked.

4) The passage of information in a reflex (from receptor to effector) is called a <u>reflex arc</u>.

The Reflex Arc Goes Through the Central Nervous System

5. Impulses travel along a motor neurone, via a synapse.

4. Impulses are passed along a relay neurone, via a synapse.

6. When impulses reach muscle, it contracts.

!... OW!

3. Impulses travel along the sensory neurone.

2. Stimulation of the pain receptor.

1. Cheeky bee stings finger.

1) The neurones in reflex arcs go through the <u>spinal cord</u> or through an <u>unconscious part of the brain</u>.

2) When a <u>stimulus</u> (e.g. a painful bee sting) is detected by receptors, <u>impulses</u> are sent along a <u>sensory neurone</u> to the CNS.

3) When the impulses reach a <u>synapse</u> between the sensory neurone and a relay neurone, they trigger chemicals to be released (see above). These chemicals cause impulses to be sent along the <u>relay neurone</u>.

4) When the impulses reach a <u>synapse</u> between the relay neurone and a motor neurone, the same thing happens. Chemicals are released and cause impulses to be sent along the <u>motor neurone</u>.

5) The impulses then travel along the motor neurone to the <u>effector</u> (in this example it's a muscle).

6) The <u>muscle</u> then <u>contracts</u> and moves your hand away from the bee.

7) Because you don't have to think about the response (which takes time) it's <u>quicker</u> than normal responses.

Here's a <u>block diagram</u> of a <u>reflex arc</u> — it shows what happens, from stimulus to response.

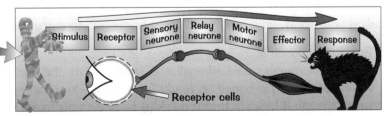

| Stimulus | Receptor | Sensory neurone | Relay neurone | Motor neurone | Effector | Response |

Receptor cells

Don't get all twitchy — just learn it...

Reflexes bypass your conscious brain completely when a quick response is essential — your body just gets on with things. Reflex actions can be used to assess the condition of <u>unconscious</u> casualties or those with <u>spinal injuries</u>. So... if you're asked <u>which bodily system</u> doctors are examining when they tap your knee with a hammer and check that you kick, just work it out. (They're checking parts of your nervous system.)

Hormones

The other way to send information around the body (apart from along nerves) is by using <u>hormones</u>.

Hormones **Are** Chemical Messengers **Sent in the Blood**

1) <u>Hormones</u> are <u>chemicals</u> released directly into the <u>blood</u>. They are carried in the <u>blood plasma</u> to other parts of the body, but only affect particular cells (called <u>target cells</u>) in particular places. Hormones control things in organs and cells that need <u>constant adjustment</u>.

2) Hormones are produced in (and secreted by) various <u>glands</u>, as shown on the diagram. They travel through your body at "<u>the speed of blood</u>".

3) Hormones tend to have relatively <u>long-lasting</u> effects.

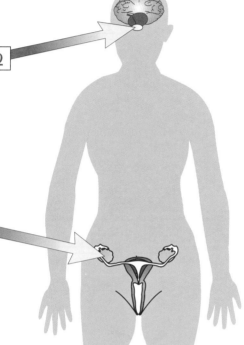

Learn this definition:
HORMONES...
are <u>chemical messengers</u>
which <u>travel in the blood</u>
to <u>activate target cells</u>.

THE PITUITARY GLAND
This produces many important hormones including <u>FSH</u> and <u>LH</u>, which are involved in the <u>menstrual cycle</u> (see page 23).

OVARIES — females only
Produce <u>oestrogen</u>, which is involved in the <u>menstrual cycle</u> (see page 23).

These are just examples — there are loads more, each doing its own thing.

Hormones **and** Nerves **Do Similar Jobs, but There Are** Differences

NERVES:
1) Very <u>FAST</u> action.
2) Act for a very <u>SHORT TIME</u>.
3) Act on a very <u>PRECISE AREA</u>.

HORMONES:
1) <u>SLOWER</u> action.
2) Act for a <u>LONG TIME</u>.
3) Act in a more <u>GENERAL</u> way.

So if you're not sure whether a response is nervous or hormonal, have a think...

1) If the response is <u>really quick</u>, it's <u>probably nervous</u>. Some information needs to be passed to effectors really quickly (e.g. pain signals, or information from your eyes telling you about the lion heading your way), so it's no good using hormones to carry the message — they're too slow.

2) But if a response <u>lasts for a long time</u>, it's <u>probably hormonal</u>. For example, when you get a shock, a hormone called adrenaline is released into the body (causing the fight-or-flight response, where your body is hyped up ready for action). You can tell it's a hormonal response (even though it kicks in pretty quickly) because you feel a bit wobbly for a while afterwards.

Nerves, hormones — no wonder revision makes me tense...

Hormones control various <u>organs</u> and <u>cells</u> in the body, though they tend to control things that aren't <u>immediately</u> life-threatening. For example, they take care of all things to do with sexual development, pregnancy, birth, breast-feeding, blood sugar level, water content... and so on. Pretty amazing really.

The Menstrual Cycle

The <u>monthly</u> release of an <u>egg</u> from a woman's <u>ovaries</u>, and the build-up and breakdown of the protective lining in the <u>uterus</u> (womb), is called the <u>menstrual cycle</u>.

The Menstrual Cycle Has Four Stages

<u>Stage 1</u>
<u>Day 1 is when the</u>
<u>bleeding starts.</u>
The uterus lining
breaks down for
about four days.

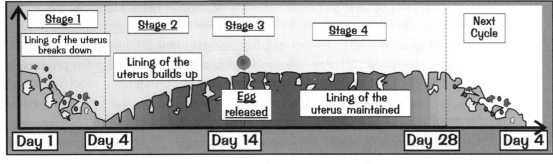

<u>Stage 2</u>
<u>The lining of the</u>
<u>uterus builds up</u>
<u>again</u>, from day 4 to day 14, into a thick spongy layer full of blood vessels, ready to receive a fertilised egg.

<u>Stage 3</u>   <u>An egg is released</u> from the ovary at day 14.

<u>Stage 4</u>   <u>The wall is then maintained</u> for about 14 days, until day 28.
If no fertilised egg has landed on the uterus wall by day 28, the spongy
lining starts to break down again and the whole cycle starts again.

Hormones Control the Different Stages

There are <u>three main hormones</u> involved:

1) <u>FSH</u> (Follicle-Stimulating Hormone):
   1) Produced by the <u>pituitary gland</u>.
   2) Causes an <u>egg to mature in one of the ovaries</u>.
   3) Stimulates the <u>ovaries to produce oestrogen</u>.

2) <u>Oestrogen</u>:
   1) Produced in the <u>ovaries</u>.
   2) Causes <u>pituitary</u> to produce <u>LH</u>.
   3) <u>Inhibits</u> the further release of <u>FSH</u>.

3) <u>LH</u> (Luteinising Hormone):
   1) Produced by the <u>pituitary gland</u>.
   2) Stimulates the <u>release of an egg</u> at
      around the middle of the menstrual cycle.

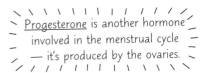

<u>Progesterone</u> is another hormone
involved in the menstrual cycle
— it's produced by the ovaries.

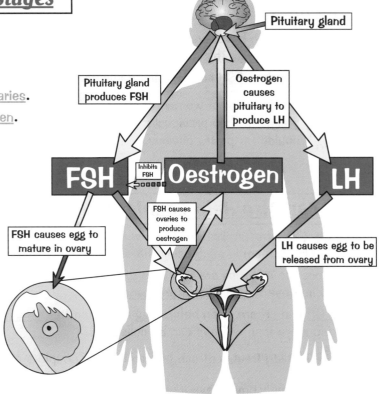

What do you call a fish with no eye — FSH...

In the exam you could be given a <u>completely new</u> situation and have to answer questions about it.
For example, say you're told that certain women with epilepsy suffer <u>more seizures</u> at certain points of the
<u>menstrual cycle</u> and you have to suggest a reason why. Sounds scary, but the key is not to panic.
You know that during the menstrual cycle, <u>hormone</u> levels change — so maybe it's these hormone changes
that are <u>triggering</u> the seizures. There are no guarantees, but that'd be a pretty good answer.

Controlling Fertility

The hormones FSH, LH, oestrogen and progesterone can be used to artificially change how fertile a woman is.

Hormones Can Be Used to Reduce Fertility...

1) Oestrogen can be used to prevent the release of an egg — so it can be used as a method of contraception.

2) This may seem kind of strange (since naturally oestrogen helps stimulate the release of eggs). But if oestrogen is taken every day to keep the level of it permanently high, it inhibits the production of FSH, and after a while egg development and production stop and stay stopped.

3) Progesterone (see page 23) also reduces fertility e.g. by stimulating the production of thick cervical mucus which prevents any sperm getting through and reaching an egg.

4) The pill is an oral contraceptive. The first version was made in the 1950s and contained high levels of oestrogen and progesterone (known as the combined oral contraceptive pill).

5) But there were concerns about a link between oestrogen in the pill and side effects like blood clots. The pill now contains lower doses of oestrogen so has fewer side effects.

PROS
1) The pill's over 99% effective at preventing pregnancy.
2) It reduces the risk of getting some types of cancer.

CONS
1) It isn't 100% effective — there's still a very slight chance of getting pregnant.
2) It can cause side effects like headaches, nausea, irregular menstrual bleeding, and fluid retention.
3) It doesn't protect against STDs (sexually transmitted diseases).

6) There's also a progesterone-only pill — it has fewer side effects than the pill (but it's not as effective).

...or Increase It

1) Some women have levels of FSH (Follicle-Stimulating Hormone) that are too low to cause their eggs to mature. This means that no eggs are released and the women can't get pregnant.

2) The hormones FSH and LH can be injected by these women to stimulate egg release in their ovaries.

PROS
It helps a lot of women to get pregnant when previously they couldn't... pretty obvious.

CONS
1) It doesn't always work — some women may have to do it many times, which can be expensive.
2) Too many eggs could be stimulated, resulting in unexpected multiple pregnancies (twins, triplets etc.).

IVF Can Also Help Couples to Have Children

1) IVF ("in vitro fertilisation") involves collecting eggs from the woman's ovaries and fertilising them in a lab using the man's sperm. These are then grown into embryos.

2) Once the embryos are tiny balls of cells, one or two of them are transferred to the woman's uterus (womb) to improve the chance of pregnancy.

3) FSH and LH are given before egg collection to stimulate egg production (so more than one egg can be collected).

PRO Fertility treatment can give an infertile couple a child — a pretty obvious benefit.

CONS
1) Some women have a strong reaction to the hormones — e.g. abdominal pain, vomiting, dehydration.
2) There have been some reports of an increased risk of cancer due to the hormonal treatment (though others have reported no such risk — the position isn't really clear at the moment).
3) Multiple births can happen if more than one embryo grows into a baby — these are risky for the mother and babies (there's a higher risk of miscarriage, stillbirth...).

Different hormones — VERY different effects...

You need to know all the facts and all the issues here. Probably the best way to be sure you know it all is to write 3 mini-essays covering all the stuff. And if you miss bits out, go back and try again.

Plant Hormones

You may not have expected <u>plants</u> to turn up in a human biology section... but hey, plants have hormones too. Hormones make sure plants grow in a <u>useful direction</u> (e.g. towards light).

Auxin *is a Plant* Growth Hormone

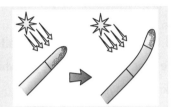

1) <u>Auxin</u> is a <u>plant hormone</u> that controls <u>growth</u> near the <u>tips</u> of <u>shoots</u> and <u>roots</u>.

2) It controls the growth of a plant in response to <u>light</u> (<u>phototropism</u>), <u>gravity</u> (<u>gravitropism</u> or <u>geotropism</u>) and <u>moisture</u>.

3) Auxin is produced in the <u>tips</u> and <u>moves backwards</u> to stimulate the <u>cell elongation (enlargement) process</u> which occurs in the cells <u>just behind</u> the tips.

4) If the tip of a shoot is <u>removed</u>, no auxin is available and the shoot may <u>stop growing</u>.

5) Extra auxin <u>promotes</u> growth in the <u>shoot</u> but <u>inhibits</u> growth in the <u>root</u> — producing the <u>desired result</u>...

Shoots grow towards light

1) When a <u>shoot tip</u> is exposed to <u>light</u>, <u>more auxin</u> accumulates on the side that's in the <u>shade</u> than the side that's in the <u>light</u>.

2) This makes the cells grow (elongate) <u>faster</u> on the <u>shaded side</u>, so the shoot bends <u>towards</u> the light.

Shoots grow away from gravity

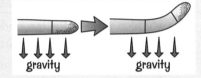

1) When a <u>shoot</u> is growing sideways, <u>gravity</u> produces an unequal distribution of auxin in the tip, with <u>more auxin</u> on the <u>lower side</u>.

2) This causes the lower side to grow <u>faster</u>, bending the shoot <u>upwards</u>.

Roots grow towards gravity

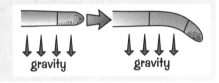

1) A <u>root</u> growing sideways will also have more auxin on its <u>lower side</u>.

2) But in a root the <u>extra</u> auxin <u>inhibits</u> growth. This means the cells on <u>top</u> elongate faster, and the root bends <u>downwards</u>.

Roots grow towards moisture

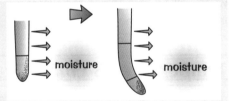

1) An uneven amount of moisture either side of a root produces <u>more auxin</u> on the side with <u>more moisture</u>.

2) This <u>inhibits</u> growth on that side, causing the root to bend in that direction, <u>towards the moisture</u>.

Plant Hormones have Uses in Agriculture

Plant hormones can be <u>extracted</u> and used by people, or <u>artificial versions</u> can be made — dead useful.

1) Most <u>weeds</u> in crop fields are <u>broad-leaved</u>, unlike <u>grasses</u> and <u>cereals</u> which have very <u>narrow leaves</u>. <u>Selective weedkillers</u> are made of <u>plant growth hormones</u> — they only affect the <u>broad-leaved plants</u>. They <u>disrupt</u> their normal growth patterns, which soon <u>kills</u> them, but leave the crops <u>untouched</u>.

2) Plant cuttings <u>won't always grow</u> in soil. If you add <u>rooting powder</u>, which contains the plant hormone <u>auxin</u>, they'll <u>produce roots</u> rapidly and start growing as <u>new plants</u>. This helps growers to produce lots of <u>clones</u> of a really good plant <u>very quickly</u>.

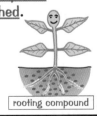

boring old soil

rooting compound

A plant auxin to a bar — 'ouch'...

Learn the page. Learn the <u>whole darn page</u>. There's no getting out of it folks.

Homeostasis

Homeostasis is a fancy word, but it covers lots of things, so maybe that's fair enough.
It means all the functions of your body which try to maintain a "constant internal environment".

Your Body Needs Some Things to Be Kept Constant

To keep all your cells working properly, certain things must be kept at the right level
— not too high, and not too low.

Bodily levels that need
to be controlled include:

1) Ion content
2) Water content
3) Sugar content
4) Temperature

Ion Content Is Regulated by the Kidneys

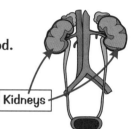

Kidneys

1) Ions (e.g. sodium, Na$^+$) are taken into the body in food, then absorbed into the blood.

2) If the food contains too much of any kind of ion then the excess ions
need to be removed. E.g. a salty meal will contain far too much Na$^+$.

3) Some ions are lost in sweat (which tastes salty, you'll have noticed).

4) The kidneys will remove the excess from the blood — this is then got rid of in urine.

Water Is Lost from the Body in Various Ways

There's also a need for the body to constantly balance the water coming in against the water going out.
Water is taken into the body as food and drink and is lost from the body in these ways:

1) through the SKIN as SWEAT...
2) via the LUNGS in BREATH...
3) via the kidneys as URINE.

Some water is
also lost in faeces.

The balance between sweat and urine can depend on what you're doing, or what the weather's like...

On a COLD DAY, or when you're
NOT EXERCISING, you don't sweat
much, so you'll produce more urine,
which will be pale (since the waste
carried in the urine is more diluted).

On a HOT DAY, or when you're EXERCISING,
you sweat a lot, and so you will produce less urine,
but this will be more concentrated (and hence a deeper
colour). You will also lose more water through your
breath when you exercise because you breathe faster.

Body Temperature Is Controlled by the Brain

1) All enzymes work best at a certain temperature. The enzymes within the human body
work best at about 37 °C — and so this is the temperature your body tries to maintain.

2) A part of the brain acts as your own personal thermostat. It's sensitive to the blood temperature in
the brain, and it receives messages from the skin that provide information about skin temperature.

Blood Sugar Level Needs to Be Controlled Too

1) Eating foods containing carbohydrate puts glucose into the blood from the gut.

2) The normal metabolism of cells removes glucose from the blood.
But if you do a lot of vigorous exercise, then much more glucose is removed.

3) A hormone called insulin helps to maintain the right level of glucose in your blood,
so your cells get a constant supply of energy.

My sister never goes out — she's got homeostasis...

Sports drinks (which usually contain electrolytes and carbohydrates) can help your body keep things in order.
The electrolytes replace those lost in sweat, while the carbohydrates can give a bit of an energy boost.

Drugs

Drugs alter what goes on in your body. Your body's essentially a seething mass of chemical reactions — drugs can interfere with these reactions, sometimes for the better, sometimes not.

Drugs Change Your Body Chemistry

Some of the chemical changes caused by drugs can lead to the body becoming addicted to the drug. If the drug isn't taken, an addict can suffer physical withdrawal symptoms — and these are sometimes very unpleasant. E.g. heroin, cocaine, nicotine and caffeine are all very addictive.

Drugs can be Medicinal, Recreational or Performance-Enhancing

1) Medicinal drugs are medically useful, like antibiotics. For some of these drugs you don't need a prescription (e.g. paracetamol), but for others you do (e.g. morphine) because they can be dangerous if misused.

2) Recreational drugs are used for fun. These can be legal or illegal (see page 29).

3) Performance-enhancing drugs can improve a person's performance in sport (see below).

Performance-Enhancing Drugs have Health and Ethical Impacts

1) Some athletes take performance-enhancing drugs to make them better at sport.

2) There are several different types, including anabolic steroids (that increase muscle size) and stimulants (that increase heart rate).

3) But these drugs can have negative health effects, e.g. steroids can cause high blood pressure.

4) Some of these drugs are banned by law, some are prescription-only, but all are banned by sporting bodies.

5) There are also ethical problems with taking performance-enhancing drugs:

Against drugs...
1) It's unfair if people gain an advantage by taking drugs, not just through training.
2) Athletes may not be fully informed of the serious health risks of the drugs they take.

For drugs...
1) Athletes have the right to make their own decision about whether taking drugs is worth the risk or not.
2) Drug-free sport isn't really fair anyway — different athletes have access to different training facilities, coaches, equipment, etc.

Claims About Drugs need to be Carefully Looked At

Claims about the effects of drugs (both prescribed and non-prescribed) need to be looked at critically. E.g:

STATINS
1) Statins are prescribed drugs used to lower the risk of heart and circulatory disease.
2) There's evidence that statins lower blood cholesterol and significantly lower the risk of heart disease in diabetic patients.
3) The original research was done by government scientists with no connection to the manufacturers. And the sample was big — 6000 patients.
4) It compared two groups of patients — those who had taken statins and those who hadn't. Other studies have since backed up these findings.

So control groups were used. And the results were reproducible.

But research findings are not always so clear cut...

CANNABIS
1) Cannabis is an illegal drug. Scientists have investigated whether the chemicals in cannabis smoke cause mental health problems. The results vary, and are sometimes open to different interpretations.
2) Basically, until more definite scientific evidence is found, no one's sure.

Drugs can kill you or cure you (or anything in between)...

Many people take drugs of some kind, e.g. caffeine in coffee, headache tablets, alcohol, hayfever medicine or an inhaler for asthma. Most of these are okay if you're careful with them and don't go mad. It's misuse that can get you into trouble (e.g. a paracetamol overdose can kill you). Read the packet.

Testing Medicinal Drugs

New drugs are constantly being developed. But before they can be given to the general public, they have to go through a thorough testing procedure. This is what usually happens...

There are Three Main Stages in Drug Testing

1) Drugs are tested on human cells and tissues in the lab.
2) However, you can't use human cells and tissues to test drugs that affect whole or multiple body systems, e.g. testing a drug for blood pressure must be done on a whole animal because it has an intact circulatory system.

② 1) The next step is to test the drug on live animals. This is to see whether the drug works (produces the effect you're looking for), to find out about its toxicity (how harmful it is) and the best dosage (the dose at which it's most effective).
2) The law in Britain states that any new drug must be tested on two different live mammals. Some people think it's cruel to test on animals, but others believe this is the safest way to make sure a drug isn't dangerous before it's given to humans.

But some people think that animals are so different from humans that testing on animals is pointless.

③ 1) If the drug passes the tests on animals then it's tested on human volunteers in a clinical trial.
2) First, the drug is tested on healthy volunteers. This is to make sure that it doesn't have any harmful side effects when the body is working normally. At the start of the trial, a very low dose of the drug is given and this is gradually increased.
3) If the results of the tests on healthy volunteers are good, the drugs can be tested on people suffering from the illness. The optimum dose is found — this is the dose of drug that is the most effective and has few side effects.
4) To test how well the drug works, patients are put into two groups. One is given the new drug, the other is given a placebo (a substance that's like the drug being tested). This is so the doctor can see the actual difference the drug makes — it allows for the placebo effect (when the patient expects the treatment to work and so feels better, even though the treatment isn't doing anything).
5) Clinical trials are blind — the patient in the study doesn't know whether they're getting the drug or the placebo. In fact, they're often double-blind — neither the patient nor the doctor knows until all the results have been gathered. This is so the doctors monitoring the patients and analysing the results aren't subconsciously influenced by their knowledge.

Things Have Gone Wrong in the Past

An example of what can happen when drugs are not thoroughly tested is the case of thalidomide — a drug developed in the 1950s.

1) Thalidomide was intended as a sleeping pill, and was tested for that use. But later it was also found to be effective in relieving morning sickness in pregnant women.
2) Unfortunately, thalidomide hadn't been tested as a drug for morning sickness, and so it wasn't known that it could pass through the placenta and affect the fetus, causing abnormal limb development. In some cases, babies were born with no arms or legs at all.
3) About 10,000 babies were affected by thalidomide, and only about half of them survived.
4) The drug was banned, and more rigorous testing procedures were introduced.
5) More recently thalidomide has been used in the treatment of leprosy and other diseases, e.g. some cancers.

A little learning is a dangerous thing...

The thalidomide story is an example of an attempt to improve people's lives which then caused some pretty tragic knock-on effects. Could the same thing happen today? Well, maybe not the exact same thing, but there's no such thing as perfect knowledge — we're learning all the time, and you can never eliminate risk completely.

Recreational Drugs

Not all drugs are used by people with illnesses — some are just used for <u>fun</u>. But fun comes with <u>risk</u>. Everyone knows that. Just like the time I thought it'd be fun to roller skate around the office. Not advisable.

Recreational Drugs Can Be Illegal or Legal

1) <u>Illegal</u> drugs are often divided into two main classes — <u>soft</u> and <u>hard</u>. Hard drugs are usually thought of as being seriously <u>addictive</u> and generally more <u>harmful</u>.

2) But the terms "soft" and "hard" are a bit <u>vague</u> — they're <u>not</u> scientific descriptions, and you can certainly have problems with <u>soft</u> drug use. E.g. <u>heroin</u> and <u>ecstasy</u> (hard drugs) and <u>cannabis</u> (a soft drug) can all cause <u>heart</u> and <u>circulatory system</u> problems.

There Are Various Reasons Why People Use Recreational Drugs

So if all these recreational drugs are so dangerous, why do so many people use them...

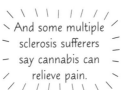

And some multiple sclerosis sufferers say cannabis can relieve pain.

1) When asked why they use cannabis, most <u>users</u> quote either simple <u>enjoyment</u>, <u>relaxation</u> or <u>stress relief</u>. Some say they do it to <u>get stoned</u> or for <u>inspiration</u>.

2) But very often this turns out to be <u>not</u> the <u>whole</u> story. There may be other factors in the user's <u>background</u> or <u>personal life</u> which influence them in choosing to use drugs. It's a <u>personal</u> thing, and often pretty <u>complicated</u>.

Some Studies Link Cannabis and Hard Drug Use — Others Don't

Almost all users of <u>hard drugs</u> have tried <u>cannabis</u> first (though <u>most</u> users of cannabis do <u>not</u> go on to use hard drugs). The <u>link</u> between cannabis and hard drugs isn't clear, but <u>three</u> opinions are common...

Cannabis is a "stepping stone": The effects of cannabis create a desire to try harder drugs.

Cannabis is a "gateway drug": Cannabis use brings people into contact with drug dealers.

It's all down to genetics: Certain people are more likely to take drugs generally, so cannabis users will also try other drugs.

Some Legal Drugs have More of an Impact than Illegal Drugs

1) <u>Tobacco</u> and <u>alcohol</u> are both <u>legal</u> recreational drugs but have a massive impact on people and society:

SMOKING
1) Smoking causes <u>disease</u> of the <u>heart</u>, <u>blood vessels</u> and <u>lungs</u>.
2) Tobacco smoke also causes <u>cancer</u>.
3) <u>Nicotine</u> is the drug found in <u>cigarettes</u> — it's <u>addictive</u> so it's hard to stop smoking.

ALCOHOL
1) Alcohol affects the <u>nervous system</u> and slows down the body's reactions.
2) Too much alcohol leads to <u>impaired judgement</u>, <u>poor coordination</u> and <u>unconsciousness</u>.
3) And excessive drinking can cause <u>liver disease</u> and <u>brain damage</u>.
4) Alcohol is also <u>addictive</u>.

2) <u>Tobacco</u> and <u>alcohol</u> have a bigger impact in the UK than illegal drugs, as <u>so many</u> people take them.

3) The National Health Service spends loads on treating people with <u>lung diseases</u> caused by <u>smoking</u>. Add to this the cost to businesses of people missing days from work, and the figures get pretty scary.

4) The same goes for <u>alcohol</u>. The costs to the NHS are huge, but are pretty small compared to the costs related to <u>crime</u> (police time, damage to people/property) and the <u>economy</u> (lost working days etc.).

5) And in addition to the financial costs, alcohol and tobacco cause <u>sorrow</u> and <u>anguish</u> to people affected by them, either directly or indirectly.

Drinking and smoking — it's so big and clever...

So it's <u>legal</u> drugs that have the most impact on the country as a <u>whole</u>, when you take everything into consideration. Some legal drugs are <u>prescribed</u> by doctors — but these can also have a <u>massive impact</u> on health if people <u>misuse</u> them, e.g. people can become addicted to prescribed <u>painkillers</u> if they're overused.

Revision Summary for Biology 1a

Congratulations, you've made it to the end of the first section. I reckon that section wasn't too bad, there's some pretty interesting stuff there — diets, vaccinations, nerves, drugs, booze... what more could you want? Actually, I know what more you could want, some questions to make sure you know it all.

1) Name all the food groups you should eat to have a balanced diet.
2)* Put these jobs in order of how much energy they would need from their food (from highest to lowest): a) mechanic, b) professional runner, c) secretary.
3) Name five health problems that are associated with obesity.
4) In terms of energy, what does a person have to do to lose weight?
5) Describe three ways in which your immune system defends the body against disease.
6) Describe how the MMR vaccine prevents you getting measles, mumps or rubella.
7) Why shouldn't your doctor give you antibiotics for the flu?
8) Name one type of bacteria that has developed resistance to antibiotics.
9) What practice did Semmelweis introduce in the 1840s? Explain why this reduced death rates on his ward.
10) Describe the structure of the central nervous system and explain what it does.
11) Where would you find the following receptors in a dog: a) smell b) taste c) light d) pressure e) sound?
12) What is a synapse?
13) What is the purpose of a reflex action?
14) Describe the pathway of a reflex arc from stimulus to response.
15) Define "hormone".
16)* Here's a table of data about response times.
    a) Which response (A or B) is carried by nerves?
    b) Which is carried by hormones?

Response	Reaction time (s)	Response duration (s)
A	0.005	0.05
B	2	10

17) Draw a timeline of the 28 day menstrual cycle. Label the four stages of the cycle and label when the egg is released.
18) Describe two effects of FSH on the body.
19) State two advantages and two disadvantages of using the contraceptive pill.
20) Briefly describe how IVF is carried out.
21) What is auxin? Explain how auxin causes plant shoots to grow towards light.
22) Water content is kept steady by homeostasis. Describe how the amount and concentration of urine you produce varies depending on how much exercise you do and how hot it is.
23) Why might an athlete use performance-enhancing drugs like steroids? Why might they not use them?
24) Briefly describe how a double blind drug trial works.
25) Name a drug that was not tested thoroughly enough and describe the consequences of its use.
26) Describe three opinions about the link between cannabis and hard drug use.
27) Which has the bigger impact on society in the UK, legal or illegal drugs? Explain your answer.

* Answers on page 108.

Adaptations

Organisms survive in many <u>different environments</u> because they have <u>adapted</u> to them.

Desert Animals *Have* Adapted *to Save Water* and *Keep Cool*

LARGE SURFACE AREA COMPARED TO VOLUME	This lets desert animals <u>lose more body heat</u> — which helps to stop them overheating.

EFFICIENT WITH WATER
1) Desert animals <u>lose less water</u> by producing small amounts of <u>concentrated urine</u>.
2) They also make very little <u>sweat</u>. Camels are able to do this by tolerating <u>big changes</u> in <u>body temperature</u>, while kangaroo rats live in <u>burrows</u> underground where it's <u>cool</u>.

GOOD IN HOT, CONDITIONS
Desert animals have very <u>thin layers</u> of <u>body fat</u> and a <u>thin coat</u> to help them <u>lose</u> body heat. E.g. camels keep nearly all their fat in their <u>humps</u>.

CAMOUFLAGE
A <u>sandy colour</u> gives <u>good camouflage</u> — to help them <u>avoid predators</u>, or <u>sneak up on prey</u>.

Arctic Animals *Have* Adapted *to Reduce Heat Loss*

SMALL SURFACE AREA COMPARED TO VOLUME
Animals living in <u>cold</u> conditions have a <u>compact</u> (rounded) shape to keep their <u>surface area</u> to a minimum — this <u>reduces heat loss</u>.

WELL INSULATED
1) They also have a thick layer of <u>blubber</u> for <u>insulation</u> — this also acts as an <u>energy store</u> when food is scarce.
2) <u>Thick hairy coats</u> keep body heat in, and <u>greasy fur</u> sheds water (this <u>prevents cooling</u> due to evaporation).

CAMOUFLAGE
Arctic animals have <u>white fur</u> to help them <u>avoid predators</u>, or <u>sneak up on prey</u>.

Desert Plants *Have* Adapted *to Having* Little Water

SMALL SURFACE AREA COMPARED TO VOLUME
1) Plants <u>lose water vapour</u> from the surface of their leaves. Cacti have <u>spines instead of leaves</u> — to <u>reduce water loss</u>.
2) They also have a <u>small surface area</u> compared to their size (about 1000 times smaller surface area than normal plants), which also <u>reduces water loss</u>.

WATER STORAGE TISSUES
For example, a cactus <u>stores water</u> in its thick stem.

MAXIMISING WATER ABSORPTION
Some cacti have <u>shallow</u> but <u>extensive roots</u> to <u>absorb</u> water quickly over a large area. Others have <u>deep roots</u> to access <u>underground water</u>.

Some *Plants* and *Animals* Are Adapted *to Deter Predators*

There are various <u>special features</u> used by animals and plants to help <u>protect</u> them against being <u>eaten</u>:
1) Some plants and animals have <u>armour</u> — like roses (<u>thorns</u>), cacti (<u>sharp spines</u>) and tortoises (<u>shells</u>).
2) Others produce <u>poisons</u> — like bees and poison ivy.
3) And some have amazing <u>warning colours</u> to scare off predators — like wasps.

Microorganisms *Have a Huge Variety* of Adaptations...

...so that they can live in a <u>wide range</u> of environments, for example:

Some <u>microorganisms</u> (e.g. bacteria) are known as <u>extremophiles</u> — they're adapted to live in seriously <u>extreme conditions</u> like super <u>hot</u> volcanic vents, in very <u>salty</u> lakes or at <u>high pressure</u> on the sea bed.

In a nutshell, it's horses for courses...

By looking at an animal or plant's <u>characteristics</u>, you should be able to have a pretty good guess at the kind of <u>environment</u> it lives in (or vice versa). Why does it have a large/small surface area... what are those spines for..?

Competition and Environmental Change

It's tough in the wild — there's always competition for food and other resources. So if the environment changes, e.g. there's not enough food or it's too hot, that can be the last straw and populations can decline.

Organisms Compete for Resources to Survive

Organisms need things from their environment and from other organisms in order to survive and reproduce:

1) Plants need light, space, water and minerals (nutrients) from the soil.

2) Animals need space (territory), food, water and mates.

Organisms compete with other species (and members of their own species) for the same resources. E.g. red and grey squirrels live in the same habitat and eat the same food. Competition with the grey squirrels for these resources means there's not enough food for the reds — so the population of red squirrels is decreasing.

Environmental Changes are Caused by Different Factors

The environment in which plants and animals live changes all the time. These changes are caused by living and non-living factors, such as:

A change could be an increase or a decrease.

LIVING FACTORS

1) A change in the occurrence of infectious diseases.
2) A change in the number of predators.
3) A change in the number of prey or the availability of food sources.
4) A change in the number or types of competitors.

NON-LIVING FACTORS

1) A change in average temperature.
2) A change in average rainfall.
3) A change in the level of air or water pollution.

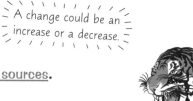

Environmental Changes Affect Populations in Different Ways

Environmental changes can affect animals and plants in these three ways:

1) Population SIZE INCREASES

E.g. if the number of prey increases, then there's more food available for predators, so more predators survive and reproduce, and their numbers increase too.

2) Population SIZE DECREASES

E.g. the number of bees in the US is falling rapidly.
Experts aren't sure why but they think it could be because:

1) Some pesticides may be having a negative effect on bees.
2) There's less food available — there aren't as many nectar-rich plants around any more.
3) There's more disease — bees are being killed by new pathogens or parasites.

3) Population DISTRIBUTION CHANGES A change in distribution means a change in where an organism lives.

For example, the distribution of bird species in Germany is changing because of a rise in average temperature. E.g. the European Bee-Eater bird is a Mediterranean species but it's now present in parts of Germany.

I compete with my brother for the front seat of the car...

In the exam you might be given some data and asked about the change in distribution of any organism. But don't panic — just think about what that organism would need to survive and any environmental changes that have occurred. And remember, if things are in limited supply then there's going to be competition.

Measuring Environmental Change

It's difficult to <u>measure accurately</u> just how much our environment is changing.
But there are some <u>useful indicators</u> that can be used...

Environmental Changes can be Measured Using Living Indicators...

1) Some <u>organisms</u> are very <u>sensitive to changes</u> in their environment and so can be studied to see the effect of human activities — these organisms are known as <u>indicator species</u>.

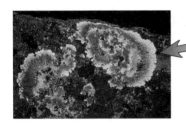

2) For example, <u>air pollution</u> can be monitored by looking at particular types of <u>lichen</u> that are very sensitive to the concentration of <u>sulfur dioxide</u> in the atmosphere (and so can give a good idea about the level of pollution from <u>car exhausts</u>, power stations, etc.). The number and type of lichen at a particular location will indicate <u>how clean</u> the air is (e.g. the air is <u>clean</u> if there are <u>lots of lichen</u>).

3) If <u>raw sewage</u> is released into a <u>river</u>, the <u>bacterial population</u> in the water increases and <u>uses up</u> the <u>oxygen</u>. Some invertebrate animals, like <u>mayfly larvae</u>, are <u>good indicators</u> for water pollution because they're <u>very sensitive</u> to the concentration of <u>dissolved oxygen</u> in the water. If you find mayfly larvae in a river, it <u>indicates</u> that the <u>water is clean</u>.

4) Other <u>invertebrate</u> species have adapted to live in <u>polluted conditions</u> — so if you see a lot of them you know there's a problem. E.g. <u>rat-tailed maggots</u> and <u>sludgeworms</u> indicate a <u>very high level of water pollution</u>.

...and Non-Living Indicators

To find out about <u>environmental change</u>, scientists are busy collecting <u>data</u> about the environment.

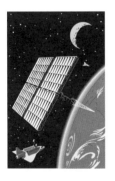

1) They use <u>satellites</u> to measure the <u>temperature</u> of the <u>sea surface</u> and the <u>amount of snow</u> and ice cover. These are modern, accurate instruments and give us a global coverage.

2) <u>Automatic weather stations</u> tell us the <u>atmospheric temperature</u> at various locations. They contain thermometers that are sensitive and accurate — they can measure to very small fractions of a degree.

3) They measure <u>rainfall</u> using <u>rain gauges</u>, to find out how much the average rainfall changes <u>year on year</u>.

4) They use <u>dissolved oxygen meters</u>, which measure the concentration of dissolved oxygen in water, to discover how the level of <u>water pollution</u> is changing.

Teenagers are an indicator species — not found in clean rooms...

Recording the levels of <u>living</u> and <u>non-living</u> things helps scientists to have a good idea of how our environment is changing. In your exam, you might get given some <u>data</u> about lichen or mayfly larvae as an <u>indirect measure</u> of pollution — and you'll have to figure out what the data means. (Easy — lots of lichen indicates clean air, lots of mayfly larvae indicates clean water. Nothing to it.)

Pyramids of Biomass

A <u>trophic level</u> is a <u>feeding</u> level. It comes from the Greek word <u>trophe</u> meaning 'nourishment'. So there.

You Need to Be Able to Construct Pyramids of Biomass

There's <u>less energy</u> and <u>less biomass</u> every time you move <u>up</u> a stage (<u>trophic level</u>) in a food chain.
There are usually <u>fewer organisms</u> every time you move up a level too:

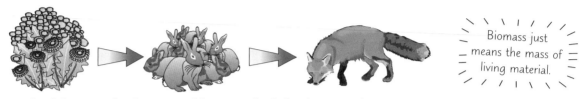

Biomass just means the mass of living material.

100 dandelions... feed... 10 rabbits... which feed... one fox.

This <u>isn't</u> always true though — for example, if <u>500 fleas</u> are feeding on the fox, the number of organisms has <u>increased</u> as you move up that stage in the food chain. So a better way to look at the food chain is often to think about <u>biomass</u> instead of number of organisms. You can use information about biomass to construct a <u>pyramid of biomass</u> to represent the food chain:

1) Each bar on a <u>pyramid of biomass</u> shows the <u>mass of living material</u> at that stage of the food chain — basically how much all the organisms at each level would "<u>weigh</u>" if you put them <u>all together</u>.

2) So the one fox above would have a <u>big biomass</u> and the <u>hundreds of fleas</u> would have a <u>very small biomass</u>. Biomass pyramids are practically <u>always pyramid-shaped</u> (unlike number pyramids):

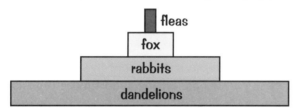

You need to be able to <u>construct</u> pyramids of biomass. Luckily it's pretty simple — they'll give you <u>all</u> the <u>information</u> you need to do it in the exam.

The big bar along the bottom of the pyramid always represents the <u>producer</u> (i.e. a plant).
The next bar will be the <u>primary consumer</u> (the animal that eats the plant), then the <u>secondary consumer</u> (the animal that eats the primary consumer) and so on up the food chain. Easy.

You Need to be Able to Interpret Pyramids of Biomass

You also need to be able to look at pyramids of biomass and <u>explain</u> what they show about the <u>food chain</u>. Also very easy. For example:

```
        partridge
      ladybirds
    aphids
  pear tree
```

Even if you know nothing about the natural world, you're probably aware that a <u>tree</u> is quite a bit <u>bigger</u> than an <u>aphid</u>. So what's going on here is that <u>lots</u> (probably thousands) of aphids are feeding on a <u>few</u> great big trees. Quite a lot of <u>ladybirds</u> are then eating the aphids, and a few <u>partridges</u> are eating the ladybirds. <u>Biomass</u> and <u>energy</u> are still <u>decreasing</u> as you go up the levels — it's just that <u>one tree</u> can have a very <u>big biomass</u>, and can fix a lot of the <u>Sun's energy</u> using all those leaves.

Constructing pyramids is a breeze — just ask the Egyptians...

There are actually a couple of exceptions where pyramids of <u>biomass</u> aren't quite pyramid-shaped.
It happens when the producer has a very short life but reproduces loads, like with plankton at certain times of year. But it's <u>rare</u>, and you <u>don't</u> need to know about it. Forget I ever mentioned it. Sorry.

Energy Transfer and Decay

So now you need to learn why there's less energy and biomass each time you move up a trophic level.

All That Energy Just Disappears Somehow...

1) Energy from the Sun is the source of energy for nearly all life on Earth.

2) Green plants and algae use a small percentage of the light energy from the Sun to make food during photosynthesis. This energy's stored in the substances which make up the cells of plants and algae, and then works its way through the food chain as animals eat them and each other.

3) Respiration supplies the energy for all life processes, including movement. Most of the energy is eventually lost to the surroundings as heat. This is especially true for mammals and birds, whose bodies must be kept at a constant temperature which is normally higher than their surroundings.

Material and energy are both lost at each stage of the food chain.

HEAT LOSS

MATERIALS LOST IN ANIMAL'S WASTE

4) Some of the material which makes up plants and animals is inedible (e.g. bone), so it doesn't pass to the next stage of the food chain. Material and energy are also lost from the food chain in the organisms' waste materials.

5) This explains why you get biomass pyramids. Most of the biomass is lost and so does not become biomass in the next level up.

6) It also explains why you hardly ever get food chains with more than about five trophic levels. So much energy is lost at each stage that there's not enough left to support more organisms after four or five stages.

Elements are Cycled Back to the Start of the Food Chain by Decay

1) Living things are made of materials they take from the world around them.

2) Plants take elements like carbon, oxygen, hydrogen and nitrogen from the soil or the air. They turn these elements into the complex compounds (carbohydrates, proteins and fats) that make up living organisms, and these then pass through the food chain.

3) These elements are returned to the environment in waste products produced by the organisms, or when the organisms die. These materials decay because they're broken down (digested) by microorganisms — that's how the elements get put back into the soil.

4) Microorganisms work best in warm, moist conditions. Many microorganisms also break down material faster when there's plenty of oxygen available. Compost bins recreate these ideal conditions.

5) All the important elements are thus recycled — they return to the soil, ready to be used by new plants and put back into the food chain again.

6) In a stable community the materials taken out of the soil and used are balanced by those that are put back in. There's a constant cycle happening.

A Compost Bin — Kitchen waste (e.g. food peelings) can be made into compost. Compost is decayed remains of animal and plant matter that can be used as fertiliser. It recycles nutrients back into the soil — giving you a lovely garden.

Extra decomposers added (compost maker)

Finely shredded waste is best

Warmth generated by decomposition helps it all along

Mesh sides to let air in

So when revising, put the fire on and don't take toilet breaks...

No, I'm being silly, go if you have to. But do your bit on the way — put your kitchen waste in the compost and your garden waste (e.g. hedge trimmings) into a green bin (then the council can do the composting for you).

The Carbon Cycle

As you've seen, all the nutrients in our environment are constantly being recycled — there's a nice balance between what goes in and what goes out again. This page is all about the recycling of carbon.

The Carbon Cycle Shows How Carbon is Recycled

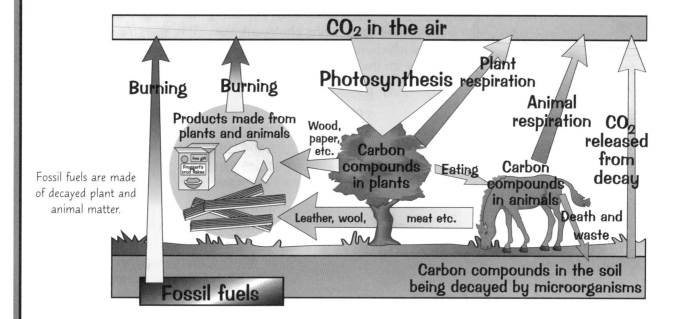

Fossil fuels are made of decayed plant and animal matter.

That can look a bit complicated at first, but it's actually pretty simple.
Learn these important points:

The energy that green plants and algae get from photosynthesis is transferred up the food chain.

1) There's only one arrow going down from the atmosphere. The whole thing is "powered" by photosynthesis. CO_2 is removed from the atmosphere by green plants and algae, and the carbon is used to make carbohydrates, fats and proteins in the plants and algae.

2) Some of the carbon is returned to the atmosphere as CO_2 when the plants and algae respire. Some of the carbon becomes part of the fats and proteins in animals when the plants and algae are eaten. The carbon then moves through the food chain.

3) Some of the carbon is returned to the atmosphere as CO_2 when the animals respire.

4) When plants, algae and animals die, other animals (called detritus feeders) and microorganisms feed on their remains. When these organisms respire, CO_2 is returned to the atmosphere.

5) Animals also produce waste, and this too is broken down by detritus feeders and microorganisms. Compounds in the waste are taken up from the soil by plants as nutrients — they're put back into the food chain again.

6) Some useful plant and animal products, e.g. wood and fossil fuels, are burnt (combustion). This also releases CO_2 back into the air.

7) So the carbon is constantly being cycled — from the air, through food chains and eventually back out into the air again.

What goes around comes around...

Carbon is very important for living things — it's the basis for all the organic molecules (fats, proteins, carbohydrates, etc.) in our bodies. In sci-fi films the aliens are sometimes silicon-based... but then by the end they've usually been defeated by some Bruce Willis type, so I don't really think they're onto a winner.

Variation

You'll probably have noticed that not all people are identical. There are reasons for this.

Organisms of the Same Species Have Differences

1) Different species look... well... different — my dog definitely doesn't look like a daisy.
2) But even organisms of the same species will usually look at least slightly different — e.g. in a room full of people you'll see different colour hair, individually shaped noses, a variety of heights etc.
3) These differences are called the variation within a species — and there are two types of variation: genetic variation and environmental variation.

Different Genes Cause Genetic Variation

1) All plants and animals have characteristics that are in some ways similar to their parents' (e.g. I've got my dad's nose, apparently).
2) This is because an organism's characteristics are determined by the genes inherited from their parents. (Genes are the codes inside your cells that control how you're made — more about these on page 38).
3) These genes are passed on in sex cells (gametes), which the offspring develop from (see page 39).
4) Most animals (and quite a lot of plants) get some genes from the mother and some from the father.
5) This combining of genes from two parents causes genetic variation — no two of the species are genetically identical (other than identical twins).
6) Some characteristics are determined only by genes (e.g. violet flower colour). In animals these include: eye colour, blood group and inherited disorders (e.g. haemophilia or cystic fibrosis).

Characteristics are also Influenced by the Environment

1) The environment that organisms live and grow in also causes differences between members of the same species — this is called environmental variation.
2) Environmental variation covers a wide range of differences — from losing your toes in a piranha attack, to getting a suntan, to having yellow leaves (never happened to me yet though), and so on.

A plant grown on a nice sunny windowsill would grow luscious and green.

The same plant grown in darkness would grow tall and spindly and its leaves would turn yellow — these are environmental variations.

3) Basically, any difference that has been caused by the conditions something lives in, is an environmental variation.

Most Characteristics are Due to Genes AND the Environment

1) Most characteristics (e.g. body weight, height, skin colour, condition of teeth, academic or athletic prowess, etc.) are determined by a mixture of genetic and environmental factors.
2) For example, the maximum height that an animal or plant could grow to is determined by its genes. But whether it actually grows that tall depends on its environment (e.g. how much food it gets).

My mum's got no trousers — cos I've got her jeans...

So, you are the way you are partly because of the genes you inherited off your folks. But you can't blame it all on your parents, since your environment then takes over and begins to mould you in all sorts of ways. In fact, it's often really tricky to decide which factor is more influential, your genes or the environment — a good way to study this is with identical twins.

Genes, Chromosomes and DNA

This page is a bit tricky, but it's dead important you get to grips with all the stuff on it
— because you're going to hear a lot more about it over the next few pages...

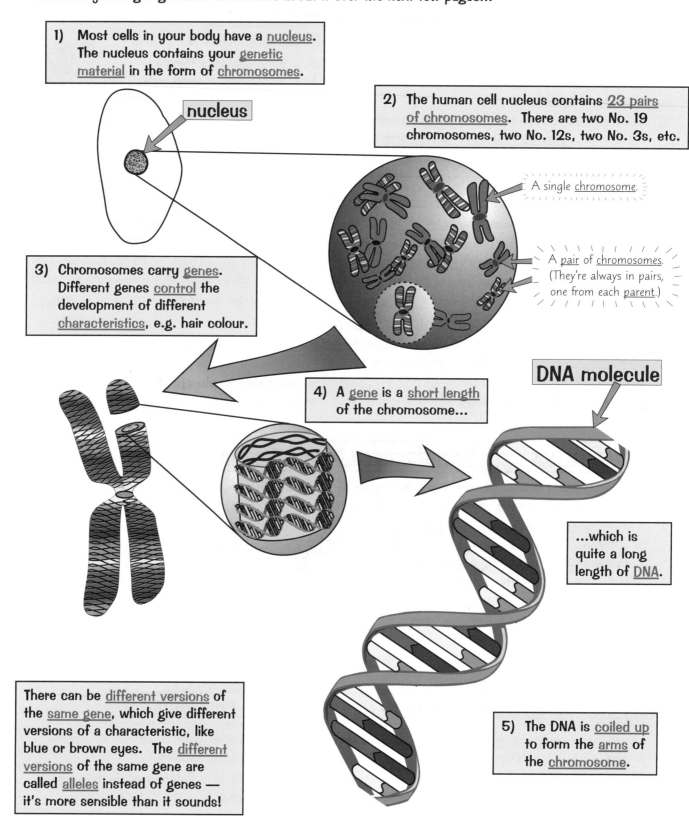

1) Most cells in your body have a nucleus. The nucleus contains your genetic material in the form of chromosomes.

nucleus

2) The human cell nucleus contains 23 pairs of chromosomes. There are two No. 19 chromosomes, two No. 12s, two No. 3s, etc.

A single chromosome.

A pair of chromosomes. (They're always in pairs, one from each parent.)

3) Chromosomes carry genes. Different genes control the development of different characteristics, e.g. hair colour.

4) A gene is a short length of the chromosome...

DNA molecule

...which is quite a long length of DNA.

There can be different versions of the same gene, which give different versions of a characteristic, like blue or brown eyes. The different versions of the same gene are called alleles instead of genes — it's more sensible than it sounds!

5) The DNA is coiled up to form the arms of the chromosome.

It's hard being a DNA molecule, there's so much to remember...

This is the bare bones of genetics, so you definitely need to understand everything on this page or you'll find the rest of this topic dead hard. The best way to get all of these important facts engraved in your mind is to cover the page, scribble down the main points and sketch out the diagrams...

Reproduction

Ooo err, reproduction... Surely you knew it'd come up at some point. It can happen in <u>two different ways</u>...

Sexual Reproduction Produces Genetically Different Cells

1) <u>Sexual reproduction</u> is where genetic information from <u>two</u> organisms (a <u>father</u> and a <u>mother</u>) is combined to produce offspring which are <u>genetically different</u> to either parent.

2) In sexual reproduction the mother and father produce <u>gametes</u> — e.g. <u>egg</u> and <u>sperm</u> cells in animals.

3) In humans, each gamete contains <u>23 chromosomes</u> — <u>half</u> the number of chromosomes in a normal cell. (Instead of having <u>two</u> of each chromosome, a <u>gamete</u> has just <u>one</u> of each.)

4) The <u>egg</u> (from the mother) and the <u>sperm</u> cell (from the father) then <u>fuse together</u> (<u>fertilisation</u>) to form a cell with the <u>full number</u> of chromosomes (<u>half from the father</u>, <u>half from the mother</u>).

> <u>SEXUAL REPRODUCTION</u> involves the fusion of male and female gametes.
> Because there are <u>TWO</u> parents, the offspring contain <u>a mixture of their parents' genes</u>.

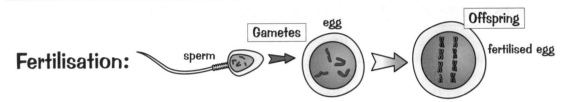

5) This is why the offspring <u>inherits features</u> from <u>both parents</u> — it's received a <u>mixture</u> of chromosomes from its mum and its dad (and it's the chromosomes that decide how you turn out).

6) This <u>mixture of genetic material</u> produces <u>variation</u> in the offspring. Pretty cool, eh.

Asexual Reproduction Produces Genetically Identical Cells

1) An <u>ordinary cell</u> can make a new cell by simply <u>dividing in two</u>. The <u>new cell</u> has <u>exactly the same</u> genetic information (i.e. genes) as the parent cell — this is known as <u>asexual reproduction</u>.

> In <u>ASEXUAL REPRODUCTION</u> there's only <u>ONE</u> parent. There's <u>no fusion</u> of gametes, <u>no mixing</u> of chromosomes and <u>no genetic variation</u> between parent and offspring. The offspring are <u>genetically identical</u> to the parent — they're <u>clones</u>.

2) Here's how it works...

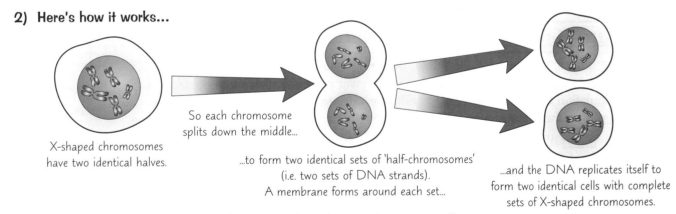

X-shaped chromosomes have two identical halves.

So each chromosome splits down the middle...

...to form two identical sets of 'half-chromosomes' (i.e. two sets of DNA strands). A membrane forms around each set...

...and the DNA replicates itself to form two identical cells with complete sets of X-shaped chromosomes.

3) This is how all plants and animals <u>grow</u> and produce <u>replacement cells</u>.

4) Some organisms also <u>produce offspring</u> using asexual reproduction, e.g. <u>bacteria</u> and certain <u>plants</u>.

You need to reproduce these facts in the exam...

The main messages on this page are that: 1) <u>sexual</u> reproduction needs <u>two</u> parents and forms cells that are <u>genetically different</u> to the parents, so there's <u>lots</u> of genetic variation. And 2) <u>asexual</u> reproduction needs just <u>one</u> parent to make genetically <u>identical</u> cells (clones), so there's <u>no genetic variation</u> in the offspring.

Cloning

We can clone plants and animals in several different ways. Cool. But some of them have potential problems...

Plants Can Be Cloned from Cuttings and by Tissue Culture

CUTTINGS

1) Gardeners can take cuttings from good parent plants, and then plant them to produce genetically identical copies (clones) of the parent plant.

2) These plants can be produced quickly and cheaply.

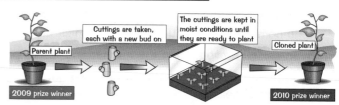

Parent plant — 2009 prize winner

Cuttings are taken, each with a new bud on

The cuttings are kept in moist conditions until they are ready to plant

Cloned plant — 2010 prize winner

TISSUE CULTURE

This is where a few plant cells are put in a growth medium with hormones, and they grow into new plants — clones of the parent plant. These plants can be made very quickly, in very little space, and be grown all year.

You Can Make Animal Clones Using Embryo Transplants

Farmers can produce cloned offspring from their best bull and cow — using embryo transplants.

1) Sperm cells are taken from a prize bull and egg cells are taken from a prize cow. The sperm are then used to artificially fertilise an egg cell. The embryo that develops is then split many times (to form clones) before any cells become specialised.

2) These cloned embryos can then be implanted into lots of other cows where they grow into baby calves (which will all be genetically identical to each other).

3) Hundreds of "ideal" offspring can be produced every year from the best bull and cow.

Adult Cell Cloning is Another Way to Make a Clone

1) Adult cell cloning involves taking an unfertilised egg cell and removing its genetic material (the nucleus). A complete set of chromosomes from an adult body cell (e.g. skin cell) is inserted into the 'empty' egg cell.

2) The egg cell is then stimulated by an electric shock — this makes it divide, just like a normal embryo.

3) When the embryo is a ball of cells, it's implanted into an adult female (the surrogate mother) to grow into a genetically identical copy (clone) of the original adult body cell.

4) This technique was used to create Dolly — the famous cloned sheep.

There are Many Issues Surrounding Cloning

1) Cloning quickly gets you lots of "ideal" offspring. But you also get a "reduced gene pool" — this means there are fewer different alleles in a population. If a population are all closely related and a new disease appears, they could all be wiped out — there may be no allele in the population giving resistance to the disease.

2) But the study of animal clones could lead to greater understanding of the development of the embryo, and of ageing and age-related disorders.

3) Cloning could also be used to help preserve endangered species.

4) However, it's possible that cloned animals might not be as healthy as normal ones, e.g. Dolly the sheep had arthritis, which tends to occur in older sheep (but the jury's still out on if this was due to cloning).

5) Some people worry that humans might be cloned in the future. If it was allowed, any success may follow many unsuccessful attempts, e.g. children born severely disabled.

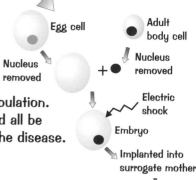

Egg cell

Adult body cell

Nucleus removed

Nucleus removed

Electric shock

Embryo

Implanted into surrogate mother

Live animal

Thank goodness they didn't do that with my little brother...

Cloning can be a controversial topic — especially when it's to do with cloning animals (and especially humans). More large-scale, long-term studies into cloned animals are needed to find out what the dangers are.

Genetic Engineering

Scientists can now <u>change</u> an organism's <u>genes</u> to alter its characteristics. This is a new science with exciting possibilities, but there might be <u>dangers</u> too...

Genetic Engineering <u>Uses</u> Enzymes <u>to Cut and Paste</u> Genes

The basic idea is to copy a <u>useful gene</u> from one organism's chromosome into the cells of another...

1) A useful gene is "<u>cut</u>" from one organism's chromosome using <u>enzymes</u>.

2) <u>Enzymes</u> are then used to <u>cut</u> another organism's chromosome and then to <u>insert</u> the useful gene.

3) Scientists use this method to do all sorts of things — for example, the human insulin gene can be inserted into <u>bacteria</u> to <u>produce human insulin</u>:

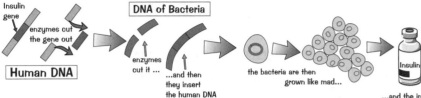

Genes <u>can be</u> Transferred <u>into</u> Animals <u>and</u> Plants

The same method can be used to <u>transfer useful genes</u> into <u>animals</u> and <u>plants</u> at the <u>very early stages</u> of their development (i.e. shortly after <u>fertilisation</u>). This means they'll develop <u>useful characteristics</u>, e.g:

1) <u>Genetically modified</u> (<u>GM</u>) <u>crops</u> have had their genes modified, e.g. to make them <u>resistant to viruses</u>, <u>insects</u> or <u>herbicides</u> (chemicals used to kill weeds).

2) <u>Sheep</u> have been genetically engineered to produce substances, like drugs, in their <u>milk</u> that can be used to treat <u>human diseases</u>.

3) <u>Genetic disorders</u> like cystic fibrosis are caused by faulty genes. Scientists are trying to treat these disorders by <u>inserting working genes</u> into sufferers. This is called <u>gene therapy</u>.

But Genetic Engineering is a <u>Controversial Topic...</u>

1) Genetic engineering is an <u>exciting new area in science</u> which has the <u>potential</u> for solving many of our problems (e.g. treating diseases, more efficient food production etc.) but not everyone thinks it's a great idea.

2) There are <u>worries</u> about the long-term effects of genetic engineering — that changing a person's genes might <u>accidentally</u> create unplanned <u>problems</u>, which could then get passed on to <u>future generations</u>.

It's the Same with GM Crops — There Are <u>Pros</u> and <u>Cons...</u>

1) Some people say that growing GM crops will affect the number of <u>weeds</u> and <u>flowers</u> (and so the population of <u>insects</u>) that live in and around the crops — <u>reducing</u> farmland <u>biodiversity</u>.

2) Not everyone is convinced that GM crops are <u>safe</u>. People are worried they may develop <u>allergies</u> to the food — although there's probably no more risk for this than for eating usual foods.

3) A big concern is that <u>transplanted genes</u> may get out into the <u>natural environment</u>. For example, the <u>herbicide resistance</u> gene may be picked up by weeds, creating a new '<u>superweed</u>' variety.

4) On the plus side, GM crops can <u>increase the yield</u> of a crop, making more food.

5) People living in developing nations often lack <u>nutrients</u> in their diets. GM crops could be <u>engineered</u> to contain the nutrient that's <u>missing</u>. For example, they're testing 'golden rice' that contains beta-carotene — lack of this substance causes <u>blindness</u>.

6) GM crops are already being grown elsewhere in the world (not the UK) often <u>without any problems</u>.

If only there was a gene to make revision easier...

At the end of the day, it's up to the <u>Government</u> to weigh up all the <u>evidence</u> for the pros and cons before <u>making a decision</u> on how this scientific knowledge is used. All scientists can do is make sure the Government has all the information it needs to make the decision. And all you need to do is to <u>learn</u> this page inside out.

Evolution

THEORY OF EVOLUTION: More than 3 billion years ago, life on Earth began as simple organisms from which all the more complex organisms evolved (rather than just popping into existence).

All Organisms are Related... even if Only Distantly

Looking at the similarities and differences between organisms allows us to classify them into groups. E.g:

1) Plants make their own food (by photosynthesis) and are fixed in the ground.

2) Animals move about the place and can't make their own food.

3) Microorganisms are different to plants and animals, e.g. bacteria are single-celled.

Studying the similarities and differences between organisms also help us to understand how all living things are related (evolutionary relationships) and how they interact with each other (ecological relationships):

EVOLUTIONARY

1) Species with similar characteristics often have similar genes because they share a recent common ancestor, so they're closely related. They often look very alike and tend to live in similar types of habitat, e.g. whales and dolphins.

2) Occasionally, genetically different species might look alike too. E.g. dolphins and sharks look pretty similar because they've both adapted to living in the same habitat. But they're not closely related — they've evolved from different ancestors.

3) Evolutionary trees show common ancestors and relationships between organisms. The more recent the common ancestor, the more closely related the two species.

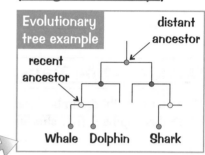

Whales and dolphins have a recent common ancestor so are closely related. They're both more distantly related to sharks.

ECOLOGICAL

1) If we see organisms in the same environment with similar characteristics (e.g. dolphins and sharks) it suggests they might be in competition (e.g for the same food source).

2) Differences between organisms in the same environment (e.g. dolphins swim in small groups, but herring swim in giant shoals) can show predator-prey relationships (e.g. dolphins hunt herring).

Natural Selection Explains How Evolution Occurs

Charles Darwin came up with the idea of natural selection. It works like this...

Genetic differences are caused by sexual reproduction (see page 39) and mutations (see below).

1) Individuals within a species show variation because of the differences in their genes, e.g. some rabbits have big ears and some have small ones.

2) Individuals with characteristics that make them better adapted to the environment have a better chance of survival and so are more likely to breed successfully. E.g. big-eared rabbits are more likely to hear a fox sneaking up on them, and so are more likely to live and have millions of babies. Small-eared rabbits are more likely to end up as fox food.

3) So, the genes that are responsible for the useful characteristics are more likely to be passed on to the next generation. E.g. all the baby rabbits are born with big ears.

Evolution can Occur Due To Mutations

1) A mutation is a change in an organism's DNA.

2) Most of the time mutations have no effect, but occasionally they can be beneficial by producing a useful characteristic. This characteristic may give the organism a better chance of surviving and reproducing.

3) If so, the beneficial mutation is more likely to be passed on to future generations by natural selection.

4) Over time, the beneficial mutation will accumulate in a population, e.g. some species of bacteria have become resistant to antibiotics due to a mutation (see page 18).

"Natural selection" — sounds like vegan chocolates...

Natural selection's all about the organisms with the best characteristics surviving to pass on their genes so that the whole species ends up adapted to its environment. It doesn't happen overnight though.

More About Evolution

There's a lot of evidence for the theory of evolution by natural selection.
But back in the day, poor Charlie Darwin didn't have half as much evidence to convince people.

Not Everyone Agreed with Darwin...

Darwin's idea was very <u>controversial</u> at the time — for various reasons...

① It went against common <u>religious beliefs</u> about how life on Earth developed — it was the first plausible explanation for our own existence <u>without</u> the need for a "Creator" (God).

② Darwin couldn't give a <u>good explanation</u> for why these new, useful characteristics <u>appeared</u> or exactly <u>how</u> individual organisms passed on their beneficial characteristics to their offspring. But then he didn't know anything about <u>genes</u> or <u>mutations</u> — they weren't discovered 'til 50 years after his theory was published.

③ There wasn't enough <u>evidence</u> to convince many <u>scientists</u>, because not many <u>other studies</u> had been done into how organisms change over time.

...and Lamarck had Different Ideas

There were <u>different scientific hypotheses</u> about evolution around at the same time, such as Lamarck's:

1) <u>Lamarck</u> (1744-1829) argued that if a <u>characteristic</u> was <u>used a lot</u> by an organism then it would become <u>more developed</u> during its <u>lifetime</u>. E.g. if a rabbit <u>used</u> its legs to run a lot (to escape predators), then its legs would get <u>longer</u>.

2) Lamarck believed that these <u>acquired characteristics</u> would be passed on to the <u>next generation</u>, e.g. the rabbit's offspring would have <u>longer legs</u>.

Scientists can Develop Different Hypotheses from Similar Observations

1) Often scientists come up with <u>different hypotheses</u> to explain <u>similar observations</u>.

2) Scientists might develop different hypotheses because they have different <u>beliefs</u> (e.g. religious) or they have been <u>influenced</u> by different people (e.g. other scientists and their way of thinking)... or they just darn well <u>think differently</u>.

There's more about how science works on page 2.

3) The only way to <u>find out</u> whose hypothesis is right is to find evidence to <u>support</u> or <u>disprove</u> each one.

4) For example, Lamarck and Darwin both had different hypotheses to explain how evolution happens. In the end...

- Lamarck's hypothesis was eventually <u>rejected</u> because experiments <u>didn't support his hypothesis</u>. You can see it for yourself, e.g. if you dye a hamster's fur <u>bright pink</u> (not recommended), its offspring will still be born with the <u>normal</u> fur colour because the new characteristic <u>won't</u> have been passed on.
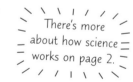
- The discovery of genetics <u>supported</u> Darwin's idea because it provided an <u>explanation</u> of how organisms born with beneficial characteristics can <u>pass them on</u> (i.e. via their genes).

5) There's so much evidence for Darwin's idea that it's now an <u>accepted hypothesis</u> (a <u>theory</u>).

Did you know that exams evolved from the Spanish Inquisition...

This is a good example of how scientific hypotheses come about — someone <u>observes</u> something and then tries to <u>explain</u> it. Their hypothesis will then be <u>tested</u> by other scientists — if their evidence supports the hypothesis, it gains in credibility. If not, it's <u>rejected</u>. Darwin's theory <u>hasn't</u> been <u>rejected</u> yet.

Revision Summary for Biology 1b

There's a lot to remember from this section and some of the topics are controversial, like cloning and genetic engineering. You need to know all sides of the story, as well as all the facts... so, here are some questions to help you figure out what you know. If you get any wrong, go back and learn the stuff.

1) Name four ways in which a desert animal may be adapted to its environment.
2) State three ways that plants and animals might be adapted to deter predators.
3) Name three things that: a) plants compete for, b) animals compete for.
4) Give two examples of non-living factors that can cause environmental changes.
5) Explain how lichen can be used as an indicator of air pollution.
6) Name an organism that can be used as an indicator of water pollution.
7) What does each bar on a pyramid of biomass represent?
8) Give two ways that energy is lost from a food chain.
9) Give one way that carbon dioxide from the air enters a food chain.
10) Give three ways that carbon compounds in a food chain become carbon dioxide in the air again.
11) Name three animal characteristics that are determined only by genes.
12) Name three animal characteristics that are determined by a mixture of genes and the environment.
13) How many pairs of chromosomes do humans have in each cell?
14) The table below compares sexual and asexual reproduction.
Complete the table by ticking whether each statement is true for sexual or asexual reproduction.

	Sexual reproduction	Asexual reproduction
Reproduction involves two parents.		
Offspring are clones of the parent.		
There is variation in the offspring.		
There is no fusion of gametes.		

15) How would you make a plant clone using tissue culture?
16) State two examples of useful applications of genetic engineering.
17) Why are some people concerned about genetic engineering?
18) Explain Darwin's theory of natural selection.
19) Why was Darwin's idea very controversial at the time?
20) Explain how Lamarck's hypothesis was different from Darwin's.

Atoms and Elements

Atoms are the building blocks of <u>everything</u> — and I mean everything.
They're <u>amazingly tiny</u> — you can only see them with an incredibly powerful microscope.

Atoms have a Small <u>Nucleus</u> Surrounded by <u>Electrons</u>

There are quite a few different (and equally useful) models of the atom — but chemists tend to like this <u>nuclear model</u> best. You can use it to explain pretty much the whole of Chemistry... which is nice.

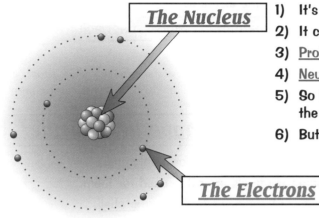

The Nucleus

1) It's in the <u>middle</u> of the atom.
2) It contains <u>protons</u> and <u>neutrons</u>.
3) <u>Protons</u> are <u>positively charged</u>.
4) <u>Neutrons</u> have <u>no charge</u> (they're neutral).
5) So the nucleus has a <u>positive charge</u> overall because of the protons.
6) But size-wise it's <u>tiny</u> compared to the rest of the atom.

The Electrons

1) Move <u>around</u> the nucleus.
2) They're <u>negatively charged</u>.
3) They're <u>tiny</u>, but they cover <u>a lot of space</u>.
4) They occupy <u>shells</u> around the nucleus.
5) These shells explain <u>the whole of Chemistry</u>.

Number of Protons <u>Equals</u> Number of Electrons

1) Atoms have <u>no charge</u> overall. They are neutral.
2) The <u>charge</u> on the electrons is the <u>same</u> size as the charge on the <u>protons</u> — but <u>opposite</u>.
3) This means the <u>number</u> of <u>protons</u> always equals the <u>number</u> of <u>electrons</u> in an <u>atom</u>.
4) If some electrons are <u>added or removed</u>, the atom becomes <u>charged</u> and is then an <u>ion</u>.

Elements <u>Consist of One Type</u> of Atom Only

1) Atoms can have different numbers of protons, neutrons and electrons.
   It's the number of <u>protons</u> in the nucleus that decides what <u>type</u> of atom it is.
2) For example, an atom with <u>one proton</u> in its nucleus is <u>hydrogen</u> and an atom with <u>two protons</u> is <u>helium</u>.
3) If a substance only contains <u>one type</u> of atom it's called an <u>element</u>.
4) There are about <u>100 different elements</u> — quite a lot of everyday substances are elements:

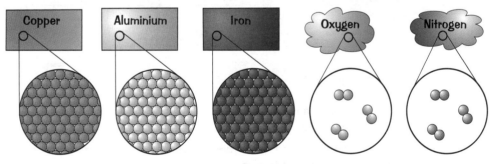

So <u>all the atoms</u> of a particular <u>element</u> (e.g. nitrogen) have the <u>same number</u> of protons...

...and <u>different elements</u> have atoms with <u>different numbers</u> of protons.

Number of protons = number of electrons...

This stuff might seem a bit useless at first, but it should be permanently engraved into your mind.
You need to <u>know these basic facts</u> — then you'll have a better chance of understanding the rest of Chemistry.

The Periodic Table

Chemistry would be really messy if it was all big lists of names and properties. So instead they've come up with a kind of shorthand for the names, and made a beautiful table to organise the elements — like a big filing system. Might not be much fun, but it makes life (and exam questions) much, much easier.

Atoms Can be Represented by Symbols

Atoms of each element can be represented by a one or two letter symbol — it's a type of shorthand that saves you the bother of having to write the full name of the element.

Some make perfect sense, e.g.

| C = carbon | O = oxygen | Mg = magnesium |

Others seem to make about as much sense as an apple with a handle.

E.g.

| Na = sodium | Fe = iron | Pb = lead |

Most of these odd symbols actually come from the Latin names of the elements.

The Periodic Table Puts Elements with Similar Properties Together

1) The periodic table is laid out so that elements with similar properties form columns.

2) These vertical columns are called groups and Roman numerals are often used for them.

3) All of the elements in a group have the same number of electrons in their outer shell.

4) This is why elements in the same group have similar properties. So, if you know the properties of one element, you can predict properties of other elements in that group.

5) For example, the Group 1 elements are Li, Na, K, Rb, Cs and Fr. They're all metals and they react the same way. E.g. they all react with water to form an alkaline solution and hydrogen gas, and they all react with oxygen to form an oxide.

6) The elements in the final column (Group 0) are the noble gases. They all have eight electrons in their outer shell, apart from helium (which has two). This means that they're stable and unreactive.

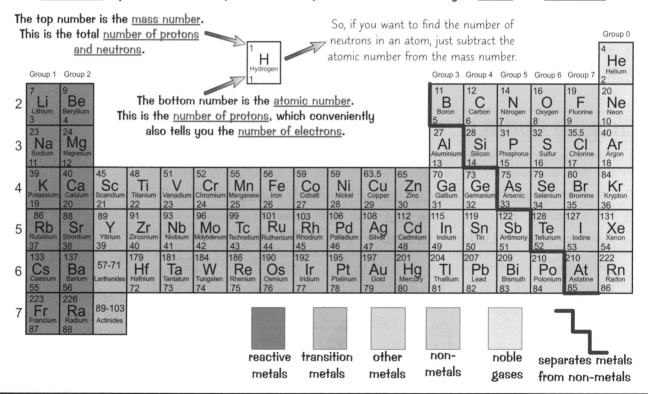

The top number is the mass number. This is the total number of protons and neutrons.

So, if you want to find the number of neutrons in an atom, just subtract the atomic number from the mass number.

The bottom number is the atomic number. This is the number of protons, which conveniently also tells you the number of electrons.

reactive metals   transition metals   other metals   non-metals   noble gases   separates metals from non-metals

I'm in a chemistry band — I play the symbols...

Scientists keep making new elements and feeling well chuffed with themselves. The trouble is, these new elements only last for a fraction of a second before falling apart. You don't need to know the properties of each group of the periodic table, but if you're told, for example, that fluorine (Group 7) forms two-atom molecules, it's a fair guess that chlorine, bromine, iodine and astatine do too.

Electron Shells

The fact that electrons occupy "shells" around the nucleus is what causes the whole of chemistry. Remember that, and watch how it applies to each bit of it. It's ace.

Electron Shell Rules:

1) Electrons always occupy <u>shells</u> (sometimes called <u>energy levels</u>).

2) The <u>lowest</u> energy levels are <u>always filled first</u> — these are the ones closest to the nucleus.

3) Only <u>a certain number</u> of electrons are allowed in each shell:
<u>1st shell</u>: 2   <u>2nd shell</u>: 8   <u>3rd shell</u>: 8

4) Atoms are much <u>happier</u> when they have <u>full electron shells</u> — like the <u>noble gases</u> in <u>Group 0</u>.

5) In most atoms the <u>outer shell</u> is <u>not full</u> and this makes the atom want to <u>react</u> to fill it.

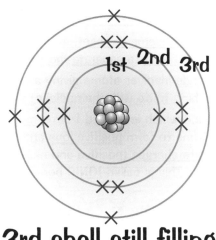

1st 2nd 3rd

3rd shell still filling

Follow the Rules to Work Out Electronic Structures

You need to know the <u>electronic structures</u> for the first <u>20</u> elements (things get a bit more complicated after that). But they're not hard to work out. For a quick example, take nitrogen. <u>Follow the steps...</u>

1) The periodic table tells us nitrogen has <u>seven</u> protons... so it must have <u>seven</u> electrons.

2) Follow the '<u>Electron Shell Rules</u>' above. The <u>first</u> shell can only take 2 electrons and the <u>second</u> shell can take a <u>maximum</u> of 8 electrons.

3) So the electronic structure for nitrogen <u>must</u> be <u>2, 5</u>. Easy peasy.

4) Now <u>you</u> try it for argon.

The periodic table has a big gap here where the transition metals fit in on row four.

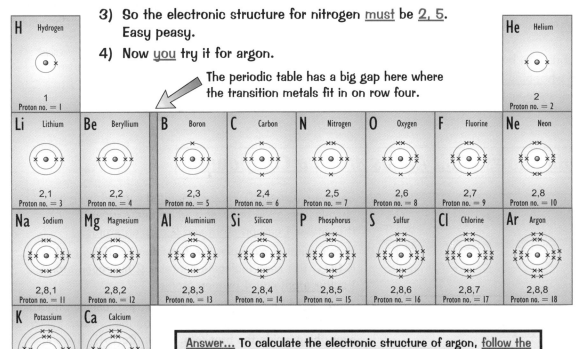

Answer... To calculate the electronic structure of argon, <u>follow the rules</u>. It's got 18 protons, so it <u>must</u> have 18 electrons. The first shell must have <u>2</u> electrons, the second shell must have <u>8</u>, and so the third shell must have <u>8</u> as well. It's as easy as <u>2, 8, 8</u>.

One little duck and two fat ladies — 2, 8, 8...

You need to know enough about electron shells to draw out that <u>whole diagram</u> at the bottom of the page without looking at it. Obviously, you don't have to learn each element separately, just <u>learn the pattern</u>. Cover the page: using a periodic table, find the atom with the electron structure 2, 8, 6.

Compounds

Life'd be oh so simple if you only had to worry about elements, even if there are a hundred or so of them. But you can mix and match elements to make lots of compounds, which complicates things no end.

Atoms Join Together to Make Compounds

1) When <u>different elements react</u>, atoms form <u>chemical bonds</u> with other atoms to form <u>compounds</u>. It's <u>usually difficult</u> to <u>separate</u> the two original elements out again.

2) <u>Making bonds</u> involves atoms giving away, taking or sharing <u>electrons</u>. Only the <u>electrons</u> are involved — it's nothing to do with the nuclei of the atoms at all.

3) A compound which is formed from a <u>metal</u> and a <u>non-metal</u> consists of <u>ions</u>. The <u>metal</u> atoms <u>lose</u> electrons to form <u>positive ions</u> and the non-metal atoms <u>gain</u> electrons to form <u>negative ions</u>. The <u>opposite charges</u> (positive and negative) of the ions mean that they're strongly <u>attracted</u> to each other. This is called <u>IONIC bonding</u>.

   E.g. NaCl
   (Na ● → Cl)   A sodium atom <u>gives</u> an electron to a chlorine atom.

4) A compound formed from <u>non-metals</u> consists of <u>molecules</u>. Each atom <u>shares</u> an <u>electron</u> with another atom — this is called a <u>COVALENT bond</u>. Each atom has to make enough covalent bonds to <u>fill up</u> its <u>outer shell</u>.

   E.g. HCl
   (H) (Cl)   A hydrogen atom bonds with a chlorine atom by <u>sharing</u> an electron with it.

5) The <u>properties</u> of a compound are <u>totally different</u> from the properties of the <u>original elements</u>. For example, if iron (a lustrous magnetic metal) and sulfur (a nice yellow powder) react, the compound formed (<u>iron sulfide</u>) is a <u>dull grey solid lump</u>, and doesn't behave <u>anything like</u> either iron or sulfur.

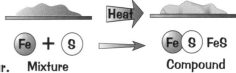

Fe + S → Fe S FeS
Mixture   Compound

6) Compounds can be <u>small molecules</u> like water, or <u>great whopping lattices</u> like sodium chloride (when I say whopping I'm talking in atomic terms).

a water molecule

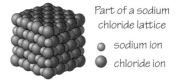
Part of a sodium chloride lattice
● sodium ion
● chloride ion

A Formula Shows What Atoms are in a Compound

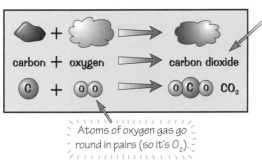

carbon + oxygen → carbon dioxide

C + O O → O C O CO₂

Atoms of oxygen gas go round in pairs (so it's O₂).

1) Carbon dioxide, CO_2, is a <u>compound</u> formed from a <u>chemical reaction</u> between carbon and oxygen. It contains <u>1 carbon atom</u> and <u>2 oxygen atoms</u>.

2) Here's another example: the formula of <u>sulfuric acid</u> is H_2SO_4. So, each molecule contains <u>2 hydrogen atoms</u>, <u>1 sulfur atom</u> and <u>4 oxygen atoms</u>.

3) There might be <u>brackets</u> in a formula, e.g. calcium hydroxide is $Ca(OH)_2$. The little number outside the bracket applies to <u>everything</u> inside the brackets. So in $Ca(OH)_2$ there is <u>1 calcium atom, 2 oxygen atoms</u> and <u>2 hydrogen atoms</u>.

Not learning this stuff will only compound your problems...

So, it turns out that <u>atoms</u> can be very caring and <u>sharing</u> little things when it comes to <u>forming compounds</u>. In fact, I know some people who could learn a lot from them. In fact, just the other day... Anyway, enough of my problems. Make sure you understand <u>what compounds are</u> and what the <u>difference</u> is between <u>covalent</u> and <u>ionic</u> bonding. It'll come in incredibly useful later on in your chemistry learnings. I promise.

Balancing Equations

Equations need a lot of practice if you're going to get them right — don't just skate over this stuff.

Atoms Aren't Lost or Made in Chemical Reactions

1) During chemical reactions, things don't appear out of nowhere and things don't just disappear.

2) You still have the same atoms at the end of a chemical reaction as you had at the start. They're just arranged in different ways.

3) Balanced symbol equations show the atoms at the start (the reactant atoms) and the atoms at the end (the product atoms) and how they're arranged. For example:

> Word equation: magnesium + oxygen → magnesium oxide
>
> Balanced symbol equation: $2Mg$ + O_2 → $2MgO$

4) Because atoms aren't gained or lost, the mass of the reactants equals the mass of the products. So, if you completely react 6 g of magnesium with 4 g of oxygen, you'd end up with 10 g of magnesium oxide.

Balancing the Equation — Match Them Up One by One

1) There must always be the same number of atoms of each element on both sides — they can't just disappear.

2) You balance the equation by putting numbers in front of the formulas where needed. Take this equation for reacting sulfuric acid (H_2SO_4) with sodium hydroxide (NaOH) to get sodium sulfate (Na_2SO_4) and water (H_2O):

$$H_2SO_4 \; + \; NaOH \; \rightarrow \; Na_2SO_4 + H_2O$$

The formulas are all correct but the numbers of some atoms don't match up on both sides. E.g. there are 3 Hs on the left, but only 2 on the right. You can't change formulas like H_2O to H_3O. You can only put numbers in front of them:

Method: Balance Just ONE Type of Atom at a Time

The more you practise, the quicker you get, but all you do is this:

> 1) Find an element that doesn't balance and pencil in a number to try and sort it out.
>
> 2) See where it gets you. It may create another imbalance — if so, just pencil in another number and see where that gets you.
>
> 3) Carry on chasing unbalanced elements and it'll sort itself out pretty quickly.

I'll show you. In the equation above you soon notice we're short of H atoms on the RHS (Right-Hand Side).

1) The only thing you can do about that is make it $2H_2O$ instead of just H_2O:

$$H_2SO_4 \; + \; NaOH \; \rightarrow \; Na_2SO_4 + 2H_2O$$

2) But that now causes too many H atoms and O atoms on the RHS, so to balance that up you could try putting 2NaOH on the LHS (Left-Hand Side):

$$H_2SO_4 \; + \; 2NaOH \; \rightarrow \; Na_2SO_4 + 2H_2O$$

3) And suddenly there it is! Everything balances. And you'll notice the Na just sorted itself out.

Balancing equations — weigh it up in your mind...

REMEMBER WHAT THOSE NUMBERS MEAN: A number in front of a formula applies to the entire formula. So, $3Na_2SO_4$ means three lots of Na_2SO_4. The little numbers in the middle or at the end of a formula only apply to the atom or brackets immediately before. So the 4 in Na_2SO_4 just means 4 Os, not 4 Ss.

Using Limestone

Limestone's often formed from sea shells, so you might not expect that it'd be useful as a building material...

Limestone *is Mainly* Calcium Carbonate

Limestone's quarried out of the ground — it's great for making into blocks for building with. Fine old buildings like cathedrals are often made purely from limestone blocks. It's pretty sturdy stuff, but don't go thinking it doesn't react with anything.

St Paul's Cathedral is made from limestone.

1) Limestone is mainly calcium carbonate — $CaCO_3$.

2) When it's heated it thermally decomposes to make calcium oxide and carbon dioxide.

> calcium carbonate → calcium oxide + carbon dioxide
> $$CaCO_{3(s)} \rightarrow CaO_{(s)} + CO_{2(g)}$$

Thermal decomposition is when one substance chemically changes into at least two new substances when it's heated.

- When magnesium, copper, zinc and sodium carbonates are heated, they decompose in the same way. E.g. magnesium carbonate → magnesium oxide + carbon dioxide (i.e. $MgCO_3 \rightarrow MgO + CO_2$)
- However, you might have difficulty doing some of these reactions in class — a Bunsen burner can't reach a high enough temperature to thermally decompose some carbonates of Group I metals.

3) Calcium carbonate also reacts with acid to make a calcium salt, carbon dioxide and water. E.g.:

> calcium carbonate + sulfuric acid → calcium sulfate + carbon dioxide + water
> $$CaCO_3 + H_2SO_4 \rightarrow CaSO_4 + CO_2 + H_2O$$

- The type of salt produced depends on the type of acid. For example, a reaction with hydrochloric acid would make a chloride (e.g. $CaCl_2$).

This reaction means that limestone is damaged by acid rain (see p.61).

- Other carbonates that react with acids are magnesium, copper, zinc and sodium.

Calcium Oxide **Reacts with** Water **to Produce** Calcium Hydroxide

1) When you add water to calcium oxide you get calcium hydroxide.

> calcium oxide + water ⟶ calcium hydroxide   or $CaO + H_2O \longrightarrow Ca(OH)_2$

2) Calcium hydroxide is an alkali which can be used to neutralise acidic soil in fields. Powdered limestone can be used for this too, but the advantage of calcium hydroxide is that it works much faster.

3) Calcium hydroxide can also be used in a test for carbon dioxide. If you make a solution of calcium hydroxide in water (called limewater) and bubble gas through it, the solution will turn cloudy if there's carbon dioxide in the gas. The cloudiness is caused by the formation of calcium carbonate.

> calcium hydroxide + carbon dioxide → calcium carbonate + water
> $$Ca(OH)_2 + CO_2 \rightarrow CaCO_3 + H_2O$$

Limestone *is Used to Make* Other Useful Things *Too*

1) Powdered limestone is heated in a kiln with powdered clay to make cement.

2) Cement can be mixed with sand and water to make mortar. Mortar is the stuff you stick bricks together with. You can also add calcium hydroxide to mortar.

3) Or you can mix cement with sand and aggregate (water and gravel) to make concrete.

Limestone — a sea creature's cementery...

Wow. It sounds like you can achieve pretty much anything with limestone, possibly apart from a bouncy castle. I wonder what we'd be using instead if all those sea creatures hadn't died and conveniently become rock?

Using Limestone

Using limestone ain't all hunky-dory — tearing it out of the ground and making stuff from it causes quite a few <u>problems</u>. You need to learn the problems... And to top it all off you've got to learn the <u>advantages</u> and <u>disadvantages</u> of using limestone, cement and concrete as building materials too. It's just not your day.

Quarrying Limestone Makes a Right Mess of the Landscape

Digging limestone out of the ground can cause environmental problems.

1) For a start, it makes <u>huge ugly holes</u> which permanently change the landscape.

2) <u>Quarrying</u> processes, like blasting rocks apart with explosives, make lots of <u>noise</u> and <u>dust</u> in quiet, scenic areas.

3) Quarrying <u>destroys the habitats</u> of animals and birds.

4) The limestone needs to be <u>transported away</u> from the quarry — usually in lorries. This causes more noise and pollution.

5) Waste materials produce unsightly <u>tips</u>.

Making Stuff from Limestone Causes Pollution Too

1) <u>Cement factories</u> make a lot of <u>dust</u>, which can cause <u>breathing problems</u> for some people.

2) <u>Energy</u> is needed to produce cement and quicklime. The energy is likely to come from burning <u>fossil fuels</u>, which causes pollution.

See page 61 for more on pollution caused by burning fossil fuels.

But on the Plus Side...

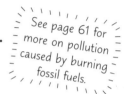

1) Limestone provides things that people want — like <u>houses</u> and <u>roads</u>. Chemicals used in making <u>dyes</u>, <u>paints</u> and <u>medicines</u> also come from limestone.

2) Limestone products are used to <u>neutralise acidic soil</u>. Acidity in lakes and rivers caused by <u>acid rain</u> is also <u>neutralised</u> by limestone products.

3) Limestone is also used in power station chimneys to <u>neutralise sulfur dioxide</u>, which is a cause of acid rain.

4) The quarry and associated businesses provide <u>jobs</u> for people and bring more money into the <u>local economy</u>. This can lead to <u>local improvements</u> in transport, roads, recreation facilities and health.

5) Once quarrying is complete, <u>landscaping</u> and <u>restoration</u> of the area is normally required as part of the planning permission.

Limestone Products Have Advantages and Disadvantages

Limestone and concrete (made from cement) are used as <u>building materials</u>. In some cases they're <u>perfect</u> for the job, but in other cases they're a bit of a compromise.

1) Limestone is <u>widely available</u> and is <u>cheaper</u> than granite or marble. It's also a fairly easy rock to <u>cut</u>.

2) Some limestone is more <u>hard-wearing</u> than marble, but it still looks <u>attractive</u>.

3) Concrete can be poured into <u>moulds</u> to make blocks or panels that can be joined together. It's a <u>very quick and cheap</u> way of constructing buildings — <u>and it shows</u>... — concrete has got to be the most <u>hideously unattractive</u> building material ever known.

4) Limestone, concrete and cement <u>don't rot</u> when they get wet like wood does. They can't be gnawed away by <u>insects</u> or <u>rodents</u> either. And to top it off, they're <u>fire-resistant</u> too.

5) Concrete <u>doesn't corrode</u> like lots of metals do. It does have a fairly <u>low tensile strength</u> though, and can crack. If it's <u>reinforced</u> with steel bars it'll be much stronger.

Tough revision here — this stuff's rock hard...

There's a <u>downside</u> to everything, including using limestone — ripping open huge quarries definitely <u>spoils the countryside</u>. But you have to find a <u>balance</u> between the environmental and ecological factors and the economic and social factors — is it worth keeping the countryside pristine if it means loads of people have nowhere to live because there's no stuff available to build houses with?

Getting Metals from Rocks

A few <u>unreactive metals</u> like <u>gold</u> are found in the Earth as the <u>metal itself</u>, rather than as a compound. The rest of the metals we get by extracting them from rocks — and I bet you're just itching to find out how...

Ores Contain Enough Metal to Make Extraction Worthwhile

1) A <u>metal ore</u> is a <u>rock</u> which contains <u>enough metal</u> to make it <u>worthwhile</u> extracting the metal from it.

2) In many cases the ore is an <u>oxide</u> of the metal. For example, the main <u>aluminium ore</u> is called <u>bauxite</u> — it's aluminium oxide (Al_2O_3).

3) <u>Most metals</u> need to be extracted from their ores using a <u>chemical reaction</u>.

4) The <u>economics</u> (profitability) of metal extraction can <u>change</u> over <u>time</u>. For example:

- If the market <u>price</u> of a metal <u>drops</u> a lot, it <u>might not</u> be worth extracting it. If the <u>price increases</u> a lot then it <u>might be worth</u> extracting <u>more</u> of it.
- As <u>technology improves</u>, it becomes possible to <u>extract more</u> metal from a sample of rock than was originally possible. So it might now be <u>worth</u> extracting metal that <u>wasn't</u> worth extracting <u>in the past</u>.

Metals Are Extracted From their Ores Chemically

1) A metal can be extracted from its ore <u>chemically</u> — by <u>reduction</u> (see below) or by <u>electrolysis</u> (splitting with electricity, see page 53).

2) Some ores may have to be <u>concentrated</u> before the metal is extracted — this just involves getting rid of the <u>unwanted rocky material</u>.

3) <u>Electrolysis</u> can also be used to <u>purify</u> the extracted metal (see page 53).

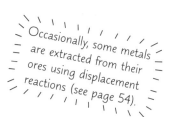

Occasionally, some metals are extracted from their ores using displacement reactions (see page 54).

Some Metals can be Extracted by Reduction with Carbon

1) A metal can be <u>extracted</u> from its ore chemically by <u>reduction</u> using <u>carbon</u>.

2) When an ore is reduced, <u>oxygen is removed</u> from it, e.g.

$2Fe_2O_3$	+	$3C$	$\rightarrow$	$4Fe$	+	$3CO_2$
iron(III) oxide	+	carbon	$\rightarrow$	iron	+	carbon dioxide

3) The position of the metal in the <u>reactivity series</u> determines whether it can be extracted by <u>reduction</u> with carbon.

a) Metals <u>higher than carbon</u> in the reactivity series have to be extracted using <u>electrolysis</u>, which is expensive.

b) Metals <u>below carbon</u> in the reactivity series can be extracted by <u>reduction</u> using <u>carbon</u>. For example, <u>iron oxide</u> is reduced in a <u>blast furnace</u> to make <u>iron</u>.

This is because carbon <u>can only take the oxygen</u> away from metals which are <u>less reactive</u> than carbon <u>itself</u> is.

Extracted using Electrolysis

Extracted by reduction using carbon

The Reactivity Series		
Potassium	K	more
Sodium	Na	reactive
Calcium	Ca	
Magnesium	Mg	
Aluminium	Al	
<u>CARBON</u>	<u>C</u>	
Zinc	Zn	
Iron	Fe	
Tin	Sn	less
Copper	Cu	reactive

Learn how metals are extracted — ore else...

Extracting metals isn't cheap. You have to pay for special equipment, energy and labour. Then there's the cost of getting the ore to the extraction plant. If there's a choice of extraction methods, a company always picks the <u>cheapest</u>, unless there's a good reason not to (e.g. to increase purity). They're <u>not</u> extracting it for fun.

Getting Metals from Rocks

You may think you know all you could ever want to know about how to get metals from rocks, but no — there's <u>more</u> of it. Think of each of the facts on this page as a little <u>gold nugget</u>. Or, er, a copper one.

Some Metals *have to be* Extracted *by* Electrolysis

1) Metals that are <u>more reactive</u> than carbon (see previous page) have to be extracted using electrolysis of <u>molten compounds</u>.

2) An example of a metal that has to be extracted this way is <u>aluminium</u>.

3) However, the process is <u>much more expensive</u> than reduction with carbon (see previous page) because it <u>uses a lot of energy</u>.

> <u>FOR EXAMPLE</u>: a <u>high temperature</u> is needed to <u>melt</u> aluminium oxide so that <u>aluminium</u> can be extracted — this requires a lot of <u>energy</u>, which makes it an <u>expensive</u> process.

Copper *is* Purified *by* Electrolysis

1) Copper can be easily extracted by <u>reduction with carbon</u> (see previous page). The ore is <u>heated</u> in a <u>furnace</u> — this is called <u>smelting</u>.

2) However, the copper produced this way is <u>impure</u> — and impure copper <u>doesn't</u> conduct electricity very well. This <u>isn't</u> very <u>useful</u> because a lot of copper is used to make <u>electrical wiring</u>.

3) So <u>electrolysis</u> is also used to <u>purify</u> it, even though it's quite <u>expensive</u>.

4) This produces <u>very pure</u> copper, which is a <u>much better conductor</u>.

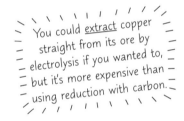

You could <u>extract</u> copper straight from its ore by electrolysis if you wanted to, but it's more expensive than using reduction with carbon.

Electrolysis Means "Splitting Up with Electricity"

1) <u>Electrolysis</u> is the <u>breaking down</u> of a substance using <u>electricity</u>.

2) It requires a <u>liquid</u> to <u>conduct</u> the <u>electricity</u>, called the <u>electrolyte</u>.

3) Electrolytes are often <u>metal salt solutions</u> made from the ore (e.g. copper sulfate) or <u>molten metal oxides</u>.

4) The electrolyte has <u>free ions</u> — these <u>conduct</u> the electricity and allow the whole thing to work.

5) Electrons are <u>taken away</u> by the <u>(positive) anode</u> and <u>given away</u> by the <u>(negative) cathode</u>. As ions gain or lose electrons they become atoms or molecules and are released.

> Here's how electrolysis is used to get <u>copper</u>:
> 1) <u>Electrons</u> are <u>pulled off</u> copper atoms at the <u>anode</u>, causing them to go into solution as <u>Cu^{2+} ions</u>.
> 2) <u>Cu^{2+} ions</u> near the <u>cathode</u> gain electrons and turn back into <u>copper atoms</u>.
> 3) The <u>impurities</u> are dropped at the <u>anode</u> as a <u>sludge</u>, whilst <u>pure copper atoms</u> bond to the <u>cathode</u>.

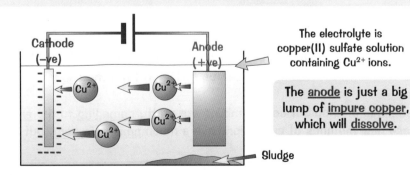

The cathode starts as a thin piece of pure copper and more pure copper adds to it.

The electrolyte is copper(II) sulfate solution containing Cu^{2+} ions.

The <u>anode</u> is just a big lump of <u>impure copper</u>, which will <u>dissolve</u>.

Someone robbed your metal? — call a copper...

The skin of the <u>Statue of Liberty</u> is made of copper — about 80 tonnes of it in fact. Its surface reacts with gases in the air to form <u>copper carbonate</u> — which is why it's that pretty shade of <u>green</u>.

Getting Metals from Rocks

Just to top it off, you need to know even more about copper extraction... sigh, it's a hard life.

You Can Extract Copper From a Solution Using a Displacement Reaction

1) More reactive metals react more vigorously than less reactive metals.

2) If you put a reactive metal into a solution of a dissolved metal compound, the reactive metal will replace the less reactive metal in the compound.

3) This is because the more reactive metal bonds more strongly to the non-metal bit of the compound and pushes out the less reactive metal.

4) For example, scrap iron can be used to displace copper from solution — this is really useful because iron is cheap but copper is expensive. If some iron is put in a solution of copper sulfate, the more reactive iron will "kick out" the less reactive copper from the solution. You end up with iron sulfate solution and copper metal.

> copper sulfate + iron → iron sulfate + copper

5) If a piece of silver metal is put into a solution of copper sulfate, nothing happens. The more reactive metal (copper) is already in the solution.

Copper-rich Ores are in Short Supply

1) The supply of copper-rich ores is limited, so it's important to recycle as much copper as possible.

2) The demand for copper is growing and this may lead to shortages in the future.

3) Scientists are looking into new ways of extracting copper from low-grade ores (ores that only contain small amounts of copper) or from the waste that is currently produced when copper is extracted.

4) Examples of new methods to extract copper are bioleaching and phytomining:

Bioleaching

This uses bacteria to separate copper from copper sulfide. The bacteria get energy from the bond between copper and sulfur, separating out the copper from the ore in the process. The leachate (the solution produced by the process) contains copper, which can be extracted, e.g. by filtering.

Phytomining

This involves growing plants in soil that contains copper. The plants can't use or get rid of the copper so it gradually builds up in the leaves. The plants can be harvested, dried and burned in a furnace. The copper can be collected from the ash left in the furnace.

5) Traditional methods of copper mining are pretty damaging to the environment (see next page). These new methods of extraction have a much smaller impact, but the disadvantage is that they're slow.

Personally, I'd rather be pound rich than copper rich...

Pure copper is expensive but exceptionally useful stuff. Just think where we'd be without good quality copper wire to conduct electricity (hmmm... how would I live without my electric pineapple corer). The fact that copper-rich ore supplies are dwindling means that scientists have to come up with ever-more-cunning methods to extract it. It also means that you have to learn all about it. Sorry about that.

Impacts of Extracting Metals

Metals are very useful. Just imagine if all knives and forks were made of plastic instead — there'd be prongs snapping all over the place at dinner time. However, metal extraction uses a lot of <u>energy</u> and is <u>bad</u> for the <u>environment</u>. And that's where recycling comes in handy.

Metal Extraction <u>can be</u> <u>Bad</u> <u>for the</u> <u>Environment</u>

1) People have to balance the <u>social</u>, <u>economic</u> and <u>environmental</u> effects of mining the ores.

2) Most of the issues are exactly the same as those to do with quarrying limestone on page 51.

So mining metal ores is <u>good</u> because it means that <u>useful</u> <u>products</u> can be made. It also provides local people with <u>jobs</u> and brings <u>money</u> into the area. This means services such as <u>transport</u> and <u>health</u> can be improved.

But mining ores is <u>bad for the environment</u> as it causes noise, scarring of the landscape and loss of habitats. Deep mine shafts can also be <u>dangerous</u> for a long time after the mine has been abandoned.

Recycling <u>Metals is</u> <u>Important</u>

1) Mining and extracting metals takes lots of <u>energy</u>, most of which comes from burning <u>fossil fuels</u>.

2) Fossil fuels are <u>running out</u> so it's important to <u>conserve</u> them. Not only this, but burning them contributes to <u>acid rain</u>, <u>global dimming</u> and <u>climate change</u> (see pages 61 and 62).

3) Recycling metals only uses a <u>small fraction</u> of the energy needed to mine and extract new metal. E.g. recycling copper only takes 15% of the energy that's needed to mine and extract new copper.

4) Energy doesn't come cheap, so recycling <u>saves money</u> too.

5) Also, there's a <u>finite amount</u> of each <u>metal</u> in the Earth. Recycling conserves these resources.

6) Recycling metal cuts down on the amount of rubbish that gets sent to <u>landfill</u>. Landfill takes up space and <u>pollutes</u> the surroundings. If all the aluminium cans in the UK were recycled, there'd be 14 million fewer dustbins to empty each year.

<u>Get back on your bike again — recycle...</u>

Recycling metals saves <u>natural resources</u> and <u>money</u> and reduces <u>environmental problems</u>. It's great. There's no limit to the number of times metals like aluminium, copper and steel can be recycled. So your humble little drink can may one day form part of a powerful robot who takes over the galaxy.

Chemistry 1a — Products from Rocks

Properties of Metals

Metals are all the <u>same</u> but slightly <u>different</u>. They have some <u>basic properties</u> in common, but each has its own <u>specific combination</u> of properties, which mean you use different ones for different purposes.

Metals are Strong and Bendy and They're Great Conductors

1) <u>Most of the elements</u> are <u>metals</u> — so they cover most of the periodic table.
   In fact, <u>only</u> the elements on the <u>far right</u> are <u>non-metals</u>.

2) All metals have some fairly similar <u>basic properties</u>:

   • Metals are <u>strong</u> (hard to break), but they can
     be <u>bent or hammered</u> into different shapes.

   • They're great at <u>conducting heat</u>.

   • They <u>conduct electricity well</u>.

The coloured elements are metals
Just look at 'em all
— there's loads of 'em!

Transition Metals

3) Metals (and especially <u>transition metals</u>, which are found in the
   <u>centre block</u> of the periodic table) have loads of <u>everyday</u> uses because of these properties...

   • Their strength and 'bendability' makes them handy for making into things like <u>bridges</u> and <u>car bodies</u>.

   • Metals are ideal if you want to make something that heat needs to travel through,
     like a <u>saucepan base</u>.

   • And their conductivity makes them great for making things like <u>electrical wires</u>.

A Metal's Exact Properties Decide How It's Best Used

1) The properties above are <u>typical properties</u> of metals.
   Not all metals are the same though — you need to learn the <u>specific</u> properties of these <u>three metals</u>:

   <u>Copper</u> is a <u>good conductor</u> of <u>electricity</u>, so it's ideal for drawing out into electrical wires.
   It's <u>hard</u> and <u>strong</u> but can be <u>bent</u>. It also <u>doesn't react with water</u>.

   <u>Aluminium</u> is <u>corrosion-resistant</u> and has a <u>low density</u>. Pure aluminium <u>isn't</u> particularly strong, but it forms hard, strong alloys (see page 57).

   <u>Titanium</u> is another <u>low density metal</u>.
   Unlike aluminium it's <u>very strong</u>.
   It is also <u>corrosion-resistant</u>.

2) <u>Different metals</u> are chosen for <u>different uses</u> because of their specific properties. For example:

   • If you were doing some <u>plumbing</u>, you'd pick a metal that could be <u>bent</u> to make pipes and tanks,
     and is below hydrogen in the reactivity series so it <u>doesn't react with water</u>. <u>Copper</u> is great for this.

   • If you wanted to make an <u>aeroplane</u>, you'd probably use metal as it's <u>strong</u> and can be
     <u>bent into shape</u>. But you'd also need it to be <u>light</u>, so <u>aluminium</u> would be a good choice.

   • And if you were making <u>replacement hips</u>, you'd pick a metal that <u>won't corrode</u> when it comes in
     contact with water. It'd also have to be <u>light</u> too, and not too bendy. <u>Titanium</u> has all of these
     properties so it's used for this.

Metals are Good — but Not Perfect

1) Metals are very useful <u>structural materials</u>, but some <u>corrode</u> when exposed to air and water, so they
   need to be <u>protected</u>, e.g. by painting. If metals corrode, they lose their strength and hardness.

2) Metals can get 'tired' when stresses and strains are repeatedly put on them over time. This is known
   as <u>metal fatigue</u> and leads to metals breaking, which can be very <u>dangerous</u>, e.g. in planes.

Metal fatigue? — yeah, I've had enough of this page too...

So, all metals <u>conduct electricity and heat</u> and can be <u>bent into shape</u>. But lots of them have <u>special properties</u>
too. You have to decide what properties you need and use the metal with those properties.

Alloys

Pure metals often aren't quite right for certain jobs. Scientists don't just make do, oh no my friend... they mix two metals together (or mix a metal with a non-metal) — creating an alloy with the properties they want.

Pure Iron Tends to be a Bit Too Bendy

1) 'Iron' straight from the blast furnace is only 96% iron. The other 4% is impurities such as carbon.

2) This impure iron is used as cast iron. It's handy for making ornamental railings, but it doesn't have many other uses because it's brittle.

3) So all the impurities are removed from most of the blast furnace iron. This pure iron has a regular arrangement of identical atoms. The layers of atoms can slide over each other, which makes the iron soft and easily shaped. This iron is far too bendy for most uses.

Most Iron is Converted into Steel — an Alloy

Most of the pure iron is changed into alloys called steels. Steels are formed by adding small amounts of carbon and sometimes other metals to the iron.

TYPE OF STEEL	PROPERTIES	USES
Low carbon steel (0.1% carbon)	easily shaped	car bodies
High carbon steel (1.5% carbon)	very hard, inflexible	blades for cutting tools, bridges
Stainless steel (chromium added, and sometimes nickel)	corrosion-resistant	cutlery, containers for corrosive substances

Alloys are Harder Than Pure Metals

1) Different elements have different sized atoms. So when an element such as carbon is added to pure iron, the smaller carbon atom will upset the layers of pure iron atoms, making it more difficult for them to slide over each other. So alloys are harder.

2) Many metals in use today are actually alloys. E.g.:

BRONZE = COPPER + TIN Bronze is harder than copper.
It's good for making medals and statues from.

CUPRONICKEL = COPPER + NICKEL This is hard and corrosion resistant.
It's used to make "silver" coins.

GOLD ALLOYS ARE USED TO MAKE JEWELLERY Pure gold is too soft. Metals such as zinc, copper, silver, palladium and nickel are used to harden the "gold".

ALUMINIUM ALLOYS ARE USED TO MAKE AIRCRAFT Aluminium has a low density, but it's alloyed with small amounts of other metals to make it stronger.

3) In the past, the development of alloys was by trial and error. But nowadays we understand much more about the properties of metals, so alloys can be designed for specific uses.

A brass band — harder than Iron Maiden...

The Eiffel Tower is made of iron — but the problem with iron is, it goes rusty if air and water get to it. So the Eiffel Tower has to be painted every seven years to make sure that it doesn't rust. This is quite a job and takes an entire year for a team of 25 painters. Too bad they didn't use stainless steel.

Fractional Distillation of Crude Oil

Crude oil is formed from the buried remains of plants and animals — it's a fossil fuel. Over millions of years, the remains turn to crude oil, which can be extracted by drilling and pumping.

Crude Oil is a Mixture of Hydrocarbons

1) A mixture consists of two (or more) elements or compounds that aren't chemically bonded to each other.

2) Crude oil is a mixture of many different compounds. Most of the compounds are hydrocarbon molecules.

3) Hydrocarbons are basically fuels such as petrol and diesel. They're made of just carbon and hydrogen.

4) There are no chemical bonds between the different parts of a mixture, so the different hydrocarbon molecules in crude oil aren't chemically bonded to one another.

5) This means that they all keep their original properties, such as their condensing points. The properties of a mixture are just a mixture of the properties of the separate parts.

6) The parts of a mixture can be separated out by physical methods, e.g. crude oil can be split up into its separate fractions by fractional distillation. Each fraction contains molecules with a similar number of carbon atoms to each other (see next page).

Crude Oil is Split into Separate Groups of Hydrocarbons

The fractionating column works continuously, with heated crude oil piped in at the bottom. The vaporised oil rises up the column and the various fractions are constantly tapped off at the different levels where they condense.

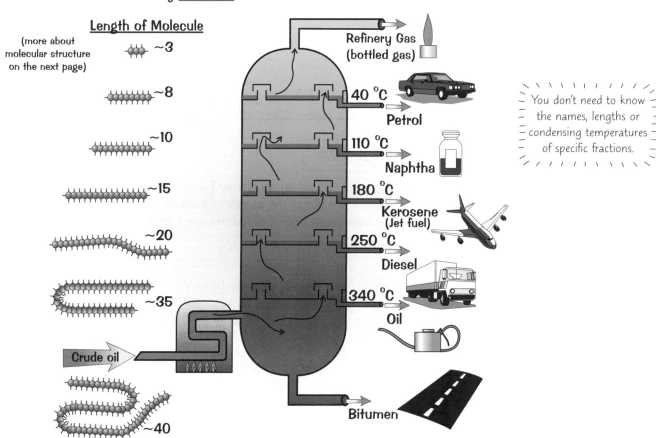

Crude oil — it's always cracking dirty jokes...

It's amazing what you get from buried dead stuff. But it has had a few hundred million years with high temperature and pressure to get into the useful state it's in now. So if we use it all, we're going to have to wait an awful long time for more to form. No one knows exactly when oil will run out, but some scientists reckon that it could be within this century. The thing is, technology is advancing all the time, so one day it's likely that we'll be able to extract oil that's too difficult and expensive to extract at the moment.

Properties and Uses of Crude Oil

The different fractions of crude oil have different properties, and it's all down to their structure. You need to know the basic structure and a few trends, so you can apply what you've learnt to exam questions.

Crude Oil is Mostly Alkanes

1) All the fractions of crude oil are hydrocarbons called alkanes.
2) Alkanes are made up of chains of carbon atoms surrounded by hydrogen atoms.
3) Different alkanes have chains of different lengths.
4) The first four alkanes are methane (natural gas), ethane, propane and butane.

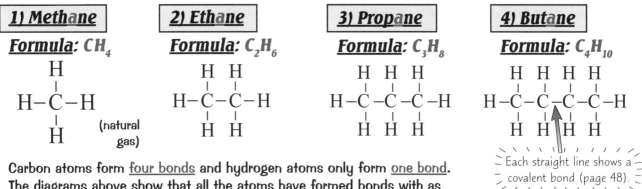

1) Methane
Formula: CH_4
(natural gas)

2) Ethane
Formula: C_2H_6

3) Propane
Formula: C_3H_8

4) Butane
Formula: C_4H_{10}

Each straight line shows a covalent bond (page 48).

5) Carbon atoms form four bonds and hydrogen atoms only form one bond. The diagrams above show that all the atoms have formed bonds with as many other atoms as they can — this means they're saturated.

6) Alkanes all have the general formula C_nH_{2n+2}. So if an alkane has 5 carbons, it's got to have $(2 \times 5) + 2 = 12$ hydrogens.

Alkanes $= C_nH_{2n+2}$

Learn the Basic Trends:

1) The shorter the molecules, the more runny the hydrocarbon is — that is, the less viscous (gloopy) it is.

2) The shorter the molecules, the more volatile they are. "More volatile" means they turn into a gas at a lower temperature. So, the shorter the molecules, the lower the temperature at which that fraction vaporises or condenses — and the lower its boiling point.

3) Also, the shorter the molecules, the more flammable (easier to ignite) the hydrocarbon is.

The Uses Of Hydrocarbons Depend on their Properties

1) The volatility helps decide what the fraction is used for. The refinery gas fraction has the shortest molecules, so it has the lowest boiling point — in fact it's a gas at room temperature. This makes it ideal for using as bottled gas. It's stored under pressure as liquid in 'bottles'. When the tap on the bottle is opened, the fuel vaporises and flows to the burner where it's ignited.

2) The petrol fraction has longer molecules, so it has a higher boiling point. Petrol is a liquid which is ideal for storing in the fuel tank of a car. It can flow to the engine where it's easily vaporised to mix with the air before it is ignited.

3) The viscosity also helps decide how the hydrocarbons are used. The really gloopy, viscous hydrocarbons are used for lubricating engine parts and for covering roads.

Alkane ya if you don't learn this...

So short-chain hydrocarbons are less viscous, more volatile and easier to ignite than longer-chain hydrocarbons. If you learn the properties of short-chain hydrocarbons, you should be able to work out the properties of longer-chain ones in the exam. These properties decide how they're used. In the real world there's more demand for stuff like petrol than there is for long gloopy hydrocarbons like bitumen — I guess there's only so many roads that need covering.

Using Crude Oil as a Fuel

Nothing as amazingly useful as crude oil would be without its problems. No, that'd be too good to be true.

Crude Oil Provides an Important Fuel for Modern Life

1) Crude oil fractions burn cleanly so they make good <u>fuels</u>. Most modern transport is fuelled by a crude oil fraction, e.g. cars, boats, trains and planes. Parts of crude oil are also burned in <u>central heating systems</u> in homes and in <u>power stations</u> to <u>generate electricity</u>.

2) There's a <u>massive industry</u> with scientists working to find oil reserves, take it out of the ground, and turn it into useful products. As well as fuels, crude oil also provides the raw materials for making various <u>chemicals</u>, including <u>plastics</u>.

3) Often, <u>alternatives</u> to using crude oil fractions as fuel are possible. E.g. electricity can be generated by <u>nuclear</u> power or <u>wind</u> power, there are <u>ethanol</u>-powered cars, and <u>solar</u> energy can be used to heat water.

4) But things tend to be <u>set up</u> for using oil fractions. For example, cars are designed for <u>petrol or diesel</u> and it's <u>readily available</u>. There are filling stations all over the country, with storage facilities and pumps specifically designed for these crude oil fractions. So crude oil fractions are often the <u>easiest and cheapest</u> thing to use.

5) Crude oil fractions are often <u>more reliable</u> too — e.g. solar and wind power won't work without the right weather conditions. Nuclear energy is reliable, but there are lots of concerns about its <u>safety</u> and the storage of radioactive waste.

But it Might Run Out One Day... Eeek

1) Most scientists think that oil will <u>run out</u> — it's a <u>non-renewable fuel</u>.

2) No one knows exactly when it'll run out but there have been heaps of <u>different predictions</u> — e.g. about 40 years ago, scientists predicted that it'd all be gone by the year 2000.

3) <u>New oil reserves</u> are discovered from time to time and <u>technology</u> is constantly improving, so it's now possible to extract oil that was once too <u>difficult</u> or <u>expensive</u> to extract.

4) In the <u>worst-case scenario</u>, oil may be pretty much gone in about 25 years — and that's not far off.

5) Some people think we should <u>immediately stop</u> using oil for things like transport, for which there are alternatives, and keep it for things that it's absolutely <u>essential</u> for, like some chemicals and medicines.

6) It will take time to <u>develop</u> alternative fuels that will satisfy all our energy needs (see page 62 for more info). It'll also take time to <u>adapt things</u> so that the fuels can be used on a wide scale. E.g. we might need different kinds of car engines, or special storage tanks built.

7) One alternative is to generate energy from <u>renewable</u> sources — these are sources that <u>won't run out</u>. Examples of renewable energy sources are <u>wind power</u>, <u>solar power</u> and <u>tidal power</u>.

8) So however long oil does last for, it's a good idea to start <u>conserving</u> it and finding <u>alternatives</u> now.

Crude Oil is NOT the Environment's Best Friend

1) <u>Oil spills</u> can happen as the oil is being transported by tanker — this spells <u>disaster</u> for the local environment. <u>Birds</u> get covered in the stuff and are <u>poisoned</u> as they try to clean themselves. Other creatures, like <u>sea otters</u> and <u>whales</u>, are poisoned too.

2) You have to <u>burn oil</u> to release the energy from it. But burning oil is thought to be a major cause of <u>global warming</u>, <u>acid rain</u> and <u>global dimming</u> — see pages 61 and 62.

If oil alternatives aren't developed, we might get caught short...

Crude oil is <u>really important</u> to our lives. Take <u>petrol</u> for instance — at the first whisper of a shortage, there's mayhem. Loads of people dash to the petrol station and start filling up their tanks. This causes a queue, which starts everyone else panicking. I don't know what they'll do when it runs out totally.

Environmental Problems

We burn fuels all the time to release the energy stored inside them — e.g. 90% of crude oil is used as fuel.

Burning Fossil Fuels Releases Gases and Particles

1) Power stations burn huge amounts of fossil fuels to make electricity. Cars are also a major culprit in burning fossil fuels.

Pure hydrogen can also be used as a fuel (see next page). It only produces water vapour when burnt.

2) Most fuels, such as crude oil and coal, contain carbon and hydrogen. During combustion, the carbon and hydrogen are oxidised so that carbon dioxide and water vapour are released into the atmosphere. Energy (heat) is also produced.
   E.g.:

   > hydrocarbon + oxygen → carbon dioxide + water vapour

3) If the fuel contains sulfur impurities, the sulfur will be released as sulfur dioxide when the fuel is burnt.

4) Oxides of nitrogen will also form if the fuel burns at a high temperature.

5) When there's plenty of oxygen, all the fuel burns — this is called complete combustion.

6) If there's not enough oxygen, some of the fuel doesn't burn — this is called partial combustion. Under these conditions, solid particles (called particulates) of soot (carbon) and unburnt fuel are released. Carbon monoxide (a poisonous gas) is also released.

Sulfur Dioxide Causes Acid Rain

1) Sulfur dioxide is one of the gases that causes acid rain.

2) When the sulfur dioxide mixes with clouds it forms dilute sulfuric acid. This then falls as acid rain.

3) In the same way, oxides of nitrogen cause acid rain by forming dilute nitric acid in clouds.

4) Acid rain causes lakes to become acidic and many plants and animals die as a result.

5) Acid rain kills trees and damages limestone buildings and ruins stone statues. It's shocking.

6) Links between acid rain and human health problems have been suggested.

7) The benefits of electricity and travel have to be balanced against the environmental impacts. Governments have recognised the importance of this and international agreements have been put in place to reduce emissions of air pollutants such as sulfur dioxide.

You can Reduce Acid Rain by Reducing Sulfur Emissions

1) Most of the sulfur can be removed from fuels before they're burnt, but it costs more to do it.

2) Also, removing sulfur from fuels takes more energy. This usually comes from burning more fuel, which releases more of the greenhouse gas carbon dioxide.

3) However, petrol and diesel are starting to be replaced by low-sulfur versions.

4) Power stations now have Acid Gas Scrubbers to take the harmful gases out before they release their fumes into the atmosphere.

5) The other way of reducing acid rain is simply to reduce our usage of fossil fuels.

Eee, problems, problems — there's always summat goin' wrong...

Pollutants like sulfur dioxide can be carried a long way in the atmosphere. So a country might suffer from acid rain that it didn't cause, which doesn't seem very fair. It's not just up to big industries though — there's lots of things you can do to reduce the amount of fossil fuels burnt. Putting an extra jumper on instead of turning up the heating helps. As does walking places instead of cadging a lift.

More Environmental Problems

More doom and gloom on this page I'm afraid... You've got to know it all though.

Increasing Carbon Dioxide Causes Climate Change

1) The level of carbon dioxide in the atmosphere is increasing — because of the large amounts of fossil fuels humans burn.

2) There's a scientific consensus that this extra carbon dioxide has caused the average temperature of the Earth to increase — global warming.

3) Global warming is a type of climate change and causes other types of climate change, e.g. changing rainfall patterns. It could also cause severe flooding due to the polar ice caps melting.

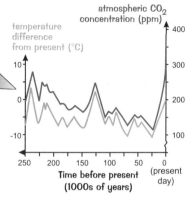

Particles Cause Global Dimming

1) In the last few years, some scientists have been measuring how much sunlight is reaching the surface of the Earth and comparing it to records from the last 50 years.

2) They have been amazed to find that in some areas nearly 25% less sunlight has been reaching the surface compared to 50 years ago. They have called this global dimming.

3) They think that it is caused by particles of soot and ash that are produced when fossil fuels are burnt. These particles reflect sunlight back into space, or they can help to produce more clouds that reflect the sunlight back into space.

4) There are many scientists who don't believe the change is real and blame it on inaccurate recording equipment.

Alternative Fuels are Being Developed

Some alternative fuels have already been developed, and there are others in the pipeline (so to speak). Many of them are renewable fuels so, unlike fossil fuels, they won't run out. However, none of them are perfect — they all have pros and cons. For example:

> ETHANOL can be produced from plant material so is known as a biofuel. It's made by fermentation of plants and is used to power cars in some places. It's often mixed with petrol to make a better fuel.
>
> PROS: The CO_2 released when it's burnt was taken in by the plant as it grew, so it's 'carbon neutral'. The only other product is water.
>
> CONS: Engines need to be converted before they'll work with ethanol fuels. And ethanol fuel isn't widely available. There are worries that as demand for it increases farmers will switch from growing food crops to growing crops to make ethanol — this will increase food prices.

> BIODIESEL is another type of biofuel. It can be produced from vegetable oils such as rapeseed oil and soybean oil. Biodiesel can be mixed with ordinary diesel fuel and used to run a diesel engine.
>
> PROS: Biodiesel is 'carbon neutral'. Engines don't need to be converted. It produces much less sulfur dioxide and 'particulates' than ordinary diesel or petrol.
>
> CONS: We can't make enough to completely replace diesel. It's expensive to make. It could increase food prices like using more ethanol could (see above).

> HYDROGEN GAS can also be used to power vehicles. You get the hydrogen from the electrolysis of water — there's plenty of water about but it takes electrical energy to split it up. This energy can come from a renewable source, e.g. solar.
>
> PROS: Hydrogen combines with oxygen in the air to form just water — so it's very clean.
>
> CONS: You need a special, expensive engine and hydrogen isn't widely available. You still need to use energy from another source to make it. Also, hydrogen's hard to store.

Global dimming — romantic lighting all day...

Alternative fuels are the shining light at the end of a long tunnel of problems caused by burning fuels (and I mean long). But nothing's perfect (except my quiff... and maybe my golf swing), so get learnin' those disadvantages.

Revision Summary for Chemistry 1a

There wasn't anything too ghastly in this section, and a few bits were even quite interesting I reckon. But you've got to make sure the facts are all firmly embedded in your brain and that you really understand the issues. These questions will let you see what you know and what you don't. If you get stuck on any, you need to look at that stuff again. Keep going till you can do them all without coming up for air.

1) Sketch an atom. Label the nucleus and the electrons.
2) What are the symbols for: a) calcium, b) carbon, c) sodium?
3)* Which element's properties are more similar to magnesium's: calcium or iron?
4) Describe how you would work out the electronic structure of an atom given its atomic number.
5) Describe the process of ionic bonding.
6) What is covalent bonding?
7)* Say which of the diagrams on the right show:
   a) an element   and   b) a compound
   Suggest what elements or compounds could be in each.
8)* Balance these equations:
   a) $CaCO_3 + HCl \rightarrow CaCl_2 + H_2O + CO_2$ b) $Ca + H_2O \rightarrow Ca(OH)_2 + H_2$

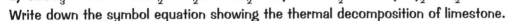

9) Write down the symbol equation showing the thermal decomposition of limestone.
10) What products are produced when limestone reacts with an acid?
11) What is calcium hydroxide used for?
12) Name three building materials made from limestone.
13) Plans to develop a limestone quarry and a cement factory on some hills next to your town are announced. Describe the views that the following might have:
   a) dog owners   b) a mother of young children
   c) the owner of a cafe   d) a beetle
14) What's the definition of an ore?
15) Explain why zinc can be extracted by reduction with carbon but magnesium can't.
16) Give a reason why aluminium is an expensive metal.
17) What is electrolysis?
18) Describe the process of purifying copper by electrolysis.
19) Describe how scrap iron is used to displace copper from solution.
20) What is the name of the method where plants are used to extract metals from soil?
21) Give three reasons why it's good to recycle metal.
22) Give three properties of metals.
23) Briefly describe two problems with metals.
24) What is the problem with using a) iron straight from the blast furnace, b) very pure iron?
25) Give two examples of alloys and say what's in them.
26) What does crude oil consist of? What does fractional distillation do to crude oil?
27) What's the general formula for an alkane?
28) Is a short-chain hydrocarbon more viscous than a long-chain hydrocarbon? Is it more volatile?
29)* You're going on holiday to a very cold place. The temperature will be about –10 °C. Which of the fuels shown on the right do you think will work best in your camping stove? Explain your answer.

Fuel	Boiling point (°C)
Propane	–42
Butane	–0.4
Pentane	36.2

30) Name three pollutants released into the atmosphere when fuels are burned. What environmental problems are associated with each?
31) List three ways of reducing acid rain.
32) Has the theory of global dimming been proven?
33) List three alternative ways of powering cars. What are the pros and cons of each?

* Answers on page 108.

Cracking Crude Oil

After the distillation of crude oil (see page 58), you've still got both short and long hydrocarbons, just not all mixed together. But there's <u>more demand</u> for some products, like <u>petrol</u>, than for others.

Cracking *Means Splitting Up* Long–chain Hydrocarbons...

1) <u>Long-chain hydrocarbons</u> form <u>thick gloopy liquids</u> like <u>tar</u> which aren't all that useful, so...

2) ... a lot of the longer molecules produced from <u>fractional distillation</u> are <u>turned into smaller ones</u> by a process called <u>cracking</u>.

3) Some of the products of cracking are useful as fuels, e.g. petrol for cars and paraffin for jet fuel.

4) Cracking also produces substances like <u>ethene</u>, which are needed for <u>making plastics</u> (see page 66).

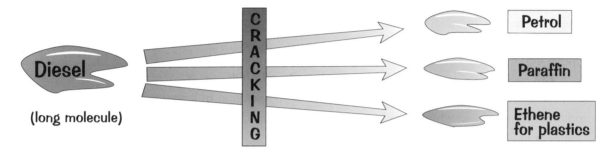

...*by Passing* Vapour *Over a Hot* Catalyst

1) <u>Cracking</u> is a <u>thermal decomposition</u> reaction — <u>breaking molecules down</u> by <u>heating</u> them.

2) The first step is to <u>heat</u> the long-chain hydrocarbon to <u>vaporise</u> it (turn it into a gas).

3) Then the <u>vapour</u> is passed over a <u>powdered catalyst</u> at a temperature of about <u>400 °C – 700 °C</u>.

4) <u>Aluminium oxide</u> is the catalyst used.

5) The <u>long-chain</u> molecules <u>split apart</u> or "crack" on the <u>surface</u> of the specks of catalyst.

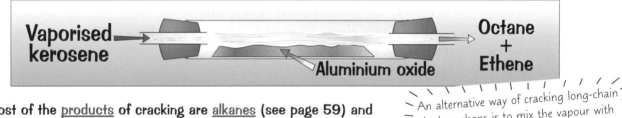

6) Most of the <u>products</u> of cracking are <u>alkanes</u> (see page 59) and unsaturated hydrocarbons called <u>alkenes</u> (see page 65)...

An alternative way of cracking long-chain hydrocarbons is to mix the vapour with steam at a very high temperature.

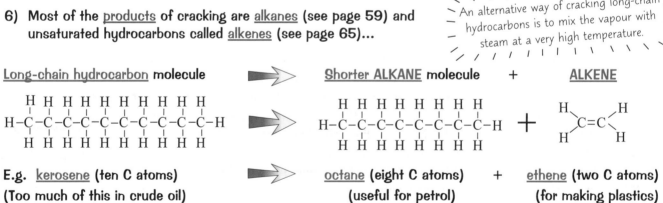

Long-chain hydrocarbon molecule	Shorter ALKANE molecule + ALKENE
E.g. <u>kerosene</u> (ten C atoms) (Too much of this in crude oil)	<u>octane</u> (eight C atoms) + <u>ethene</u> (two C atoms) (useful for petrol) (for making plastics)

Get cracking — there's a lot to learn...

Crude oil is <u>useful stuff</u>, there's no doubt about it. But using it is not without its problems (see page 60 for more about fuels). For example, oil is shipped around the planet, which can lead to <u>slicks</u> if there's an accident. Also, burning oil is thought to cause <u>climate change</u>, <u>acid rain</u> and <u>global dimming</u>. Oil is going to start <u>running out</u> one day, which will lead to big difficulties.

Alkenes and Ethanol

Alkenes are very useful. You can use them to make all sorts of stuff.

Alkenes Have a C=C Double Bond

1) Alkenes are hydrocarbons which have a double bond between two of the carbon atoms in their chain.

2) They are known as unsaturated because they can make more bonds — the double bond can open up, allowing the two carbon atoms to bond with other atoms.

3) The first two alkenes are ethene (with two carbon atoms) and propene (three Cs).

4) All alkenes have the general formula: C_nH_{2n} — they have twice as many hydrogens as carbons.

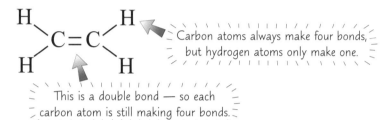

| 1) Ethene |
Formula: C_2H_4

Carbon atoms always make four bonds, but hydrogen atoms only make one.

This is a double bond — so each carbon atom is still making four bonds.

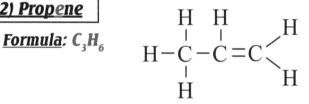

| 2) Propene |
Formula: C_3H_6

bromine water + alkene — decolourised

5) You can test for an alkene by adding the substance to bromine water. An alkene will decolourise the bromine water, turning it from orange to colourless. This is because the double bond has opened up and formed bonds with the bromine.

Ethene Can Be Reacted with Steam to Produce Ethanol

1) Ethene (C_2H_4) can be hydrated with steam (H_2O) in the presence of a catalyst to make ethanol.

2) At the moment this is a cheap process, because ethene's fairly cheap and not much of it is wasted.

3) The trouble is that ethene's produced from crude oil, which is a non-renewable resource that could start running out fairly soon. This means using ethene to make ethanol will become very expensive.

Ethanol Can Also Be Produced from Renewable Resources

The alcohol in beer and wine, etc. isn't made from ethene — it's made by fermentation.

1) The raw material for fermentation is sugar. This is converted into ethanol using yeast.
   The word equation for this is: sugar → carbon dioxide + ethanol

2) This process needs a lower temperature and simpler equipment than when using ethene.

3) Another advantage is that the raw material is a renewable resource. Sugar is grown as a major crop in several parts of the world, including many poorer countries.

4) The ethanol produced this way can also be used as quite a cheap fuel in countries which don't have oil reserves for making petrol.

5) There are disadvantages though. The ethanol you get from this process isn't very concentrated, so if you want to increase its strength you have to distil it (as in whisky distilleries). It also needs to be purified.

Make ethanol — not war...

Don't get alkenes confused with alkanes — that one letter makes all the difference. Alkenes have a C=C bond, alkanes don't. The first parts of their names are the same though — "eth-" means "two C atoms", "prop-" means "three C atoms". And remember — alkenes decolourise bromine water and alkanes don't.

Using Alkenes to Make Polymers

Before we knew how to make <u>polymers</u>, there were no <u>polythene bags</u>. Everyone used string bags for their shopping. Now we have plastic bags that hurt your hands and split halfway home.

Alkenes Can Be Used to Make Polymers

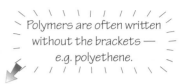
Polymers are often written without the brackets — e.g. polyethene.

1) Probably the most useful thing you can do with alkenes is <u>polymerisation</u>. This means joining together lots of <u>small alkene molecules</u> (<u>monomers</u>) to form <u>very large molecules</u> — these long-chain molecules are called <u>polymers</u>.

2) For instance, many <u>ethene</u> molecules can be joined up to produce <u>poly(ethene)</u> or "polythene".

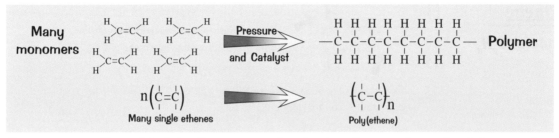

3) In the same way, if you join lots of <u>propene</u> molecules together, you've got <u>poly(propene)</u>.

Different Polymers Have Different Physical Properties...

1) The physical properties of a polymer depend on <u>what it's made from</u>. Polyamides are usually stronger than poly(ethene), for example.

2) A polymer's <u>physical properties</u> are also affected by the <u>temperature and pressure</u> of polymerisation. Poly(ethene) made at <u>200 °C</u> and <u>2000 atmospheres pressure</u> is <u>flexible</u>, and has <u>low density</u>. But poly(ethene) made at <u>60 °C</u> and a <u>few atmospheres pressure</u> with a <u>catalyst</u> is <u>rigid</u> and <u>dense</u>.

...Which Make Them Suitable for Various Different Uses

1) <u>Light, stretchable</u> polymers such as low density poly(ethene) are used to make plastic bags. <u>Elastic</u> polymer fibres are used to make super-stretchy <u>LYCRA® fibre</u> for tights.

2) <u>New uses</u> are developed all the time. <u>Waterproof</u> coatings for fabrics are made of polymers. <u>Dental polymers</u> are used in resin <u>tooth fillings</u>. Polymer <u>hydrogel wound dressings</u> keep wounds moist.

3) <u>New biodegradable packaging</u> materials made from polymers and <u>cornstarch</u> are being produced.

4) <u>Memory foam</u> is an example of a <u>smart material</u>. It's a polymer that gets <u>softer</u> as it gets <u>warmer</u>. Mattresses can be made of memory foam — they mould to your body shape when you lie on them.

Polymers Are Cheap, but Most Don't Rot — They're Hard to Get Rid Of

1) Most polymers aren't "<u>biodegradable</u>" — they're not broken down by microorganisms, so they <u>don't rot</u>.

2) It's difficult to get rid of them — if you bury them in a landfill site, they'll <u>still</u> be there <u>years later</u>. The best thing is to <u>re-use</u> them as many times as possible and then <u>recycle</u> them if you can.

3) Things made from polymers are usually <u>cheaper</u> than things made from metal. However, as <u>crude oil resources</u> get <u>used up</u>, the <u>price</u> of crude oil will rise. Crude oil products like polymers will get dearer.

4) It may be that one day there won't be <u>enough</u> oil for fuel AND plastics AND all the other uses. Choosing how to use the oil that's left means weighing up advantages and disadvantages on all sides.

Revision's like a polymer — you join lots of little facts up...

Polymers are <u>all over the place</u> — and I don't just mean all those plastic bags stuck in trees. There are <u>naturally occurring</u> polymers, like rubber and silk. That's quite a few clothing options, even without synthetic polymers like polyester and PVC. You've even got polymers <u>on the inside</u> — DNA's a polymer.

Plant Oils

If you squeeze a walnut really hard, out will ooze some walnut oil, which you could use to make walnut mayonnaise. Much better to just buy some oil from the shop though.

We Can Extract Oils from Plants

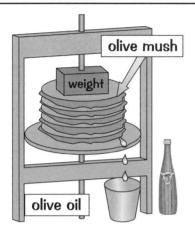

olive mush

weight

olive oil

1) Some fruits and seeds contain a lot of oil. For example, avocados and olives are oily fruits. Brazil nuts, peanuts and sesame seeds are oily seeds (a nut is just a big seed really).

2) These oils can be extracted and used for food or for fuel.

3) To get the oil out, the plant material is crushed. The next step is to press the crushed plant material between metal plates and squash the oil out. This is the traditional method of producing olive oil.

4) Oil can be separated from crushed plant material by a centrifuge — rather like using a spin-dryer to get water out of wet clothes.

5) Or solvents can be used to get oil from plant material.

6) Distillation refines oil, and removes water, solvents and impurities.

Vegetable Oils Are Used in Food

1) Vegetable oils provide a lot of energy — they have a very high energy content.

2) There are other nutrients in vegetable oils. For example, oils from seeds contain vitamin E.

3) Vegetable oils contain essential fatty acids, which the body needs for many metabolic processes.

Vegetable Oils Have Benefits for Cooking

1) Vegetable oils have higher boiling points than water. This means they can be used to cook foods at higher temperatures and at faster speeds.

2) Cooking with vegetable oil gives food a different flavour. This is because of the oil's own flavour, but it's also down to the fact that many flavours come from chemicals that are soluble in oil. This means the oil 'carries' the flavour, making it seem more intense.

3) Using oil to cook food increases the energy we get from eating it.

Vegetable Oils Can Be Used to Produce Fuels

1) Vegetable oils such as rapeseed oil and soybean oil can be processed and turned into fuels.

2) Because vegetable oils provide a lot of energy they're really suitable for use as fuels.

3) A particularly useful fuel made from vegetable oils is called biodiesel. Biodiesel has similar properties to ordinary diesel fuel — it burns in the same way, so you can use it to fuel a diesel engine.

See page 62 for more about biodiesel.

That lippie fried a few sausages back in her heyday...

Plant oils have loads of different uses, from frying bacon to fuelling cars. Even waste oil, left over from manufacturing and cooking in fast food restaurants, ends up being used in pet food and cosmetics. Grim.

Plant Oils

Oils are usually quite runny at room temperature. That's fine for salad dressing, say, but not so good for spreading in your sandwiches. For that, you could hydrogenate the oil to make margarine...

Unsaturated Oils Contain C=C Double Bonds

bromine water + unsaturated oil — decolourised

1) Oils and fats contain long-chain molecules with lots of carbon atoms.

2) Oils and fats are either saturated or unsaturated.

3) Unsaturated oils contain double bonds between some of the carbon atoms in their carbon chains.

4) So, an unsaturated oil will decolourise bromine water (as the bromine opens up the double bond and joins on).

5) Monounsaturated fats contain one C=C double bond somewhere in their carbon chains. Polyunsaturated fats contain more than one C=C double bond.

Unsaturated Oils Can Be Hydrogenated

1) Unsaturated vegetable oils are liquid at room temperature.

2) They can be hardened by reacting them with hydrogen in the presence of a nickel catalyst at about 60 °C. This is called hydrogenation. The hydrogen reacts with the double-bonded carbons and opens out the double bonds.

3) Hydrogenated oils have higher melting points than unsaturated oils, so they're more solid at room temperature. This makes them useful as spreads and for baking cakes and pastries.

4) Margarine is usually made from partially hydrogenated vegetable oil — turning all the double bonds in vegetable oil to single bonds would make margarine too hard and difficult to spread. Hydrogenating most of them gives margarine a nice, buttery, spreadable consistency.

5) Partially hydrogenated vegetable oils are often used instead of butter in processed foods, e.g. biscuits. These oils are a lot cheaper than butter and they keep longer. This makes biscuits cheaper and gives them a long shelf life.

6) But partially hydrogenating vegetable oils means you end up with a lot of so-called trans fats. And there's evidence to suggest that trans fats are very bad for you.

Vegetable Oils in Foods Can Affect Health

1) Vegetable oils tend to be unsaturated, while animal fats tend to be saturated.

2) In general, saturated fats are less healthy than unsaturated fats (as saturated fats increase the amount of cholesterol in the blood, which can block up the arteries and increase the risk of heart disease).

3) Natural unsaturated fats such as olive oil and sunflower oil reduce the amount of blood cholesterol. But because of the trans fats, partially hydrogenated vegetable oil increases the amount of cholesterol in the blood. So eating a lot of foods made with partially hydrogenated vegetable oils can actually increase the risk of heart disease.

4) Cooking food in oil, whether saturated, unsaturated or partially hydrogenated, makes it more fattening.

Double bonds — licensed to saturate...

This is tricky stuff. In a nutshell... there are saturated and unsaturated fats, which are generally bad and good for you (in that order) — easy enough. But... partially hydrogenated vegetable oil (which is unsaturated) is bad for you. Too much of the wrong types of fats can lead to heart disease. Got that...

Chemistry 1b — Oils, Earth and Atmosphere

Emulsions

Emulsions are all over the place in foods, cosmetics and paint. And in exams...

Emulsions Can Be Made from Oil and Water

1) Oils don't dissolve in water. So far so good...

2) However, you can mix an oil with water to make an emulsion. Emulsions are made up of lots of droplets of one liquid suspended in another liquid. You can have an oil-in-water emulsion (oil droplets suspended in water) or a water-in-oil emulsion (water droplets suspended in oil).

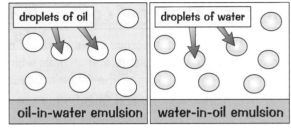

3) Emulsions are thicker than either oil or water. E.g. mayonnaise is an emulsion of sunflower oil (or olive oil) and vinegar — it's thicker than either.

4) The physical properties of emulsions make them suited to lots of uses in food — e.g. as salad dressings and in sauces. For instance, a salad dressing made by shaking olive oil and vinegar together forms an emulsion that coats salad better than plain oil or plain vinegar.

5) Generally, the more oil you've got in an oil-in-water emulsion, the thicker it is. Milk is an oil-in-water emulsion with not much oil and a lot of water — there's about 3% oil in full-fat milk. Single cream has a bit more oil — about 18%. Double cream has lots of oil — nearly 50%.

6) Whipped cream and ice cream are oil-in-water emulsions with an extra ingredient — air. Air is whipped into cream to give it a fluffy, frothy consistency for use as a topping. Whipping air into ice cream gives it a softer texture, which makes it easier to scoop out of the tub.

7) Emulsions also have non-food uses. Most moisturising lotions are oil-in-water emulsions. The smooth texture of an emulsion makes it easy to rub into the skin.

Some Foods Contain Emulsifiers to Help Oil and Water Mix

Oil and water mixtures naturally separate out. But here's where emulsifiers come in...

1) Emulsifiers are molecules with one part that's attracted to water and another part that's attracted to oil or fat. The bit that's attracted to water is called hydrophilic, and the bit that's attracted to oil is called hydrophobic.

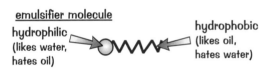

2) The hydrophilic end of each emulsifier molecule latches onto water molecules.

3) The hydrophobic end of each emulsifier molecule cosies up to oil molecules.

4) When you shake oil and water together with a bit of emulsifier, the oil forms droplets, surrounded by a coating of emulsifier... with the hydrophilic bit facing outwards. Other oil droplets are repelled by the hydrophilic bit of the emulsifier, while water molecules latch on. So the emulsion won't separate out. Clever.

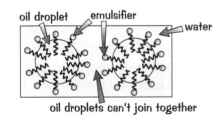

Using Emulsifiers Has Pros and Cons

1) Emulsifiers stop emulsions from separating out and this gives them a longer shelf-life.

2) Emulsifiers allow food companies to produce food that's lower in fat but that still has a good texture.

3) The down side is that some people are allergic to certain emulsifiers. For example, egg yolk is often used as an emulsifier — so people who are allergic to eggs need to check the ingredients very carefully.

Emulsion paint — spread mayonnaise all over the walls...

Before fancy stuff from abroad like olive oil, we fried our bacon and eggs in lard. Mmmm. Lard wouldn't be so good for making salad cream though. Emulsions like salad cream have to be made from shaking up two liquids — tiny droplets of one liquid are 'suspended' (NOT dissolved) in the other liquid.

Plate Tectonics

The Earth's surface is very <u>crinkly</u> — lots of mountains and valleys. Scientists used to think that these 'wrinkles' were caused by the shrinkage of the surface as it cooled down after the Earth was formed. This theory has now been replaced by one that <u>fits the facts</u> better, but most people took a lot of persuading...

Wegener's Theory of *Continental Drift...*

1) <u>Alfred Wegener</u> came across some work listing the fossils of <u>very similar</u> plants and animals which had been found on <u>opposite sides</u> of the Atlantic Ocean.

2) He investigated further, and found other cases of very similar fossils on opposite sides of oceans.

3) Other people had probably noticed this too. The accepted explanation was that there had once been <u>land bridges</u> linking the continents — so animals had been able to cross. The bridges had 'sunk' or been covered over since then.

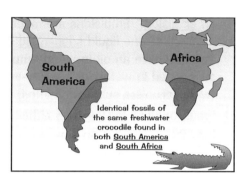

Identical fossils of the same freshwater crocodile found in both <u>South America</u> and <u>South Africa</u>

4) But Wegener had also noticed that the coastlines of Africa and South America seemed to 'match' like the pieces of a <u>jigsaw</u>. He wondered if these two continents had previously been one continent which then split. He started to look for more evidence, and found it...

5) There were <u>matching layers</u> in the rocks in different continents.

6) Fossils had been found in the 'wrong' places — e.g. fossils of tropical plants had been discovered on Arctic islands, where the present climate would clearly have killed them off.

7) In 1915, Wegener felt he had enough evidence. He published his theory of "<u>continental drift</u>".

8) Wegener said that about 300 million years ago, there had been just one '<u>supercontinent</u>'. This landmass, Pangaea, broke into smaller chunks which moved apart. He claimed that these chunks — our modern-day <u>continents</u> — were still slowly 'drifting' apart.

...Wasn't Accepted for *Many Years*

The reaction from other scientists was mostly very <u>hostile</u>. The main problem was that Wegener's explanation of <u>how</u> the '<u>drifting</u>' happened wasn't very convincing.

1) Wegener thought that the continents were 'ploughing through' the sea bed, and that their movement was caused by tidal forces and the earth's rotation.

2) Other geologists said this was <u>impossible</u>. One scientist calculated that the forces needed to move the continents like this would also have stopped the Earth rotating. (Which it hadn't.)

3) Wegener had used <u>inaccurate data</u> in his calculations, so he'd made some rather <u>wild predictions</u> about how fast the continents ought to be moving apart.

4) A few scientists supported Wegener, but most of them didn't see any reason to believe such a strange theory. It probably didn't help that he wasn't a 'proper' geologist — he'd studied astronomy.

5) Then in the 1950s, scientists were able to investigate the <u>ocean floor</u> and found <u>new evidence</u> to support Wegener's theory. He wasn't right about everything, but his <u>main idea</u> was <u>correct</u>.

6) By the 1960s, geologists were <u>convinced</u>. We now think the Earth's crust is made of several chunks called <u>tectonic plates</u> which move about, and that colliding chunks push the land up to create mountains.

I told you so — but no one ever believes me...

Sadly, Wegener died before his theory was accepted (when hundreds of geologists had to rewrite their textbooks). His story is a classic example of how science progresses — someone puts forward an idea, everyone else points out why it's nonsense, and eventually the really <u>good</u> ideas are accepted.

The Earth's Structure

No one accepted the theory of plate tectonics for ages. Almost everyone does now. How times change.

The Earth Has a Crust, Mantle, Outer and Inner Core

The Earth is almost spherical and it has a layered
structure, a bit like a scotch egg. Or a peach.

1) The bit we live on, the crust, is very thin (it varies between
    5 km and 50 km) and is surrounded by the atmosphere.

2) Below that is the mantle. The mantle has all the properties
    of a solid, except that it can flow very slowly.

3) Within the mantle, radioactive decay takes place.
    This produces a lot of heat, which causes
    the mantle to flow in convection currents.

4) At the centre of the Earth is the core, which we think is
    made of iron and nickel.

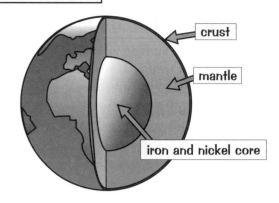

The Earth's Surface is Made Up of Tectonic Plates

1) The crust and the upper part of the mantle are cracked into a number of large pieces
    called tectonic plates. These plates are a bit like big rafts that 'float' on the mantle.

2) The plates don't stay in one place though. That's because the
    convection currents in the mantle cause the plates to drift.

3) The map shows the edges of the plates as
    they are now, and the directions
    they're moving in (red arrows).

4) Most of the plates are moving at
    speeds of a few cm per year
    relative to each other.

5) Occasionally, the plates
    move very suddenly,
    causing an earthquake.

6) Volcanoes and earthquakes
    often occur at the boundaries
    between two tectonic plates.

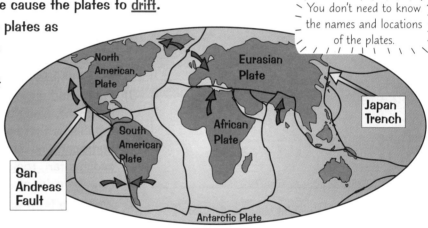

Scientists Can't Predict Earthquakes and Volcanic Eruptions

1) Tectonic plates can stay more or less put for a while and then suddenly
    lurch forwards. It's impossible to predict exactly when they'll move.

2) Scientists are trying to find out if there are any clues that an earthquake might
    happen soon — things like strain in underground rocks. Even with these clues they'll
    only be able to say an earthquake's likely to happen, not exactly when it'll happen.

3) There are some clues that say a volcanic eruption might happen soon. Before an eruption,
    molten rock rises up into chambers near the surface, causing the ground surface to bulge slightly.
    This causes mini-earthquakes near the volcano.

4) But sometimes molten rock cools down instead of erupting, so mini-earthquakes can be a false alarm.

Plate Tectonics — it's a smashing theory...

There's a mixture of plain facts and scientific thinking here. Learn the details of the Earth's structure, and make
sure you can explain how tectonic plates move and what happens at plate boundaries.
It's important to remember that earthquakes are unpredictable even with the best equipment.

The Evolution of the Atmosphere

For 200 million years or so, the atmosphere has been about how it is now: 78% nitrogen, 21% oxygen, and small amounts of other gases, mainly carbon dioxide, noble gases and water vapour. But it wasn't always like this. Here's how the past 4.5 billion years may have gone:

Phase 1 — Volcanoes Gave Out Gases

1) The Earth's surface was originally molten for many millions of years. It was so hot that any atmosphere just 'boiled away' into space.

2) Eventually things cooled down a bit and a thin crust formed, but volcanoes kept erupting.

3) The volcanoes gave out lots of gas. We think this was how the oceans and atmosphere were formed.

4) The early atmosphere was probably mostly CO_2, with virtually no oxygen. There may also have been water vapour, and small amounts of methane and ammonia. This is quite like the atmospheres of Mars and Venus today.

5) The oceans formed when the water vapour condensed.

Holiday report: Not a nice place to be. Take strong walking boots and a good coat.

Phase 2 — Green Plants Evolved and Produced Oxygen

Holiday report: A bit slimy underfoot. Take wellies and a lot of suncream.

1) Green plants and algae evolved over most of the Earth. They were quite happy in the CO_2 atmosphere.

2) A lot of the early CO_2 dissolved into the oceans. The green plants and algae also absorbed some of the CO_2 and produced O_2 by photosynthesis.

3) Plants and algae died and were buried under layers of sediment, along with the skeletons and shells of marine organisms that had slowly evolved. The carbon and hydrocarbons inside them became 'locked up' in sedimentary rocks as insoluble carbonates (e.g. limestone) and fossil fuels.

4) When we burn fossil fuels today, this 'locked-up' carbon is released and the concentration of CO_2 in the atmosphere rises.

Phase 3 — Ozone Layer Allows Evolution of Complex Animals

1) The build-up of oxygen in the atmosphere killed off some early organisms that couldn't tolerate it, but allowed other, more complex organisms to evolve and flourish.

2) The oxygen also created the ozone layer (O_3) which blocked harmful rays from the Sun and enabled even more complex organisms to evolve — us, eventually.

3) There is virtually no CO_2 left now.

Holiday report: A nice place to be. Visit before the crowds ruin it.

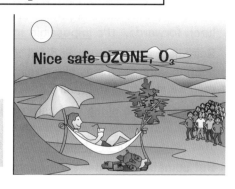

The atmosphere's evolving — shut the window will you...

We've learned a lot about the past atmosphere from Antarctic ice cores. Each year, a layer of ice forms and bubbles of air get trapped inside it, then it's buried by the next layer. So the deeper the ice, the older the air — and if you examine the bubbles in different layers, you can see how the air has changed.

Life, Resources and Atmospheric Change

Life on Earth began billions of years ago, but there's no way of knowing for definite how it all started.

Primordial Soup is Just One Theory of How Life was Formed

1) The primordial soup theory states that billions of years ago, the Earth's atmosphere was rich in nitrogen, hydrogen, ammonia and methane.

2) Lightning struck, causing a chemical reaction between the gases, resulting in the formation of amino acids.

3) The amino acids collected in a 'primordial soup' — a body of water out of which life gradually crawled.

4) The amino acids gradually combined to produce organic matter which eventually evolved into simple living organisms.

5) In the 1950s, Miller and Urey carried out an experiment to prove this theory. They sealed the gases in their apparatus, heated them and applied an electrical charge for a week.

6) They found that amino acids were made, but not as many as there are on Earth. This suggests the theory could be along the right lines, but isn't quite right.

The Earth Has All the Resources Humans Need

The Earth's crust, oceans and atmosphere are the ultimate source of minerals and resources — we can get everything we need from them. For example, we can fractionally distil air to get a variety of products (e.g. nitrogen and oxygen) for use in industry:

1) Air is filtered to remove dust.

2) It's then cooled to around -200 °C and becomes a liquid.

3) During cooling water vapour condenses and is removed.

4) Carbon dioxide freezes and is removed.

5) The liquified air then enters the fractionating column and is heated slowly.

6) The remaining gases are separated by fractional distillation. Oxygen and argon come out together so another column is used to separate them.

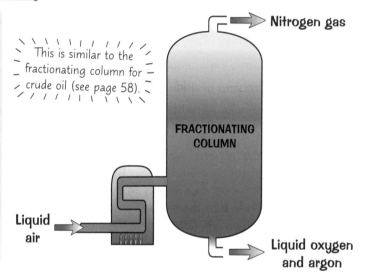

This is similar to the fractionating column for crude oil (see page 58).

Increasing Carbon Dioxide Level Affects the Climate and the Oceans

Burning fossil fuels releases CO_2 — and as the world's become more industrialised, more fossil fuels have been burnt in power stations and in car engines. This CO_2 is thought to be altering our planet...

1) An increase in carbon dioxide is causing global warming — a type of climate change (see page 62).

2) The oceans are a natural store of CO_2 — they absorb it from the atmosphere. However the extra CO_2 we're releasing is making them too acidic. This is bad news for coral and shellfish, and also means that in the future they won't be able to absorb any more carbon dioxide.

Waiter, waiter, there's a primate in my soup...

No-one was around billions of years ago, so our theories about how life formed are just that — theories. We're also still guessing about the exact effects of global warming on things like the oceans.

Revision Summary for Chemistry 1b

Cracking alkanes, making mayonnaise, food additives and earthquakes — can they really belong in the same section, I almost hear you ask. Whether you find the topics easy or hard, interesting or dull, you need to learn it all before the exam. Try these questions and see how much you really know:

1) What is "cracking"? Why is it done?

2) Give a typical example of a substance that is cracked, and the products that you get from cracking it.

3) What kind of carbon-carbon bond do alkenes have?

4) What is the general formula for alkenes?

5) Draw the chemical structure of ethene.

6) When ethene is hydrated with steam, what substance is formed?

7) What are polymers? What kinds of substances can form polymers?

8) Give two factors which affect the physical properties of a polymer.

9) List four uses of polymers.

10) Why might polymers become more expensive in the future?

11) Why do some oils need to be distilled after they have been extracted?

12) List two advantages of cooking with oil.

13) Apart from cooking, list a use of vegetable oils.

14) What kind of carbon-carbon bond do unsaturated oils contain?

15) What happens when you react unsaturated oils with hydrogen?

16) Why do some foods contain partially hydrogenated vegetable oil instead of butter?

17) What is an emulsion? Give an example.

18) How do emulsifiers keep emulsions stable?

19) Suggest one problem of adding emulsifiers to food.

20) Give one reason why Alfred Wegener's theory of continental drift wasn't accepted for a long time.

21) What can be found beneath the Earth's crust?

22) A geologist places a very heavy marker on the seabed in the middle of the Atlantic ocean. She records the marker's position over a period of four years. The geologist finds that the marker moves in a straight-line away from its original position. Her measurements are shown in the graph on the right.

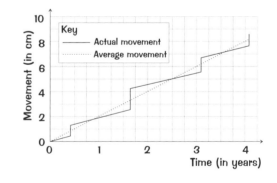

a) Explain the process that has caused the marker to move.

b)*What is the marker's average movement each year?

c)*On average, how many years will it take for the marker to move 7 cm?

23) Why can't scientists accurately predict volcanoes and earthquakes?

24) Name the two main gases that make up the Earth's atmosphere today.

25) Explain why today's atmosphere is different from the Earth's early atmosphere.

26) What is meant by 'primordial soup'?

27) Why do we fractionally distil air?

28) The burning of fossils fuels is causing a rise in the level of carbon dioxide in the atmosphere. How is this affecting the oceans and the climate?

* Answers on page 108.

Heat Radiation

Heat energy tends to flow away from a hotter object to its cooler surroundings.
But then you knew that already. I would hope.

Heat Is Transferred in Three Different Ways

1) Heat energy can be transferred by radiation, conduction or convection.
2) Heat radiation is the transfer of heat energy by infrared (IR) radiation (see below).
3) Conduction and convection involve the transfer of energy by particles.
4) Conduction is the main form of heat transfer in solids (see p.76).
5) Convection is the main form of heat transfer in liquids and gases (see p.77).
6) Infrared radiation can be emitted by solids, liquids and gases.
7) Any object can both absorb and emit infrared radiation,
   whether or not conduction or convection are also taking place.
8) The bigger the temperature difference between a body and its surroundings,
   the faster energy is transferred by heating. Kinda makes sense.

Infrared Radiation — Emission of Electromagnetic Waves

1) All objects are continually emitting and absorbing infrared radiation.
   Infrared radiation is emitted from the surface of an object.
2) An object that's hotter than its surroundings emits more radiation than it absorbs (as it cools down).
   And an object that's cooler than its surroundings absorbs more radiation than it emits (as it warms up).
3) The hotter an object is, the more
   radiation it radiates in a given time.
4) You can feel this infrared radiation if
   you stand near something hot like a
   fire or if you put your hand just above
   the bonnet of a recently parked car.

(recently parked car)

(after an hour or so)

Radiation Depends an Awful Lot on Surface Colour and Texture

1) Dark, matt surfaces absorb infrared radiation falling on them much better than light, shiny surfaces, such
   as gloss white or silver. They also emit much more infrared radiation (at any given temperature).
2) Light, shiny surfaces reflect a lot of the infrared radiation falling on them. E.g. vacuum flasks (see p.79)
   have silver inner surfaces to keep heat in or out, depending on whether it's storing hot or cold liquid.

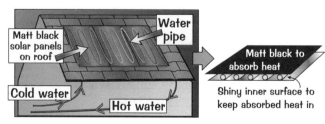

Water pipe

Matt black solar panels on roof

Cold water

Hot water

Matt black to absorb heat

Shiny inner surface to keep absorbed heat in

3) Solar hot water panels contain water pipes under a
   black surface (or black painted pipes under glass).
4) Radiation from the Sun is absorbed by the black
   surface to heat the water in the pipes.
5) This water can be used for washing or pumped
   to radiators to heat the building.

Feelin' hot hot hot...

You might be asked about an example of IR radiation that you've not come across before. As long as you
remember that light, shiny surfaces reflect IR radiation and dark, matt surfaces absorb it — you should be able to
figure out what's going on. If this stuff on radiation is floating your boat, you're going to love conduction...

Kinetic Theory and Conduction

Kinetic theory sounds complicated but it's actually pretty simple. It just describes how particles move in solids, liquids and gases. The energy an object (or particle) has because of its movement is called its kinetic energy.

Kinetic Theory Can Explain the Three States of Matter

The three states of matter are solid (e.g. ice), liquid (e.g. water) and gas (e.g. water vapour). The particles of a particular substance in each state are the same — only the arrangement and energy of the particles are different.

SOLIDS — strong forces of attraction hold the particles close together in a fixed, regular arrangement. The particles don't have much energy so they can only vibrate about their fixed positions.

LIQUIDS — there are weaker forces of attraction between the particles. The particles are close together, but can move past each other, and form irregular arrangements. They have more energy than the particles in a solid — they move in random directions at low speeds.

GASES — There are almost no forces of attraction between the particles. The particles have more energy than those in liquids and solids — they are free to move, and travel in random directions and at high speeds.

When you heat a substance, you give its particles more kinetic energy (KE) — they vibrate or move faster. This is what eventually causes solids to melt and liquids to boil.

Conduction of Heat — Occurs Mainly in Solids

Heat carries on conducting through metal pan handle

Heat conducts through pan to water

CONDUCTION OF HEAT ENERGY is the process where VIBRATING PARTICLES pass on their EXTRA KINETIC ENERGY to NEIGHBOURING PARTICLES.

This process continues throughout the solid and gradually some of the extra kinetic energy (or heat) is passed all the way through the solid, causing a rise in temperature at the other side of the solid. And hence an increase in the heat radiating from its surface.

Usually conduction is faster in denser solids, because the particles are closer together and so will collide more often and pass energy between them. Materials that have larger spaces between their particles conduct heat energy much more slowly — these materials are insulators.

Metals are Good Conductors Because of Their Free Electrons

Heat carried in metals by colliding free electrons

Conduction is more efficient through a short, fat rod than through a long, thin rod. It all comes down to how far the electrons have to transfer the energy.

1) Metals "conduct" so well because the electrons are free to move inside the metal.

2) At the hot end the electrons move faster and collide with other free electrons, transferring energy. These other electrons then pass on their extra energy to other electrons, etc.

3) Because the electrons can move freely, this is obviously a much faster way of transferring the energy through the metal than slowly passing it between jostling neighbouring atoms.

4) This is why heat energy travels so fast through metals.

Good conductors are always metals? — what about Henry Wood...

You'll notice that if a spade has been left in the sun for a while, the metal part will always feel much hotter than the wooden handle. But IT ISN'T HOTTER — it just conducts the heat into your hand much quicker than the wood, so your hand heats up much quicker. In cold weather, the metal bits of a spade, or anything else, always feel colder because they take the heat away from your hand quicker. But they're NOT COLDER... Remember that.

Convection

Gases and liquids are usually free to slosh about — and that allows them to transfer heat by convection, which is a much more effective process than conduction.

Convection of Heat — Liquids and Gases Only

> **CONVECTION** occurs when the more energetic particles **MOVE** from the **HOTTER REGION** to the **COOLER REGION** — **AND TAKE THEIR HEAT ENERGY WITH THEM.**

This is how immersion heaters in kettles and hot water tanks and (unsurprisingly) convector heaters work. Convection simply can't happen in solids because the particles can't move.

The Immersion Heater Example

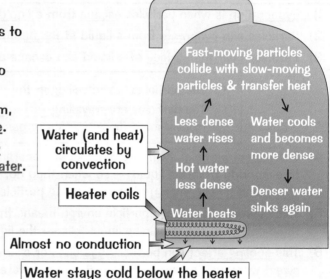

In a bit more detail:

1) Heat energy is transferred from the heater coils to the water by conduction (particle collisions).

2) The particles near the coils get more energy, so they start moving around faster.

3) This means there's more distance between them, i.e. the water expands and becomes less dense.

4) This reduction in density means that the hotter water tends to rise above the denser, cooler water.

5) As the hot water rises it displaces (moves) the colder water out of the way, making it sink towards the heater coils.

6) This cold water is then heated by the coils and rises — and so it goes on. You end up with convection currents going up, round and down, circulating the heat energy through the water.

Labels in diagram:
- Fast-moving particles collide with slow-moving particles & transfer heat
- Less dense water rises
- Water cools and becomes more dense
- Hot water less dense
- Denser water sinks again
- Water heats
- Water (and heat) circulates by convection
- Heater coils
- Almost no conduction
- Water stays cold below the heater

Note that convection is most efficient in roundish or squarish containers, because they allow the convection currents to work best. Shallow, wide containers or tall, thin ones just don't work quite so well.

Also note that because the hot water rises (because of the lower density) you only get convection currents in the water above the heater. The water below it stays cold because there's almost no conduction.

> **CONVECTION CURRENTS** are all about **CHANGES IN DENSITY**. Remember that.

The Radiator Example

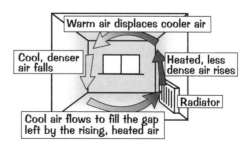

1) Heating a room with a radiator relies on convection currents too.

2) Hot, less dense air by the radiator rises and denser, cooler air flows to replace it.

Labels in diagram:
- Warm air displaces cooler air
- Cool, denser air falls
- Heated, less dense air rises
- Radiator
- Cool air flows to fill the gap left by the rising, heated air

There's a great experiment with purple crystals to show this...

You stick some potassium permanganate crystals in the bottom of a beaker of cold water, then heat it gently over a Bunsen flame. The potassium permanganate starts to dissolve and make a gorgeous bright purple solution that gets moved around the beaker by the convection currents as the water heats. It's real pretty. ☺

Condensation and Evaporation

Here are <u>a couple more</u> things about particles in <u>gases</u> and <u>liquids</u> you need to think about. It's party-cle time...

Condensation <u>is When</u> Gas <u>Turns to Liquid</u>

1) When a <u>gas cools</u>, the particles in the gas <u>slow down</u> and <u>lose kinetic energy</u>.
   The attractive forces between the particles pull them <u>closer together</u>.

2) If the temperature gets <u>cold enough</u> and the gas particles get <u>close enough</u>
   <u>together</u> that <u>condensation</u> can take place, the gas becomes a <u>liquid</u>.

3) Water vapour in the air <u>condenses</u> when it comes
   into contact with <u>cold surfaces</u> e.g. drinks glasses.

4) The <u>steam</u> you see rising from a boiling kettle is actually <u>invisible</u> water
   vapour <u>condensing</u> to form tiny water droplets as it spreads into cooler air.

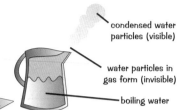

condensed water particles (visible)

water particles in gas form (invisible)

boiling water

Evaporation <u>is When</u> Liquid <u>Turns to Gas</u>

1) <u>Evaporation</u> is when particles <u>escape</u> from a <u>liquid</u>.

2) Particles can <u>evaporate</u> from a liquid at <u>temperatures</u> that are much <u>lower</u> than the liquid's <u>boiling point</u>.

3) Particles <u>near the surface</u> of a liquid can escape and become gas particles if:

> • The particles are travelling in the <u>right direction</u> to escape the liquid.
> • The particles are travelling <u>fast enough</u> (they have enough kinetic energy)
>   to overcome the <u>attractive forces</u> of the <u>other particles</u> in the liquid.

4) The <u>fastest particles</u> (with the most kinetic energy) are <u>most likely</u>
   to evaporate from the liquid — so when they do, the <u>average</u>
   <u>speed</u> and <u>kinetic energy</u> of the remaining particles <u>decreases</u>.

5) This decrease in average particle energy means the
   <u>temperature</u> of the remaining liquid <u>falls</u> — the liquid <u>cools</u>.

6) This <u>cooling effect</u> can be really <u>useful</u>. For example, you
   <u>sweat</u> when you exercise or get hot. As the water from
   the sweat on your skin <u>evaporates</u>, it <u>cools</u> you down.

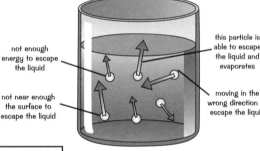

not enough energy to escape the liquid

not near enough the surface to escape the liquid

this particle is able to escape the liquid and evaporates

moving in the wrong direction to escape the liquid

Rates <u>of</u> Evaporation and Condensation <u>can</u> Vary

The <u>RATE OF EVAPORATION</u> will be <u>faster</u> if the...

• <u>TEMPERATURE is higher</u> — the <u>average</u>
  <u>particle energy</u> will be <u>higher</u>, so <u>more</u>
  <u>particles</u> will have enough energy to escape.

• <u>DENSITY is lower</u> — the <u>forces</u> between the particles will
  usually be <u>weaker</u>, so more particles will have enough
  energy to overcome these forces and escape the liquid.

• <u>SURFACE AREA is larger</u> — more particles will be
  <u>near enough to the surface</u> to escape the liquid.

• <u>AIRFLOW over the liquid is greater</u> — the <u>lower the</u>
  <u>concentration</u> of an evaporating substance <u>in the air it's</u>
  <u>evaporating into</u>, the <u>higher</u> the rate of <u>evaporation</u>.
  A greater airflow means air above the liquid is <u>replaced</u>
  <u>more quickly</u>, so the concentration in the air will be <u>lower</u>.

The <u>RATE OF CONDENSATION</u> will be <u>faster</u> if the...

• <u>TEMPERATURE OF THE GAS is lower</u> —
  the average particle energy in the gas is <u>lower</u>
  — so more particles will slow down enough
  to clump together and form liquid droplets.

• <u>TEMPERATURE OF THE SURFACE</u>
  <u>THE GAS TOUCHES is lower</u>.

• <u>DENSITY is higher</u> — the <u>forces</u> between
  the particles will be <u>stronger</u>. Fewer
  particles will have enough energy to
  overcome these forces and will instead
  clump together and form a liquid.

• <u>AIRFLOW is less</u> — the <u>concentration</u> of
  the substance in the air will be <u>higher</u>, and
  so the rate of condensation will be <u>greater</u>.

A little less condensation, a little more action...

The people who make adverts for drinks know what customers like to see — <u>condensation</u> on the outside of the bottle. It makes the drink look <u>nice and cold</u> and extra-refreshing. Mmmm. If it wasn't for condensation, you'd <u>never</u> be able to draw pictures on the <u>bus window</u> with your finger either — you've got a lot to be thankful for...

Rate of Heat Transfer

There are loads of factors that affect the rate of heat transfer.
Different objects can lose or gain heat much faster than others — even in the same conditions. Read on...

The Rate of Heat Energy Transfer Depends on Many Things...

1) Heat energy is radiated from the surface of an object.

2) The bigger the surface area, the more infrared waves that can be emitted from (or absorbed by) the surface — so the quicker the transfer of heat. E.g. radiators have large surface areas to maximise the amount of heat they transfer.

3) This is why car and motorbike engines often have 'fins' — they increase the surface area so heat is radiated away quicker. So the engine cools quicker.

Cooling fins on engines increase surface area to speed up cooling.

4) Heat sinks are devices designed to transfer heat away from objects they're in contact with, e.g. computer components. They have fins and a large surface area so they can emit heat as quickly as possible.

5) If two objects at the same temperature have the same surface area but different volumes, the object with the smaller volume will cool more quickly — as a higher proportion of the object will be in contact with its surroundings.

6) Other factors, like the type of material, affect the rate too. Objects made from good conductors (see p.76) transfer heat away more quickly than insulating materials, e.g. plastic. It also matters whether the materials in contact with it are insulators or conductors. If an object is in contact with a conductor, the heat will be conducted away much faster than if it is in contact with a good insulator.

Some Devices are Designed to Limit Heat Transfer

You need to know about heat energy transfers and how products can be designed to reduce them.

Vacuum Flasks

1) The glass bottle is double-walled with a vacuum between the two walls. This stops all conduction and convection through the sides.

2) The walls either side of the vacuum are silvered to keep heat loss by radiation to a minimum.

3) The bottle is supported using insulating foam. This minimises heat conduction to or from the outer glass bottle.

4) The stopper is made of plastic and filled with cork or foam to reduce any heat conduction through it.

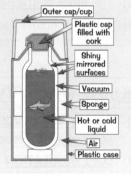

Outer cap/cup
Plastic cap filled with cork
Shiny mirrored surfaces
Vacuum
Sponge
Hot or cold liquid
Air
Plastic case

Humans and Animals Have Ways of Controlling Heat Transfer Too

1) In the cold, the hairs on your skin 'stand up' to trap a thicker layer of insulating air around the body. This limits the amount of heat loss by convection. Some animals do the same using fur.

2) When you're too warm, your body diverts more blood to flow near the surface of your skin so that more heat can be lost by radiation — that's why some people go pink when they get hot.

3) Generally, animals in warm climates have larger ears than those in cold climates to help control heat transfer.

For example, Arctic foxes have evolved small ears, with a small surface area to minimise heat loss by radiation and conserve body heat.

Desert foxes on the other hand have huge ears with a large surface area to allow them to lose heat by radiation easily and keep cool.

Don't call me 'Big Ears' — call me 'Large Surface Area'...

Examiners are like small children — they ask some barmy questions. If they ask you one about heat transfer, you must always say which form of heat transfer is involved at any point, either conduction, convection or radiation. You've got to show them that you know your stuff — it's the only way to get top marks.

Energy Efficiency in the Home

There are lots of things you can do to a building to reduce the amount of heat energy that escapes. Some are more effective than others, and some are better for your pocket than others. The most obvious examples are in the home, but you could apply this to any situation where you're trying to cut down energy loss.

Effectiveness and Cost-effectiveness are Not the Same...

Loft Insulation
Initial Cost: £200
Annual Saving: £50
Payback time: 4 years

Hot Water Tank Jacket
Initial Cost: £15
Annual Saving: £30
Payback time: 6 months

Double Glazing
Initial Cost: £3000
Annual Saving: £60
Payback time: 50 years

Cavity Wall Insulation
Initial Cost: £500
Annual Saving: £70
Payback time: 7 years

Draught-proofing
Initial Cost: £100
Annual Saving: £50
Payback time: 2 years

$$\text{payback time} = \frac{\text{initial cost}}{\text{annual saving}}$$

1) The most effective methods of insulation are ones that give you the biggest annual saving (they save you the most money each year on your heating bills).

2) Eventually, the money you've saved on heating bills will equal the initial cost of putting in the insulation (the amount it cost to buy). The time it takes is called the payback time.

3) The most cost-effective methods tend to be the cheapest.

4) They are cost-effective because they have a short payback time — this means the money you save covers the amount you paid really quickly.

Know Which Types of Heat Transfer Are Involved

1) CAVITY WALL INSULATION — foam squirted into the gap between the bricks reduces convection and radiation across the gap. Pockets of air in the foam reduce heat transfer by conduction.

2) LOFT INSULATION — a thick layer of fibreglass wool laid out across the loft floor and ceiling reduces heat loss from the house by conduction and convection.

3) DRAUGHT-PROOFING — strips of foam and plastic around doors and windows stop draughts of cold air blowing in, i.e. they reduce heat loss due to convection.

4) HOT WATER TANK JACKET — lagging such as fibreglass wool reduces conduction and radiation.

5) THICK CURTAINS — big bits of cloth over the window to reduce heat loss by conduction and radiation.

U-Values Show How Fast Heat can Transfer Through a Material

1) Heat transfers faster through materials with higher U-values than through materials with low U-values.

2) So the better the insulator (see p.76) the lower the U-value. E.g. The U-value of a typical duvet is about $0.75 \text{ W/m}^2\text{K}$, whereas the U-value of loft insulation material is around $0.15 \text{ W/m}^2\text{K}$.

It's payback time...

And it's the same with, say, cars. Buying a more fuel-efficient car might sound like a great idea — but if it costs loads more than a clapped-out old fuel-guzzler, you might still end up out of pocket. If it's cost-effectiveness you're thinking about, you always have to offset initial cost against annual savings.

Specific Heat Capacity

Specific heat capacity is one of those topics that puts people off just because it has a weird name. If you can get over that, it's actually not too bad — it sounds a lot harder than it is. Go on. Give it a second chance.

Specific Heat Capacity Tells You How Much Energy Stuff Can Store

1) It takes more heat energy to increase the temperature of some materials than others.
   E.g. you need 4200 J to warm 1 kg of water by 1 °C, but only 139 J to warm 1 kg of mercury by 1 °C.

2) Materials which need to gain lots of energy to warm up also release loads
   of energy when they cool down again. They can 'store' a lot of heat.

3) The measure of how much energy a substance can store is called its specific heat capacity.

4) Specific heat capacity is the amount of energy needed to raise the temperature of
   1 kg of a substance by 1 °C. Water has a specific heat capacity of 4200 J/kg°C.

There's a Handy Formula for Specific Heat Capacity

You'll have to do calculations involving specific heat capacity. This is the equation to learn:

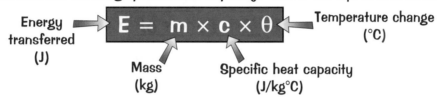

Energy transferred (J) ➡ $E = m \times c \times \theta$ ⬅ Temperature change (°C)

Mass (kg) — Specific heat capacity (J/kg°C)

EXAMPLE: How much energy is needed to heat 2 kg of water from 10 °C to 100 °C?

ANSWER: Energy needed = $2 \times 4200 \times 90 = \underline{756\ 000\ J}$

If you're not working out the energy, you'll have to rearrange
the equation, so this formula triangle will come in dead handy.

You cover up the thing you're trying to find. The parts of the
formula you can still see are what it's equal to.

$$\frac{E}{m \times c \times \theta}$$

EXAMPLE: An empty 200 g aluminium kettle cools down from 115 °C to 10 °C, losing 19 068 J of
heat energy. What is the specific heat capacity of aluminium?

Remember — you need to convert
the mass to kilograms first.

ANSWER: $SHC = \dfrac{Energy}{Mass \times Temp\ Ch} = \dfrac{19\ 068}{0.2 \times 105} = \underline{908\ J/kg°C}$

Heaters Have High Heat Capacities to Store Lots of Energy

1) The materials used in heaters usually have high specific heat
   capacities so that they can store large amounts of heat energy.

2) Water has a really high specific heat capacity. It's also a liquid, so it can easily
   be pumped around in pipes — ideal for central heating systems in buildings.

3) Electric storage heaters are designed to store heat energy at night
   (when electricity is cheaper), and then release it during the day. They store the heat using
   concrete or bricks, which (surprise surprise) have a high specific heat capacity (around 880 J/kg°C).

4) Some heaters are filled with oil, which has a specific heat capacity of around 2000 J/kg°C.
   Because this is lower than water's specific heat capacity, oil heating systems are often not as good as
   water-based systems. Oil does have a higher boiling point though, which usually means oil-filled heaters
   can safely reach higher temperatures than water-based ones.

I've just eaten five sausages — I have a high specific meat capacity...

I'm sure you'll agree that this isn't the most exciting part of GCSE physics — it's not about space travel, crashing
cars or even using springs — but it is likely to come up in your GCSEs. Sadly you just have to knuckle down and
get that formula triangle learnt — then you'll be well on the way to breezing through this question in the exam.

Energy Transfer

Heat is just one type of energy, but there are lots more as well:

Learn These Nine Types of Energy

You should know all of these <u>well enough</u> by now to list them <u>from memory</u>, including the examples:

1) <u>ELECTRICAL</u> Energy.................................... — whenever a <u>current</u> flows.
2) <u>LIGHT</u> Energy.. — from the <u>Sun</u>, <u>light bulbs</u>, etc.
3) <u>SOUND</u> Energy.. — from <u>loudspeakers</u> or anything <u>noisy</u>.
4) <u>KINETIC</u> Energy, or <u>MOVEMENT</u> Energy........ — anything that's <u>moving</u> has it.
5) <u>NUCLEAR</u> Energy...................................... — released only from <u>nuclear reactions</u>.
6) <u>THERMAL</u> Energy or <u>HEAT</u> Energy............... — <u>flows</u> from <u>hot objects</u> to colder ones.
7) <u>GRAVITATIONAL POTENTIAL</u> Energy............... — possessed by anything which can <u>fall</u>.
8) <u>ELASTIC POTENTIAL</u> Energy....................... — stretched <u>springs</u>, <u>elastic</u>, <u>rubber bands</u>, etc.
9) <u>CHEMICAL</u> Energy..................................... — possessed by <u>foods</u>, <u>fuels</u>, <u>batteries</u> etc.

Potential- and Chemical-Energy Are Forms of Stored Energy

The <u>last three</u> above are forms of <u>stored energy</u> because the energy is not obviously <u>doing</u> anything, it's kind of <u>waiting to happen</u>, i.e. waiting to be turned into one of the <u>other</u> forms.

You Need to Know the Conservation of Energy Principle

There are plenty of different <u>types</u> of energy, but <u>they all obey the principle below</u>:

> **ENERGY CAN BE <u>TRANSFERRED</u> USEFULLY FROM ONE FORM TO ANOTHER, <u>STORED</u> OR <u>DISSIPATED</u> — BUT IT CAN NEVER BE <u>CREATED OR DESTROYED</u>.**

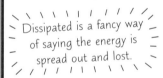
Dissipated is a fancy way of saying the energy is spread out and lost.

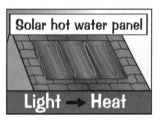
Solar hot water panel
Light → Heat

falling object
Gravitational Potential → Kinetic

Another <u>important principle</u> which you need to <u>learn</u> is this one:

> Energy is <u>only useful</u> when it can be <u>converted</u> from one form to another.

They Like Giving Exam Questions on Energy Transfers

In the exam, they can ask you about <u>any device</u> or <u>energy transfer system</u> they feel like. If you understand a few different <u>examples</u>, it'll be easier to think through whatever they ask you about in the exam.

EXAMPLES:
   <u>Electrical Devices, e.g. televisions</u>: Electrical energy ⟹ Light, sound and heat energy
   <u>Batteries</u>: Chemical energy ⟹ Electrical and heat energy
   <u>Electrical Generation, e.g. wind turbines</u>: Kinetic energy ⟹ Electrical and heat energy
   <u>Potential Energy, e.g. firing a bow and arrow</u>: Elastic potential energy ⟹ Kinetic and heat energy

Energy can't be created or destroyed — only talked about a lot...

<u>Chemical</u> energy → <u>kinetic</u> energy → <u>electrical</u> energy → <u>kinetic</u> energy → <u>chemical</u> energy.
 (me thinking)   (me typing)   (my computer) (printing machine) (you reading this)

Efficiency of Machines

More! More! Tell me more about energy transfers please! OK, since you insist:

Most Energy Transfers Involve Some Losses, Often as Heat

1) <u>Useful devices</u> are only <u>useful</u> because they can <u>transform energy</u> from <u>one form</u> to <u>another</u>.

2) In doing so, some of the useful <u>input energy</u> is always <u>lost or wasted</u>, often as <u>heat</u>.

3) The <u>less energy</u> that is '<u>wasted</u>', the <u>more efficient</u> the device is said to be.

4) The <u>energy flow diagram</u> is pretty much the same for <u>all devices</u>.

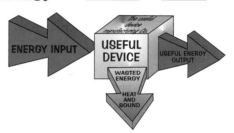

It's Really Simple to Calculate the Efficiency...

A <u>machine</u> is a device which turns <u>one type of energy</u> into <u>another</u>. The <u>efficiency</u> of any device is defined as:

$$\text{Efficiency} = \frac{\text{Useful Energy out}}{\text{Total Energy in}}$$

You might not know the <u>energy</u> inputs and outputs of a machine, but you can <u>still</u> calculate the machine's <u>efficiency</u> as long as you know the <u>power</u> input and output:

$$\text{Efficiency} = \frac{\text{Useful Power out}}{\text{Total Power in}}$$

You can give efficiency as a <u>decimal</u> or you can <u>multiply</u> <u>your answer</u> by 100 to get a <u>percentage</u>, i.e. <u>0.75 or 75%</u>.

As usual, a <u>formula triangle</u> will come handy for rearranging the formulas:

$$\frac{\text{Useful Out}}{\text{Efficiency} \times \text{Total In}}$$

How to Use the Formula — Nothing to It

1) You find how much energy is <u>supplied</u> to a machine. (The Total Energy <u>IN</u>.)

2) You find how much <u>useful energy</u> the machine <u>delivers</u>. (The Useful Energy <u>OUT</u>.) An exam question either tells you this directly or tells you how much it <u>wastes</u> as heat/sound.

3) Either way, you get those <u>two important numbers</u> and then just <u>divide</u> the <u>smaller one</u> by the <u>bigger one</u> to get a value for <u>efficiency</u> somewhere between <u>0 and 1</u> (or <u>0 and 100%</u>). Easy.

4) The other way they might ask it is to tell you the <u>efficiency</u> and the <u>input energy</u> and ask for the <u>energy output</u> — so you need to be able to swap the formula round.

Useful Energy Input Isn't Usually Equal to Total Energy Output

For any <u>given example</u> you can talk about the <u>types of energy</u> being <u>input</u> and <u>output</u>, but <u>remember this</u>:

> <u>No</u> device is 100% efficient and the <u>wasted energy</u> is usually <u>spread out</u> as <u>heat</u>.

<u>Electric heaters</u> are the <u>exception</u> to this. They're usually <u>100% efficient</u> because <u>all</u> the electricity is converted to "<u>useful</u>" heat. Ultimately, <u>all</u> energy <u>ends up as heat energy</u>. If you use an electric drill, it gives out <u>various types</u> of energy but they all quickly end up as <u>heat</u>.

Don't waste your energy — turn the TV off while you revise...

And for <u>10 bonus points</u>, calculate the efficiency of these machines:

TV — energy in = 220 J, light energy out = 5 J, sound energy out = 2 J, heat energy out = 213 J.

Loudspeaker — energy in = 35 J, sound energy out = 0.5 J, heat energy out = 34.5 J. Answers p.108.

Efficiency of Machines

I know what you're thinking — those inefficient machines are causing senseless waste. I'm pretty darn angry too. But sometimes efficiency isn't everything — there are other factors to consider too.

We Call It Wasted Heat Because We Can't Do Anything Useful with It

1) Useful energy is concentrated energy. As you know, the entire energy output by a machine, both useful and wasted, eventually ends up as heat.

2) This heat is transferred to cooler surroundings, which then become warmer. As the heat is transferred to cooler surroundings, the energy becomes less concentrated — it dissipates.

3) The total amount of energy stays the same. The energy is still there, but as it becomes increasingly spread out, it can't be easily used or collected back in again.

You Need to Think About Cost-Effectiveness and Efficiency...
...When Choosing Appliances

Example: Light Bulbs

1) A low-energy bulb is about 4 times as efficient as an ordinary light bulb.

2) Energy-efficient light bulbs are more expensive to buy but they last much longer.

3) If an energy-saving light bulb cost £3 and saved £12 of energy a year, its payback time (see p.80) would be 3 months.

4) Energy-saving light bulbs are normally more cost-effective than ordinary bulbs.

5) LED light bulbs are even more efficient than low-energy bulbs, and can last even longer.

6) But they are more expensive to buy and don't give out as much light as the other two types of bulb.

Example: Replacing Old Appliances with Newer Energy-Efficient Ones

1) New, efficient appliances are cheaper to run than older, less efficient appliances. But new appliances can be expensive to buy.

2) You've got to work out if it's cost-effective (p.80) to buy a new appliance.

3) To work out how cost-effective a new appliance will be you need to work out its payback time.

Sometimes 'Waste' Energy Can Actually Be Useful

1) Heat exchangers reduce the amount of heat energy that is 'lost'.

2) They do this by pumping a cool fluid through the escaping heat.

3) The temperature of this fluid rises as it gains heat energy.

4) The heat energy in the fluid can then be converted into a form of energy that's useful again — either in the original device, or for other useful functions. For example, some of the heat from a car's engine can be transferred to the air that's used to warm the passenger compartment.

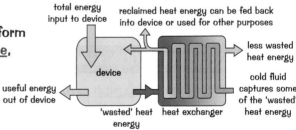

total energy input to device

reclaimed heat energy can be fed back into device or used for other purposes

device

useful energy out of device

less wasted heat energy

cold fluid captures some of the 'wasted' heat energy

'wasted' heat energy

heat exchanger

Let there be light — and a bit of wasted heat...

The thing about loss of energy is it's always the same — it always disappears as heat and sound, and even the sound ends up as heat pretty quickly. So when they ask, "Why is the input energy more than the output energy?", the answer is always the same... Learn and enjoy.

Energy Transformation Diagrams

This is another opportunity for a MATHS question. Fantastic.
So best prepare yourself — here's what those energy transformation diagrams are all about...

The Thickness of the Arrow Represents the Amount of Energy

The idea of Sankey diagrams is to make it easy to see at a glance how much of the total energy in is being usefully employed compared with how much is being wasted.

The thicker the arrow, the more energy it represents — so you see a big thick arrow going in, then several smaller arrows going off it to show the different energy transformations taking place.

You can have either a little sketch or a properly detailed diagram where the width of each arrow is proportional to the number of joules it represents.

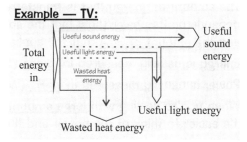

Example — TV:

Example — Sankey Diagram for a Simple Motor:

HERE'S THE SKETCH VERSION:

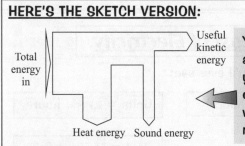

You don't know the actual amounts, but you can see that most of the energy is being wasted, and that it's mostly wasted as heat.

EXAM QUESTIONS:

With sketches, they're likely to ask you to compare two different devices and say which is more efficient. You generally want to be looking for the one with the thickest useful energy arrow(s).

AND HERE'S THE DETAILED ONE:

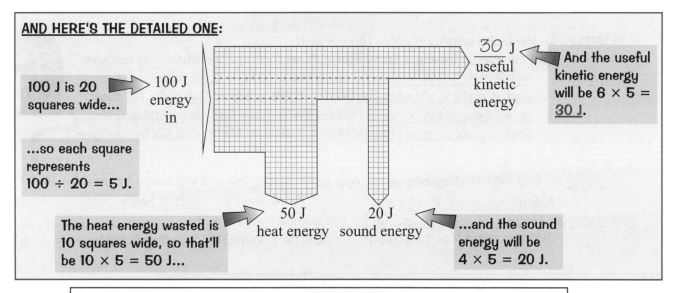

100 J is 20 squares wide...

...so each square represents 100 ÷ 20 = 5 J.

The heat energy wasted is 10 squares wide, so that'll be 10 × 5 = 50 J...

And the useful kinetic energy will be 6 × 5 = 30 J.

...and the sound energy will be 4 × 5 = 20 J.

EXAM QUESTIONS:

In an exam, the most likely question you'll get about detailed Sankey diagrams is filling in one of the numbers or calculating the efficiency. The efficiency is straightforward enough if you can work out the numbers (see p.83).

Skankey diagrams — to represent the smelliness of your socks...

If they ask you to draw your own Sankey diagram in the exam, and don't give you the figures, a sketch is all they'll expect. Just give a rough idea of where the energy goes. E.g. a filament lamp turns most of the input energy into heat, and only a tiny proportion goes to useful light energy.

The Cost of Electricity

Isn't electricity great — generally, I mean. You can power all sorts of toys and gadgets with electricity. But it'll cost you. 'How much?' I hear you cry... Read and learn.

Kilowatt-hours (kWh) are "UNITS" of Energy

1) Electrical appliances transfer electrical energy into other forms (see page 82) — e.g. sound and heat energy in a radio.

2) The amount of energy that is transferred by an appliance depends on its power (how fast the appliance can transfer it) and the amount of time that the appliance is switched on.

ENERGY = POWER x TIME

3) Energy is usually measured in joules (J) — 1 J is the amount of energy transferred by a 1 W appliance in 1 s.

4) Power is usually measured in watts (W) or kilowatts (kW). A 5 kW appliance transfers 5000 J in 1 s.

5) When you're dealing with large amounts of electrical energy (e.g. the energy used by a home in one week), it's easier to think of the power and time in kilowatts and hours — rather than in watts and seconds.

6) So the standard units of electrical energy are kilowatt-hours (kWh) — not joules.

> A **KILOWATT-HOUR** is the amount of electrical energy used by a **1 kW appliance** left on for **1 HOUR**.

The Two Easy Formulas for Calculating the Cost of Electricity

These must surely be the two most trivial and obvious formulas you'll ever see:

> No. of **UNITS** (kWh) used = **POWER** (in kW) × **TIME** (in hours)

> Units = kW × hours

> **COST** = No. of **UNITS** × **PRICE** per **UNIT**

> Cost = Units × Price

EXAMPLE: An electricity supplier charges 14p per unit.
Find the cost of leaving a 60 W light bulb on for: a) 30 minutes b) one year.
ANSWER: a) No. of units = kW × hours = 0.06 kW × ½ hr = 0.03 units.
Cost = units × price per unit(14p) = 0.03 × 14p = 0.42p for 30 mins.
b) No. of units = kW × hours = 0.06 kW × (24×365) hr = 525.6 units.
Cost = units × price per unit(14p) = 525.6 × 14p = £73.58 for one year.

EXAMPLE 2: Each unit of electricity costs 14p. For how long can a 6 kW heater be used for 14p?
A 6 hours   B 1 hour   C 10 minutes   D 7 hours
ANSWER 2: The cost of 1 unit is 14p. So for 14p you can use 1 unit.
UNITS = POWER × TIME, so TIME = UNITS ÷ POWER = 1 ÷ 6 = 0.167 hours = 10 mins

You Need to Know How to Read an Electricity Meter

1) They might ask you to read values off an electricity meter in the exam — but don't worry, it's pretty straightforward. The units are usually in kWh — but make sure you check.

2) You could be given two meter readings and be asked to work out the total energy that's been used over a particular time period. Just subtract the meter reading at the start of the time (the smaller one) from the reading at the end to work this out.

500 kWh doesn't mean much to anyone — £70 is far more real...

In reality most electricity suppliers have complicated formulas for working out the cost of electricity. Luckily in the exam you'll just be told how much a particular energy supplier charges per unit or something, phew.

Choosing Electrical Appliances

Unfortunately, this isn't about what colour MP3 player to get, but know it you must I'm afraid...

Sometimes You Have a Choice of Electrical Equipment

1) There are often a few different appliances that do the same job. In the exam, they might ask you to weigh up the pros and cons of different appliances and decide which one is most suitable for a particular situation.

2) You might need to work out whether one appliance uses less energy or is more cost-effective than another.

3) You might also need to think about the practical advantages and disadvantages of using different appliances. E.g. 'Can an appliance be used in areas with limited electricity supplies?'

4) You might get asked to compare two appliances that you haven't seen before. Just take your time and think about the advantages and disadvantages — you should be able to make a sensible judgement.

E.G. CLOCKWORK RADIOS AND BATTERY RADIOS

1) Battery radios and clockwork radios are both handy in areas where there is no mains electricity supply.

2) Clockwork radios work by storing elastic potential energy in a spring when someone winds them up. The elastic potential energy is slowly released and used to power the radio.

3) Batteries can be expensive, but powering a clockwork radio is free.

4) Battery power is also only useful if you can get hold of some new batteries when the old ones run out. You don't get that problem with clockwork radios — but it can get annoying to have to keep winding them up every few hours to recharge them.

5) Clockwork radios are also better for the environment — a lot of energy and harmful chemicals go into making batteries, and they're often tricky to dispose of safely.

You Might Be Asked to Use Data to Compare Two Appliances

EXAMPLE

A company is deciding whether to install a 720 W low-power heater, or a high-power 9 kW heater. The heater they choose will be on for 30 hours each week. Their electricity provider charges 7p per kWh of electricity. How much money per week would they save by choosing the low-power heater?

ANSWER: Weekly electricity used by the low-power heater = 0.720 kW × 30 h = 21.6 kWh
Weekly electricity used by the high-power heater = 9 kW × 30 h = 270 kWh
Total saving = (270 – 21.6) × 7 = £17.39 (to the nearest penny)

Standard of Living is Affected by Access to Electricity

1) Most people in developed countries have access to mains electricity. However, many people living in the world's poorest countries don't — this has a big effect on their standard of living.

2) In the UK, our houses are full of devices that transform electrical energy into other useful types of energy. For example, not only is electric lighting useful and convenient, but it can also help improve safety at night.

3) Refrigerators keep food fresh for longer by slowing down the growth of bacteria. Refrigerators are also used to keep vaccines cold. Without refrigeration it's difficult to distribute important vaccines — this can have devastating effects on a country's population.

4) Electricity also plays an important role in improving public health in other ways. Hospitals in developed countries rely heavily on electricity, e.g. for X-ray machines. Without access to these modern machines, the diagnosis and treatment of patients would be poorer and could reduce life expectancy.

5) Communications are also affected by a lack of electricity. No electricity means no internet or phones — making it hard for people to keep in touch, or for people to send or receive news and information.

I'm definitely a fan of things running like clockwork...

Make sure you're happy with comparing electrical devices, and you know how important access to electricity can be.

Revision Summary for Physics 1a

It's all very well reading the pages and looking at the diagrams — but you won't have a hope of remembering it for your exam if you don't understand it. Have a go at these questions to see how much has gone in so far. If you struggle with any of them, have another read through the section and give the questions another go.

1) Describe the three ways that heat energy can be transferred.
2) True or false? An object that's cooler than its surroundings emits more radiation than it absorbs.
3) Explain why solar hot water panels have a matt black surface.
4) Describe the arrangement and movement of the particles in a) solids   b) liquids   c) gases
5) What is the name of the process where vibrating particles pass on their extra kinetic energy to neighbouring particles?
6) Which type of heat transfer can't take place in solids — convection or conduction?
7) Describe how the heat from heater coils is transferred throughout the water in a kettle. What is this process called?
8) How do the densities of liquids and gases change as you heat them?
9) What happens to the particles of a gas as it turns to a liquid?
10) What is the name given to the process where a gas turns to a liquid?
11) Why does evaporation have a cooling effect on a liquid?
12) The two designs of car engine shown are made from the same material. Which engine will transfer heat quicker? Explain why.

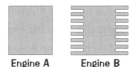
Engine A   Engine B

13) Describe two features of a vacuum flask that make it good at keeping hot liquids hot.
14) Do animals that live in hot climates tend to have large or small ears? Give one reason why this might be an advantage in a hot climate.
15)*If it costs £4000 to double glaze your house and the double glazing saves you £100 on energy bills every year, calculate the payback time for double glazing.
16) Name five ways of improving energy efficiency in the home. Explain how each improvement reduces the amount of heat lost from a house.
17) What can you tell from a material's U-value?
18) Would you expect copper or cotton wool to have a higher U-value?
19) What property of a material tells you how much energy it can store?
20)*An ornament has a mass of 0.5 kg. The ornament is made from a material that has a specific heat capacity of 1000 J/kg°C. How much energy does it take to heat the ornament from 20 °C to 200 °C?
21) Do heaters use materials that have a high or low heat capacity?
22) Name nine types of energy and give an example of each.
23) State the principle of the conservation of energy.
24) List the energy transformations that occur in a battery-powered toy car.
25) What is the useful type of energy delivered by a motor? In what form is energy wasted?
26)*What is the efficiency of a motor that converts 100 J of electrical energy into 70 J of useful kinetic energy?
27)*The following Sankey diagram shows how energy is converted in a catapult.

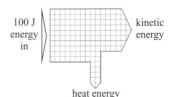
100 J energy in — kinetic energy — heat energy

a) How much energy is converted into kinetic energy?
b) How much energy is wasted?
c) What is the efficiency of the catapult?

28) What are the standard units of electrical energy?
29)*Calculate how many kWh of electrical energy are used by a 0.5 kW heater used for 15 minutes.
30) Would a battery-powered radio or a clockwork radio be more suitable to use when camping? Why?

Energy Sources & Power Stations

There are 12 different types of energy resource.
They fit into two broad types: renewable and non-renewable.

Non-Renewable Energy Resources Will Run Out One Day

The non-renewables are the three FOSSIL FUELS and NUCLEAR:

1) Coal
2) Oil
3) Natural gas
4) Nuclear fuels (uranium and plutonium)

a) They will all 'run out' one day.
b) They all do damage to the environment.
c) But they provide most of our energy.

Renewable Energy Resources Will Never Run Out

The renewables are:

1) Wind   5) Solar
2) Waves   6) Geothermal
3) Tides   7) Food
4) Hydroelectric 8) Biofuels

a) These will never run out.
b) Most of them do damage the environment, but in less nasty ways than non-renewables.
c) The trouble is they don't provide much energy and some of them are unreliable because they depend on the weather.

Energy Sources can be Burned to Drive Turbines in Power Stations

Most of the electricity we use is generated from the four NON-RENEWABLE sources of energy (coal, oil, gas and nuclear) in big power stations, which are all pretty much the same apart from the boiler.

Learn the basic features of the typical power station shown here and also the nuclear reactor below.

1) The fossil fuel is burned to convert its stored chemical energy into heat (thermal) energy.

2) The heat energy is used to heat water (or air in some fossil-fuel power stations) to produce steam.

3) The steam turns a turbine, converting heat energy into kinetic energy.

4) The turbine is connected to a generator, which transfers kinetic energy into electrical energy.

Nuclear Reactors are Just Fancy Boilers

1) A nuclear power station is mostly the same as the one above, but with nuclear fission of uranium or plutonium producing the heat to make steam to drive turbines, etc. The difference is in the boiler, as shown here:

2) Nuclear power stations take the longest time of all the power stations to start up. Natural gas power elations take the shortest time of all the fossil fuel power stations.

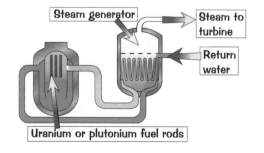

It all boils down to steam...

Steam engines were invented as long ago as the 17th century, and yet we're still using that idea to produce most of our electricity today, over 300 years later. Amazing...

Renewable Energy Sources

Renewable energy sources, like wind, waves and solar energy, will not run out. What's more, they do a lot less damage to the environment. They don't generate as much electricity as non-renewables though — if they did we'd all be using solar-powered toasters by now.

Wind Power — Lots of Little Wind Turbines

1) This involves putting lots of windmills (wind turbines) up in exposed places like on moors or round coasts.

2) Each wind turbine has its own generator inside it. The electricity is generated directly from the wind turning the blades, which turn the generator.

3) There's no pollution (except for a little bit when they're manufactured).

4) But they do spoil the view. You need about 1500 wind turbines to replace one coal-fired power station and 1500 of them cover a lot of ground — which would have a big effect on the scenery.

5) And they can be very noisy, which can be annoying for people living nearby.

6) There's also the problem of no power when the wind stops, and it's impossible to increase supply when there's extra demand.

7) The initial costs are quite high, but there are no fuel costs and minimal running costs.

8) There's no permanent damage to the landscape — if you remove the turbines, you remove the noise and the view returns to normal.

Solar Cells — Expensive but No Environmental Damage

1) Solar cells generate electric currents directly from sunlight. Solar cells are often the best source of energy for calculators and watches which don't use much electricity.

(well, there may be a bit caused by making the cells)

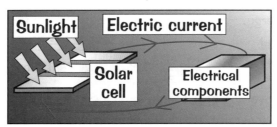

2) Solar power is often used in remote places where there's not much choice (e.g. the Australian outback) and to power electric road signs and satellites.

3) There's no pollution. (Although they do use quite a lot of energy to manufacture in the first place.)

4) In sunny countries solar power is a very reliable source of energy — but only in the daytime. Solar power can still be cost-effective even in cloudy countries like Britain.

5) Initial costs are high but after that the energy is free and running costs almost nil.

6) Solar cells are usually used to generate electricity on a relatively small scale, e.g. powering individual homes.

7) It's often not practical or too expensive to connect them to the National Grid — the cost of connecting them to the National Grid can be enormous compared with the value of the electricity generated.

People love the idea of wind power — just not in their back yard...

Did you know you can now get rucksacks with built-in solar cells to charge up your mobile phone, MP3 player and digital camera while you're wandering around. Pretty cool, huh.

Renewable Energy Sources

Good ol' water. Not only can we drink it — we can also use it to turn turbines in the same way as wind. Wherever water is moving — in waves, rivers and tides, we can transfer its kinetic energy into electrical energy.

Hydroelectric Power Uses Falling Water

1) Hydroelectric power usually requires the flooding of a valley by building a big dam.

2) Rainwater is caught and allowed out through turbines. There is no pollution (as such).

3) But there is a big impact on the environment due to the flooding of the valley (rotting vegetation releases methane and CO_2) and possible loss of habitat for some species (sometimes the loss of whole villages). The reservoirs can also look very unsightly when they dry up. Putting hydroelectric power stations in remote valleys tends to reduce their impact on humans.

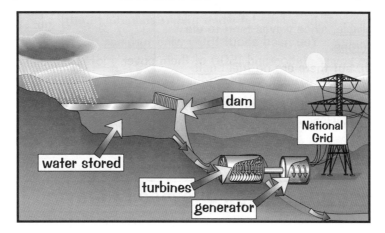

4) A big advantage is it can provide an immediate response to an increased demand for electricity.

5) There's no problem with reliability except in times of drought — but remember this is **Great Britain** we're talking about.

6) Initial costs are high, but there's no fuel and minimal running costs.

7) It can be a useful way to generate electricity on a small scale in remote areas.

Pumped Storage Gives Extra Supply Just When It's Needed

1) Most large power stations have huge boilers which have to be kept running all night even though demand is very low. This means there's a surplus of electricity at night.

2) It's surprisingly difficult to find a way of storing this spare energy for later use.

3) Pumped storage is one of the best solutions.

4) In pumped storage, 'spare' night-time electricity is used to pump water up to a higher reservoir.

5) This can then be released quickly during periods of peak demand such as at teatime each evening, to supplement the steady delivery from the big power stations.

6) Remember, pumped storage uses the same idea as hydroelectric power, but it isn't a way of generating power — it's simply a way of storing energy which has already been generated.

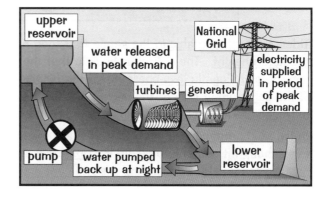

The hydroelectric power you're supplying — it's electrifying...

In Britain only a pretty small percentage of our electricity comes from hydroelectric power at the moment, but in some other parts of the world they rely much more heavily on it. For example, in the last few years, 99% of Norway's energy came from hydroelectric power. 99% — that's huge!

Renewable Energy Sources

Don't worry — I haven't forgotten about <u>wave power</u> and <u>tidal power</u>. It's easy to get confused between these two just because they're both to do with the seaside — but don't. They are <u>completely different</u>.

Wave Power — Lots of Little Wave-Powered Turbines

1) You need lots of small <u>wave-powered turbines</u> located <u>around the coast</u>.

2) As waves come in to the shore they provide an <u>up and down motion</u> which can be used to drive a <u>generator</u>.

3) There is <u>no pollution</u>. The main problems are <u>spoiling the view</u> and being a <u>hazard to boats</u>.

4) They are <u>fairly unreliable</u>, since waves tend to die out when the <u>wind drops</u>.

5) <u>Initial costs are high</u>, but there are <u>no fuel costs</u> and <u>minimal running costs</u>. Wave power is never likely to provide energy on a <u>large scale</u>, but it can be <u>very useful</u> on <u>small islands</u>.

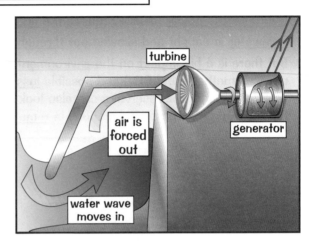

Tidal Barrages — Using the Sun and Moon's Gravity

1) <u>Tidal barrages</u> are <u>big dams</u> built across <u>river estuaries</u>, with <u>turbines</u> in them.

2) As the <u>tide comes in</u> it fills up the estuary to a height of <u>several metres</u> — it also drives the <u>turbines</u>. This water can then be allowed out <u>through the turbines</u> at a controlled speed.

3) The source of the energy is the <u>gravity</u> of the <u>Sun</u> and the <u>Moon</u>.

4) There is <u>no pollution</u>. The main problems are <u>preventing free access by boats</u>, <u>spoiling the view</u> and <u>altering the habitat</u> of the wildlife, e.g. wading birds, sea creatures and beasties who live in the sand.

5) Tides are <u>pretty reliable</u> in the sense that they happen <u>twice a day without fail</u>, and always near to the <u>predicted height</u>. The only drawback is that the <u>height</u> of the tide is <u>variable</u> so lower (neap) tides will provide <u>significantly less energy</u> than the bigger 'spring' tides. They also don't work when the water level is the <u>same</u> either side of the barrage — this happens four times a day because of the tides. But tidal barrages are <u>excellent</u> for <u>storing energy</u> ready for periods of <u>peak demand</u>.

6) <u>Initial costs are moderately high</u>, but there are <u>no fuel costs</u> and <u>minimal running costs</u>. Even though it can only be used in <u>some</u> of the <u>most suitable estuaries</u> tidal power has the potential for generating a <u>significant amount</u> of energy.

Learn about Wave Power — and bid your cares goodbye...

I do hope you appreciate the <u>big big differences</u> between <u>tidal power</u> and <u>wave power</u>. They both involve salty seawater, sure — but there the similarities end. Lots of jolly details then, just waiting to be absorbed into your cavernous intracranial void. Smile and enjoy. And <u>learn</u>.

Renewable Energy Sources

Well, who'd know it — there's <u>yet more energy</u> lurking about in piles of rubbish and deep underground. Makes you wonder sometimes why we even need to use oil. (If you are wondering about that, page 95 is all about comparing energy resources, so <u>sit tight</u> for now.)

Geothermal Energy — Heat **from** Underground

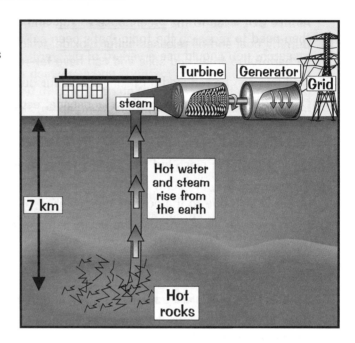

1) This is <u>only possible</u> in <u>volcanic areas</u> where <u>hot rocks</u> lie quite near to the <u>surface</u>. The source of much of the heat is the <u>slow decay</u> of various <u>radioactive elements</u>, including <u>uranium</u>, deep inside the Earth.

2) <u>Steam</u> and <u>hot water</u> rise to the surface and are used to drive a <u>generator</u>.

3) This is actually <u>brilliant free energy</u> with no real environmental problems.

4) In some places, geothermal heat is used to <u>heat buildings directly</u>, without being converted to electrical energy.

5) The <u>main drawback</u> with geothermal energy is there <u>aren't</u> very many <u>suitable locations</u> for power plants.

6) Also, the <u>cost</u> of building a power plant is often <u>high</u> compared to the <u>amount</u> of energy we can get out of it.

Biofuels **are** Made from **Plants and** Waste

1) Biofuels are <u>renewable energy resources</u>. They're used to generate electricity in <u>exactly</u> the same way as fossil fuels (see p.89) — they're <u>burnt</u> to heat up <u>water</u>.

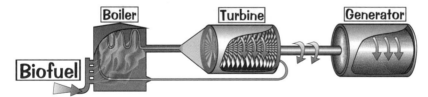

2) They can be also used in some <u>cars</u> — just like fossil fuels.

3) Biofuels can be <u>solids</u> (e.g. straw, nutshells and woodchips), <u>liquids</u> (e.g. ethanol) or <u>gases</u> (e.g. methane 'biogas' from sludge digesters).

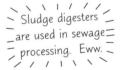

Sludge digesters are used in sewage processing. Eww.

4) We can get <u>biofuels</u> from organisms that are <u>still alive</u> or from dead organic matter — like fossil fuels, but from <u>organisms</u> that have been living much more <u>recently</u>.

5) E.g. <u>crops</u> like sugar cane can be fermented to produce <u>ethanol</u>, or plant oils can be modified to produce <u>biodiesel</u>.

Sugar cane to ethanol — a terrible waste in my opinion...

Biofuels sound quite futuristic. But believe it or not, biofuel mixed with petrol or diesel was actually used in some cars before WW2. Biofuel never really became massively successful though because of <u>cheap oil</u>. One big advantage of biofuels is they don't release as much <u>greenhouse gas</u> compared with common transport fuels like petrol and diesel. They aren't completely innocent in the pollution game though, as you'll see on the next page.

Energy Sources and the Environment

They might fly you to Spain for your holidays and power your games consoles, but using <u>non-renewable energy sources</u> and <u>biofuels</u> to generate electricity can have <u>damaging effects</u> on the <u>environment</u>.

Non-Renewables are Also Linked to Other Environmental Problems

1) All three <u>fossil fuels</u> (coal, oil and gas) release CO_2 into the atmosphere when they're burned. For the same amount of energy produced, coal releases the most CO_2, followed by oil then gas. All this CO_2 adds to the <u>greenhouse effect</u>, and contributes to <u>global warming</u>.

2) Burning coal and oil releases <u>sulfur dioxide</u>, which causes <u>acid rain</u>. Acid rain can be harmful to trees and soils and can have far-reaching effects in ecosystems.

3) Acid rain can be reduced by taking the sulfur out <u>before</u> the fuel is burned, or cleaning up the <u>emissions</u>.

4) <u>Coal mining</u> makes a <u>mess</u> of the <u>landscape</u>, especially "open-cast mining".

5) <u>Oil spillages</u> cause <u>serious environmental problems</u>, affecting mammals and birds that live in and around the sea. We try to avoid them, but they'll always happen.

6) <u>Nuclear power</u> is <u>clean</u> but the <u>nuclear waste</u> is very <u>dangerous</u> and difficult to <u>dispose of</u>.

7) Nuclear <u>fuel</u> (i.e. uranium) is <u>relatively cheap</u> but the <u>overall cost</u> of nuclear power is <u>high</u> due to the cost of the <u>power plant</u> and final <u>decommissioning</u>.

8) <u>Nuclear power</u> always carries the risk of a <u>major catastrophe</u> like the <u>Chernobyl disaster</u> in 1986.

Biofuels Have Their Disadvantages Too

1) Biofuels (see p.93) are a relatively <u>quick</u> and 'natural' source of energy and are supposedly <u>carbon neutral</u>.

2) There is still debate into the impact of biofuels on the environment, once the <u>full energy</u> that goes into the <u>production</u> is considered.

The <u>plants</u> that grew to <u>produce the waste</u> (or to <u>feed the animals</u> that produced the dung) <u>absorbed carbon dioxide</u> from the atmosphere as they were growing. When the waste is burnt, this CO_2 is <u>re-released</u> into the <u>atmosphere</u>. So it has a <u>neutral effect</u> on atmospheric CO_2 levels (although this only really works if you keep growing plants at the same rate you're burning things). Biofuel production also creates <u>methane</u> emissions — a lot of this comes from the <u>animals</u>. Nice.

Huge areas of land are needed to produce biofuels on a large scale.

3) In some regions, large areas of <u>forest</u> have been <u>cleared</u> to make room to grow <u>biofuels</u>, resulting in lots of species losing their <u>natural habitats</u>. The <u>decay</u> and <u>burning</u> of this vegetation also increases CO_2 and <u>methane</u> emissions.

4) Biofuels have <u>potential</u>, but their use is limited by the amount of available <u>farmland</u> that can be dedicated to their production.

Carbon Capture can Reduce the Impact of Carbon Dioxide

1) <u>Carbon capture and storage</u> (CCS) is used to <u>reduce</u> the amount of CO_2 building up in the atmosphere and <u>reduce</u> the strength of the <u>greenhouse effect</u>.

2) CCS works by <u>collecting</u> the CO_2 from power stations <u>before</u> it is released into the atmosphere.

3) The captured CO_2 can then be <u>pumped</u> into empty <u>gas fields</u> and <u>oil fields</u> like those under the North Sea. It can be safely <u>stored</u> without it adding to the greenhouse effect.

4) CCS is a <u>new technology</u> that's <u>developing quickly</u>. New ways of storing CO_2 are being explored, including <u>storing</u> CO_2 dissolved in <u>seawater</u> at the bottom of the ocean and <u>capturing</u> CO_2 with <u>algae</u>, which can then be used to <u>produce oil</u> that can be used as a <u>biofuel</u>.

Biofuels are great — but don't burn your biology notes just yet...

<u>Wowsers</u>. There certainly is a lot to bear in mind with all the different energy sources and all the good things and nasty things associated with each of them. The next page is <u>really handy</u> for making <u>comparisons</u> between different energy sources — it'll tell you everything you need to know. (Secret hint: you should definitely read it.)

Comparison of Energy Resources

Setting Up a Power Station

Because coal and oil are running out fast, many old <u>coal- and oil-fired power stations</u> are being <u>taken out of use</u>. Often they're being <u>replaced</u> by <u>gas-fired power stations</u> because they're <u>quick</u> to <u>set up</u>, there's still quite a lot of <u>gas left</u> and gas <u>doesn't pollute as badly</u> as coal and oil.

But gas is <u>not</u> the <u>only option</u>, as you really ought to know if you've been concentrating at all over the last few pages.

When looking at the options for a <u>new power station</u>, there are <u>several factors</u> to consider: How much it <u>costs</u> to set up and run, <u>how long</u> it takes to <u>build</u>, <u>how much power</u> it can generate, etc. Then there are also the trickier factors like <u>damage to the environment</u> and <u>impact on local communities</u>. And because these are often <u>very contentious</u> issues, getting <u>permission</u> to build certain types of power station can be a <u>long-running</u> process, and hence <u>increase</u> the overall <u>set-up time</u>. The time and <u>cost</u> of <u>decommissioning</u> (shutting down) a power plant can also be a crucial factor.

Set-Up Costs

<u>Renewable</u> resources often need <u>bigger power stations</u> than non-renewables for the <u>same output</u>. And as you'd expect, the <u>bigger</u> the power station, the <u>more expensive</u>.

<u>Nuclear reactors</u> and <u>hydroelectric dams</u> also need <u>huge</u> amounts of <u>engineering</u> to make them <u>safe</u>, which bumps up the cost.

Set-Up/Decommissioning Time

These are both affected by the <u>size</u> of the power station, the <u>complexity</u> of the engineering and also the <u>planning issues</u> (e.g. <u>discussions</u> over whether a nuclear power station should be built on a stretch of <u>beautiful coastline</u> can last <u>years</u>). <u>Gas</u> is one of the <u>quickest</u> to set up. <u>Nuclear</u> power stations take by far the <u>longest</u> (and cost the most) to <u>decommission</u>.

Reliability Issues

All the <u>non-renewables</u> are <u>reliable energy providers</u> (until they run out).

Many of the <u>renewable</u> sources <u>depend on the weather</u>, which means they're pretty <u>unreliable</u> here in the UK. The <u>exceptions</u> are <u>tidal</u> power and <u>geothermal</u> (which <u>don't</u> depend on weather).

Running/Fuel Costs

<u>Renewables</u> usually have the <u>lowest running costs</u>, because there's <u>no</u> actual <u>fuel</u> involved.

Location Issues

This is fairly <u>common sense</u> — a <u>power station</u> has to be <u>near</u> to the <u>stuff it runs on</u>.

<u>Solar</u> — pretty much <u>anywhere</u>, though the sunnier the better

<u>Gas</u> — pretty much <u>anywhere</u> there's piped gas (most of the UK)

<u>Hydroelectric</u> — <u>hilly</u>, <u>rainy</u> places with <u>floodable valleys</u>, e.g. the Lake District, Scottish Highlands

<u>Wind</u> — <u>exposed</u>, <u>windy</u> places like moors and coasts or out at sea

<u>Oil</u> — near the <u>coast</u> (oil transported by sea)

<u>Waves</u> — on the <u>coast</u>

<u>Coal</u> — near <u>coal mines</u>, e.g. Yorkshire, Wales

<u>Nuclear</u> — <u>away from people</u> (in case of disaster), <u>near water</u> (for cooling)

<u>Tidal</u> — big <u>river estuaries</u> where a dam can be built

<u>Geothermal</u> — fairly limited, only in places where <u>hot rocks</u> are <u>near the Earth's surface</u>

Environmental Issues

If there's a <u>fuel</u> involved, there'll be <u>waste pollution</u> and you'll be <u>using up resources</u>.

If it <u>relies on the weather</u>, it's often got to be in an <u>exposed place</u> where it sticks out like a <u>sore thumb</u>.

Atmospheric Pollution
Coal, Oil, Gas, (+ others, though less so)

Visual Pollution
Coal, Oil, Gas, Nuclear, Tidal, Waves, Wind, Hydroelectric,

Other Problems
Nuclear (dangerous waste, explosions, contamination), Hydroelectric (dams bursting)

Using Up Resources
Coal, Oil, Gas, Nuclear

Noise Pollution
Coal, Oil, Gas, Nuclear, Wind,

Disruption of Habitats
Hydroelectric, Tidal, Biofuels.

Disruption of Leisure Activities (e.g. boats) Waves, Tidal

Of course — the biggest problem is we need too much electricity...

It would be <u>lovely</u> if we could get rid of all the <u>nasty polluting power stations</u> and replace them with clean, green fuel, just like that... but it's not quite that simple. Renewable energy has its <u>own</u> problems too, and probably isn't enough to power the whole country without having a wind farm in everyone's back yard.

Electricity and the National Grid

The <u>National Grid</u> is the <u>network</u> of pylons and cables that covers <u>the whole of Britain</u>, getting electricity to homes everywhere. Whoever you pay for your electricity, it's the National Grid that gets it to you.

Electricity is Distributed via the National Grid...

1) The <u>National Grid</u> takes electrical energy from <u>power stations</u> to where it's needed in <u>homes</u> and <u>industry</u>.

2) It enables power to be <u>generated</u> anywhere on the grid, and then be <u>supplied</u> anywhere else on the grid.

3) To transmit the <u>huge</u> amount of <u>power</u> needed, you need either a <u>high voltage</u> or a <u>high current</u>.

4) The <u>problem</u> with a <u>high current</u> is that you lose <u>loads of energy</u> through <u>heat</u> in the cables.

5) It's much <u>cheaper</u> to <u>boost the voltage</u> up <u>really high</u> (to 400 000 V) and keep the current <u>very low</u>.

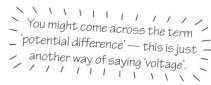
You might come across the term 'potential difference' — this is just another way of saying 'voltage'.

...With a Little Help from Pylons and Transformers

1) To get the voltage to 400 000 V to transmit power requires <u>transformers</u> as well as <u>big pylons</u> with <u>huge insulators</u> — but it's <u>still cheaper</u>.

2) The transformers have to <u>step</u> the voltage <u>up</u> at one end, for <u>efficient transmission</u>, and then bring it back down to <u>safe, usable levels</u> at the other end.

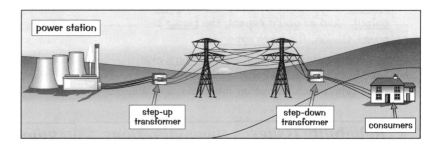

3) The <u>voltage</u> is <u>increased</u> ('<u>stepped up</u>') using a <u>step-up transformer</u>. (Yep, does what it says on the tin.)

4) It's then <u>reduced</u> again ('<u>stepped down</u>') at the consumer end using a <u>step-down transformer</u>.

There are Different Ways to Transmit Electricity

1) Electrical energy can be moved around by cables <u>buried in the ground</u>, as well as in <u>overhead</u> power lines.

2) Each of these different options has its <u>pros and cons</u>:

	Setup cost	Maintenance	Faults	How it looks	Affected by weather	Reliability	How easy to set up	Disturbance to land
Overhead Cables	lower	lots needed	easy to access	ugly	yes	less reliable	easy	minimal
Underground Cables	higher	minimal	hard to access	hidden	no	more reliable	hard	lots

Supply and Demand

1) The National Grid needs to <u>generate</u> and <u>direct</u> all the energy that the country needs — our energy demands keep on <u>increasing</u> too.

2) In order to meet these demands in the future, the <u>energy supplied</u> to the National Grid will need to <u>increase</u>, or the <u>energy demands</u> of consumers will need to <u>decrease</u>.

3) In the future, <u>supply</u> can be <u>increased</u> by opening <u>more</u> power plants or increasing their power output (or by doing <u>both</u>).

4) <u>Demand</u> can be <u>reduced</u> by consumers using more <u>energy-efficient</u> appliances, and being more <u>careful</u> not to waste energy in the home (e.g. turning off the lights or running washing machines at cooler temperatures).

Transformers — NOT robots in disguise...

You don't need to know the <u>details</u> about exactly what transformers are and how they work — just that they increase and decrease the <u>voltage</u> to <u>minimise power losses</u> in the National Grid. Make sure you know the good, bad and occasionally ugly pros and cons of <u>underground</u> and <u>over-ground</u> electricity transmission too.

Wave Basics

Waves transfer <u>energy</u> from one place to another without transferring any <u>matter</u> (stuff).

Waves **Have** Amplitude, Wavelength **and** Frequency

1) The <u>amplitude</u> is the displacement from the <u>rest position</u> to the <u>crest</u> (NOT from a trough to a crest).

2) The <u>wavelength</u> is the length of a <u>full cycle</u> of the wave, e.g. from <u>crest to crest</u>.

3) <u>Frequency</u> is the <u>number of complete waves</u> passing a certain point <u>per second</u> OR the <u>number of waves</u> produced by a source <u>each second</u>. Frequency is measured in hertz (Hz). 1 Hz is <u>1 wave per second</u>.

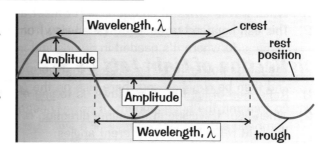

Transverse Waves **Have** Sideways **Vibrations**

<u>Most waves</u> are <u>transverse</u>:

    1) <u>Light</u> and <u>all other EM waves</u>.   3) <u>Waves</u> on <u>strings</u>.

    2) <u>Ripples</u> on water.   4) A <u>slinky spring</u> wiggled up and down.

> In <u>TRANSVERSE</u> waves the vibrations are <u>PERPENDICULAR</u> (at <u>90°</u>) to the <u>DIRECTION OF ENERGY TRANSFER</u> of the wave.

Longitudinal Waves **Have Vibrations** Along the Same Line

Examples of <u>longitudinal</u> waves are: 1) <u>Sound waves</u> and <u>ultrasound</u>.

    2) <u>Shock waves</u>, e.g. seismic waves.

    3) A <u>slinky spring</u> when you <u>push</u> the end.

Water waves, shock waves and waves in springs and ropes are all examples of <u>mechanical waves</u>.

> In <u>LONGITUDINAL</u> waves the vibrations are <u>PARALLEL</u> to the <u>DIRECTION OF ENERGY TRANSFER</u> of the wave.

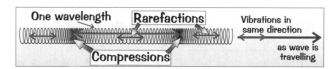

Wave Speed **=** Frequency **×** Wavelength

The equation below applies to <u>all waves</u>. You need to learn it — and <u>practise using it</u>.

> Speed = Frequency × Wavelength
> (m/s)   (Hz)   (m)

OR

> $v = f \times \lambda$

Speed (v is for <u>velocity</u>)   Frequency   Wavelength (that's the Greek letter 'lambda')

<u>EXAMPLE:</u> A radio wave has a frequency of 92.2×10^6 Hz. Find its wavelength. (The speed of all EM waves is 3×10^8 m/s.)

<u>ANSWER:</u> You're trying to find λ using f and v, so you've got to rearrange the equation. So $\lambda = v \div f = 3 \times 10^8 \div 9.22 \times 10^7 = \underline{3.25 \text{ m}}$.

$$\frac{v}{f \times \lambda}$$

The <u>speed</u> of a wave is <u>usually independent</u> of the <u>frequency</u> or <u>amplitude</u> of the wave.

Waves — dig the vibes, man...

The first thing to learn is that diagram at the top of the page. Then get that <u>$v = f \times \lambda$</u> business <u>imprinted</u> on your brain. When you've done <u>that</u>, try this question: A sound wave travelling in a solid has a frequency of <u>1.9×10^4</u> Hz and a wavelength of <u>12.5</u> cm. Find its speed.*

Waves Properties

If you're anything like me, you'll have spent hours gazing into a mirror in <u>wonder</u>. Here's why...

All Waves Can be Reflected, Refracted and Diffracted

1) When waves arrive at an obstacle (or meet a new material), their direction of travel can be changed.
2) This can happen by <u>reflection</u> (see below) or by <u>refraction</u> or <u>diffraction</u> (see page 99).

Reflection of Light Lets Us See Things

1) <u>Reflection of light</u> is what allows us to <u>see</u> objects. Light bounces off them into our eyes.
2) When light travelling in the <u>same direction</u> reflects from an <u>uneven surface</u> such as a <u>piece of paper</u>, the light reflects off <u>at different angles</u>.
3) When light travelling in the <u>same direction</u> reflects from an <u>even surface</u> (<u>smooth and shiny</u> like a <u>mirror</u>) then it's all reflected at the <u>same angle</u> and you get a <u>clear reflection</u>.

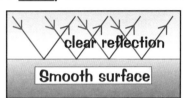

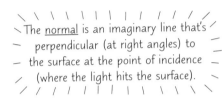

The <u>normal</u> is an imaginary line that's perpendicular (at right angles) to the surface at the point of incidence (where the light hits the surface).

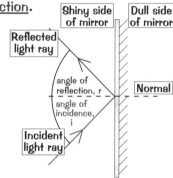

4) The <u>LAW OF REFLECTION</u> applies to <u>every reflected ray</u>:

Angle of INCIDENCE = Angle of REFLECTION

Note that these two angles are <u>ALWAYS</u> defined between the ray itself and the <u>NORMAL</u>, dotted above. <u>Don't ever</u> label them as the angle between the ray and the <u>surface</u>. Definitely uncool.

Draw a Ray Diagram for an Image in a Plane Mirror

You need to be able to <u>reproduce</u> this entire diagram of <u>how an image is formed</u> in a PLANE MIRROR. Learn these <u>important points</u>:

1) The <u>image</u> is the <u>same size</u> as the <u>object</u>.
2) It is <u>AS FAR BEHIND</u> the mirror as the object is <u>in front</u>.
3) The image is <u>virtual</u> and <u>upright</u>. The image is virtual because the object appears to be <u>behind</u> the mirror.
4) The image is <u>laterally inverted</u> — the left and right sides are <u>swapped</u>, i.e. the object's <u>left</u> side becomes its <u>right</u> side in the <u>image</u>.

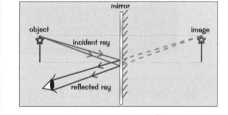

1) First off, draw the <u>virtual image</u>. <u>Don't</u> try to draw the rays first. Follow the rules in the above box — the image is the <u>same size</u>, and it's <u>as far behind</u> the mirror as the object is in <u>front</u>.

2) Next, draw a <u>reflected ray</u> going from the top of the virtual image to the top of the eye. Draw a <u>bold line</u> for the part of the ray between the mirror and eye, and a <u>dotted line</u> for the part of the ray between the mirror and virtual image.

3) Now draw the <u>incident ray</u> going from the top of the object to the mirror. The incident and reflected rays follow the <u>law of reflection</u> — but you <u>don't</u> actually have to measure any angles. Just draw the ray from the <u>object</u> to the <u>point</u> where the reflected ray <u>meets the mirror</u>.

4) Now you have an <u>incident ray</u> and <u>reflected ray</u> for the <u>top</u> of the image. Do <u>steps 2 and 3 again</u> for the <u>bottom</u> of the <u>eye</u> — a reflected ray going from the image to the bottom of the eye, then an incident ray from the object to the mirror.

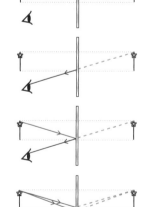

Plane mirrors — what pilots use to look behind them...

Make sure you can draw clear <u>ray diagrams</u> and you'll be well on your way to picking up lotsa marks in the exam.

Refraction and Diffraction

If you thought <u>reflection</u> was good, you'll just love <u>diffraction</u> and <u>refraction</u> — it's awesome. If you didn't find reflection interesting then I'm afraid it's tough luck — you need to know about <u>all three</u> of them. Sorry.

Diffraction and Refraction are a Bit More Complicated

1) Reflection's quite <u>straightforward</u>, but there are other ways that waves can be made to change direction.

2) They can be <u>refracted</u> — which means they go through a new material but <u>change direction</u>.

3) Or they can be <u>diffracted</u> — the waves 'bend round' obstacles, causing the waves to spread out.

Diffraction — Waves Spreading Out

1) All waves <u>spread out</u> ('diffract') at the edges when they pass through a <u>gap</u> or <u>pass an obstacle</u>.

2) The amount of diffraction depends on the size of the gap relative to the wavelength of the wave. The <u>narrower the gap</u>, or the <u>longer the wavelength</u>, the <u>more</u> the wave spreads out.

3) A <u>narrow gap</u> is one that is the same order of magnitude as the <u>wavelength</u> of the wave — i.e. they're about the <u>same size</u>.

4) So whether a gap counts as narrow or not depends on the wave in question.

5) <u>Light</u> has a very <u>small wavelength</u> (about 0.0005 mm), so it can be diffracted but it needs a <u>really small gap</u>.

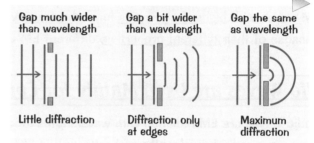

Gap much wider than wavelength — Little diffraction

Gap a bit wider than wavelength — Diffraction only at edges

Gap the same as wavelength — Maximum diffraction

Refraction — Changing the Speed of a Wave Can Change its Direction

1) When a wave crosses a boundary between two substances (from glass to air, say) it <u>changes direction</u>:

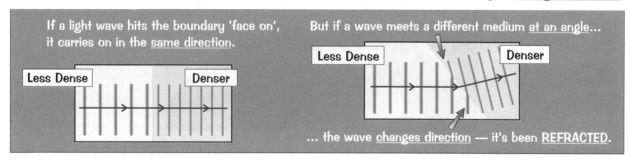

If a light wave hits the boundary 'face on', it carries on in the <u>same direction</u>.

Less Dense — Denser

But if a wave meets a different medium <u>at an angle</u>...

Less Dense — Denser

... the wave <u>changes direction</u> — it's been <u>REFRACTED</u>.

2) When light shines on a glass <u>window pane</u>, some of the light is reflected, but a lot of it passes through the glass and gets <u>refracted</u> as it does so.

3) Waves are <u>only</u> refracted if they meet a new medium <u>at an angle</u>.

4) If they're travelling <u>along the normal</u> (i.e. the angle of incidence is zero) they will <u>change speed</u>, but are <u>NOT refracted</u> — they don't change direction.

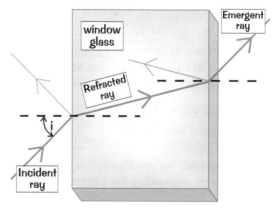

Emergent ray

window glass

Refracted ray

Incident ray

Lights, camera, refraction...

Diffraction's not too hard to get to grips with — especially if you can <u>remember those diagrams</u> at the top of the page. Also remember that <u>all</u> waves can be <u>diffracted</u> — so it doesn't matter if they're <u>longitudinal</u> or <u>transverse</u> waves. The key point to remember about <u>refraction</u> is that the wave has to meet a boundary <u>at an angle</u>.

EM Waves and Communication

Types of <u>electromagnetic</u> (EM) wave have a lot in common with one another, but their <u>differences</u> make them useful to us in different ways. These pages are packed with loads of dead important info, so pay attention...

There's a Continuous *Spectrum of EM Waves*

EM waves with <u>different wavelengths</u> (or frequencies) have different properties. We group them into <u>seven basic types</u>, but the different regions actually merge to form a <u>continuous spectrum</u>.

They're shown below with increasing frequency and energy (decreasing wavelength) from left to right.

RADIO WAVES	MICRO WAVES	INFRA RED	VISIBLE LIGHT	ULTRA VIOLET	X-RAYS	GAMMA RAYS
wavelength → $1\,m - 10^4\,m$	$10^{-2}\,m$ (1 cm)	$10^{-5}\,m$ (0.01 mm)	$10^{-7}\,m$	$10^{-8}\,m$	$10^{-10}\,m$	$10^{-15}\,m$

1) EM waves vary in <u>wavelength</u> from around $10^{-15}\,m$ to more than $10^4\,m$.

2) All the different types of EM wave travel at the <u>same speed</u> (3×10^8 m/s) in a <u>vacuum</u> (e.g. space).

3) EM waves with <u>higher frequencies</u> have <u>shorter wavelengths</u>.

4) Because of their <u>different properties</u>, different EM waves are used for <u>different purposes</u>.

Radio Waves *are Used Mainly for Communication*

1) <u>Radio waves</u> are EM radiation with wavelengths longer than about 10 cm.

2) <u>Long-wave radio</u> (wavelengths of <u>1 – 10 km</u>) can be transmitted from London, say, and received halfway round the world. That's because long wavelengths <u>diffract</u> (<u>bend</u>) (see p.99) around the curved surface of the Earth.

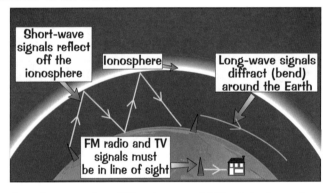

Short-wave signals reflect off the ionosphere

Ionosphere

Long-wave signals diffract (bend) around the Earth

FM radio and TV signals must be in line of sight

3) <u>Long-wave radio</u> wavelengths can also <u>diffract</u> around <u>hills</u>, into <u>tunnels</u> and all sorts.

4) This <u>diffraction effect</u> makes it possible for radio signals to be <u>received</u> even if the receiver <u>isn't</u> in <u>line of the sight</u> of the <u>transmitter</u>.

5) The radio waves used for <u>TV and FM radio</u> transmissions have very short wavelengths (10 cm – 10 m). To get reception, you must be in <u>direct sight of the transmitter</u> — the signal doesn't bend around hills or travel far <u>through</u> buildings.

6) <u>Short-wave radio</u> signals (wavelengths of about <u>10 m – 100 m</u>) can, like long-wave, be received at <u>long distances</u> from the transmitter. That's because they are <u>reflected</u> (p.98) from the <u>ionosphere</u> — an <u>electrically charged layer</u> in the Earth's upper atmosphere.

7) <u>Medium-wave</u> signals (well, the shorter ones) can also reflect from the ionosphere, depending on atmospheric conditions and the time of day.

Size matters — and my wave's longer than yours...

You'll have to be able to <u>name</u> the <u>order</u> of the different types of EM waves in terms of their <u>energy</u>, <u>frequency</u> and <u>wavelength</u>. To remember the order of <u>increasing frequency</u> and <u>energy</u>, I use the mnemonic **R**ock **M**usic **I**s **V**ery **U**seful for e**X**periments with **G**oats. It sounds stupid but it <u>does</u> work — why not make up your own...

EM Waves and Their Uses

Radio waves aren't the only waves used for communication — other EM waves come in pretty handy too. The most important thing is to think about how the properties of a wave relate to its uses.

Microwaves are Used for Satellite Communication and Mobile Phones

1) Communication to and from satellites (including satellite TV signals and satellite phones) uses microwaves. But you need to use microwaves which can pass easily through the Earth's watery atmosphere. Radio waves can't do this.

2) For satellite TV, the signal from a transmitter is transmitted into space...

3) ... where it's picked up by the satellite's receiver dish orbiting thousands of kilometres above the Earth. The satellite transmits the signal back to Earth in a different direction...

microwaves

clouds and water vapour

4) ... where it's received by a satellite dish on the ground.

5) Mobile phone calls also travel as microwaves between your phone and the nearest transmitter. Some wavelengths of microwaves are absorbed by water molecules and heat them up. If the water in question happens to be in your cells, you might start to cook — so some people think using your mobile a lot (especially next to your head), or living near a mast, could damage your health. There isn't any conclusive evidence either way yet.

6) And microwaves are used by remote-sensing satellites — to 'see' through the clouds and monitor oil spills, track the movement of icebergs, see how much rainforest has been chopped down and so on.

Infrared Waves are Used for Remote Controls and Optical Fibres

1) Infrared waves are used in lots of wireless remote controllers.

2) Remote controls work by emitting different patterns of infrared waves to send different commands to an appliance, e.g. a TV.

3) Optical fibres (e.g. those used in phone lines) can carry data over long distances very quickly.

4) They use both infrared waves and visible light.

5) The signal is carried as pulses of light or infrared radiation and is reflected off the sides of a very narrow core from one end of the fibre to the other.

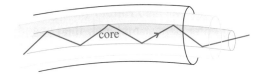

core

Visible Light is Useful for Photography

It sounds pretty obvious, but photography would be kinda tricky without visible light.

1) Cameras use a lens to focus visible light onto a light-sensitive film or electronic sensor.

2) The lens aperture controls how much light enters the camera (like the pupil in an eye).

3) The shutter speed determines how long the film or sensor is exposed to the light.

4) By varying the aperture and shutter speed (and also the sensitivity of the film or the sensor), a photographer can capture as much or as little light as they want in their photograph.

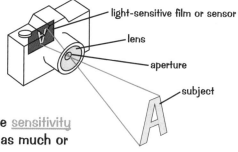

light-sensitive film or sensor

lens

aperture

subject

Microwaves are also used for making popcorn — mmm...

I bet you didn't realise that all those different types of technology — like microwaves and infrared — use waves that travel at exactly the same speed as each other (in a vacuum). It's pretty cool stuff.

Sound Waves

We hear sounds when vibrations reach our eardrums. You'll need to know how sound waves work.

Sound Travels as a Wave

1) Sound waves are caused by vibrating objects. These mechanical vibrations are passed through the surrounding medium as a series of compressions. They're a type of longitudinal wave (see page 97).

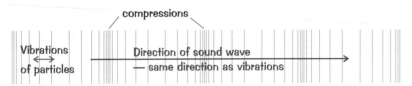

2) Sometimes the sound will eventually travel through someone's ear and reach their eardrum, at which point the person might hear it.

3) Sound generally travels faster in solids than in liquids, and faster in liquids than in gases.

4) Sound can't travel in space, because it's mostly a vacuum (there are no particles).

Sound Waves Can Reflect and Refract

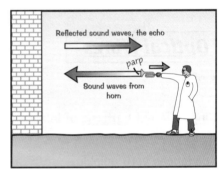

1) Sound waves will be reflected by hard flat surfaces.

2) This is very noticeable in an empty room. A big empty room sounds completely different once you've put carpet, curtains and a bit of furniture in it. That's because these things absorb the sound quickly and stop it echoing around the room. Echoes are just reflected sound waves.

3) You hear a delay between the original sound and the echo because the echoed sound waves have to travel further, and so take longer to reach your ears.

4) Sound waves will also refract (change direction) as they enter different media. As they enter denser material, they speed up. (However, since sound waves are always spreading out so much, the change in direction is hard to spot under normal circumstances.)

The Higher the Frequency, the Higher the Pitch

1) High frequency sound waves sound high pitched like a squeaking mouse.

2) Low frequency sound waves sound low pitched like a mooing cow.

3) Frequency is the number of complete vibrations each second — so a wave that has a frequency of 100 Hz vibrates 100 times each second.

4) Common units are kHz (1000 Hz) and MHz (1 000 000 Hz).

5) High frequency (or high pitch) also means shorter wavelength (see p.97).

6) The loudness of a sound depends on the amplitude (p.97) of the sound wave. The bigger the amplitude, the louder the sound.

The room always feels big and empty whenever I tell a joke... (It must be the carpets.)

The thing to do here is learn the facts. There's a simple equation that says the more you learn now, the more marks you'll get in the exam. A lot of questions just test whether you've learnt the facts. Easy marks, really. Now journey with me to a distant galaxy to explore the questions that have plagued mankind for centuries...

The Origin of the Universe

OK. Let's not kid ourselves — this is a pretty daunting topic. How the universe started is obviously open to debate, but physicists have got some neat ideas based on their observations of the stars. How romantic...

The Universe Seems to be Expanding

As big as the universe already is, it looks like it's getting even bigger.
All its galaxies seem to be moving away from each other. There's good evidence for this...

1) Light from Other Galaxies is Red-shifted

1) Different chemical elements absorb different frequencies (p.97) of light.

2) Each element produces a specific pattern of dark lines at the frequencies that it absorbs in the visible spectrum.

3) When we look at light from distant galaxies we can see the same patterns but at slightly lower frequencies than they should be — they're shifted towards the red end of the spectrum. This is called red-shift.

4) It's the same effect as the vrrroomm from a racing car — the engine sounds lower-pitched when the car's gone past you and is moving away from you. This is called the Doppler effect.

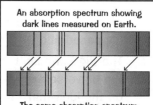

An absorption spectrum showing dark lines measured on Earth.

The same absorption spectrum measured from light from a distant galaxy. The dark lines in this spectrum are red-shifted.

The Doppler Effect

1) When something that emits waves moves towards you or away from you, the wavelengths and frequencies of the waves seem different — compared to when the source of the waves is stationary.

2) The frequency of a source moving towards you will seem higher and its wavelength will seem shorter.

3) The frequency of a source moving away from you will seem lower and its wavelength will seem longer.

4) The Doppler effect happens to both longitudinal waves (e.g. sound) and transverse waves (e.g. light and microwaves).

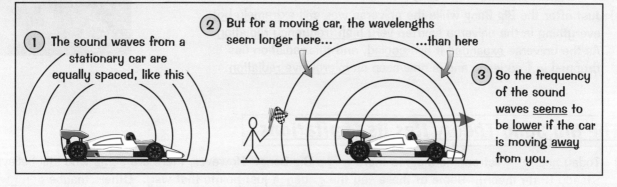

1) The sound waves from a stationary car are equally spaced, like this

2) But for a moving car, the wavelengths seem longer here... ...than here

3) So the frequency of the sound waves seems to be lower if the car is moving away from you.

2) The Further Away a Galaxy is, the Greater the Red-shift

1) Measurements of the red-shift suggest that all the galaxies are moving away from us very quickly — and it's the same result whichever direction you look in.

2) More distant galaxies have greater red-shifts than nearer ones.

3) This means that more distant galaxies are moving away from us faster than nearer ones.

4) This provides evidence that the whole universe is expanding.

If a tree falls down in the forest and you're driving away from it...

Listen out for the Doppler effect next time you hear a fast motorbike or a police siren — you should be able to work out if it's coming towards you or speeding away. You can also hear the noise in cartoons when someone falls off a cliff and it plays that classic whistling noise that gets lower, showing them accelerating away from you.

The Origin of the Universe

Once upon a time there was a really Big Bang — that's the most convincing theory we've got.

It All Started Off with a Very Big Bang (Probably)

Right now, distant galaxies are moving away from us — the further away a galaxy is from the us, the faster they're moving away. But something must have got them going. That 'something' was probably a big explosion — so they called it the Big Bang...

1) According to this theory, all the matter and energy in the universe must have been compressed into a very small space. Then it exploded from that single 'point' and started expanding.

2) The expansion is still going on. We can use the current rate of expansion of the universe to estimate its age. Our best guess is that the Big Bang happened about 14 billion years ago.

3) The Big Bang isn't the only game in town. The 'Steady State' theory says that the universe has always existed as it is now, and it always will do. It's based on the idea that the universe appears pretty much the same everywhere. This theory explains the apparent expansion by suggesting that matter is being created in the spaces as the universe expands. But there are some big problems with this theory.

4) The discovery of the cosmic microwave background radiation (CMBR) some years later was strong evidence that the Big Bang was the more likely explanation of the two.

There's a Uniform Microwave Radiation from All Directions

1) Scientists have detected low frequency electromagnetic radiation coming from all parts of the universe.

2) This radiation is largely in the microwave part of the EM spectrum (p.100). It's known as the cosmic microwave background radiation (CMBR).

3) The Big Bang theory is the only theory that can explain the CMBR.

4) Just after the Big Bang while the universe was still extremely hot, everything in the universe emitted very high frequency radiation. As the universe expanded it has cooled, and this radiation has dropped in frequency and is now seen as microwave radiation.

The Big Bang Theory Has Its Limitations

1) Today nearly all astronomers agree there was a Big Bang. However, there are some who still believe in the Steady State theory. Some of these say the evidence just points that way. Others maybe don't want to change their mind — that would mean admitting they were wrong in the first place.

2) The Big Bang theory isn't perfect. As it stands, it's not the whole explanation of the universe — there are observations that the theory can't yet explain. E.g. for complicated reasons that you don't need to know, the Big Bang theory predicts that the universe's expansion should be slowing down — but as far as we can tell it's actually speeding up.

3) The Big Bang explains the universe's expansion well, but it isn't an explanation for what actually caused the explosion in the first place, or what the conditions were like before the explosion (or if there was a 'before').

4) It seems most likely the Big Bang theory will be adapted in some way to account for its weaknesses rather than just dumped — it explains so much so well that scientists will need a lot of persuading to drop it altogether.

Time and space — it's funny old stuff isn't it...

Proving a scientific theory is impossible. If enough evidence points a certain way, then a theory can look pretty convincing. But that doesn't prove it's a fact — new evidence may change people's minds.

Revision Summary for Physics 1b

It's business time — another chance for you to see which bits went in and which bits you need to flick back and have another read over. You know the drill by now. Do as many of the questions as you can and then try the tricky ones after you've had another chance to read the pages you struggled on. You know it makes sense.

1) What is meant by a non-renewable energy resource?
   Name four different non-renewable energy resources.
2) Explain how electricity is generated in a gas-fired power station.
   Describe the useful energy transfers that occur.
3) Describe how the following renewable resources are used to generate electricity.
   State one advantage and one disadvantage for each resource.
   a) wind   b) solar energy   c) the tide   d) waves   e) geothermal energy
4) Why are hydroelectric power stations often located in remote valleys?
5) What is the purpose of pumped storage?
6) Why is wave power only a realistic major energy source on small islands?
7) What is the source of energy for tidal barrages?
8) Apart from generating electricity, how else can geothermal heat be used?
9) How are biofuels produced? Give two examples of biofuels.
10) Name two places that carbon dioxide can be stored after carbon capture.
11) Name six factors that should be considered when a new power station is being planned.
12) Which three energy sources are linked most strongly with habitat disruption?
13) Explain why a very high electrical voltage is used to transmit electricity in the National Grid.
14) Draw a diagram to illustrate frequency, wavelength and amplitude.
15)* Find the speed of a wave with frequency 50 kHz and wavelength 0.3 cm.
16) a) Sketch a diagram of a ray of light being reflected in a mirror.
    b) Label the normal and the angles of incidence and reflection.
17) Why does light bend as it moves between air and water?
18) Draw a diagram showing a wave diffracting through a gap.
19) What size should the gap be in order to maximise diffraction?
    a) much larger than the wavelength   b) the same size as the wavelength   c) a bit bigger than the wavelength
20) Sketch the EM spectrum with all its details. Put the lowest frequency waves on the left.
21) What type of wave do television remotes usually use?
22) Which two types of EM wave are commonly used to send signals along optical fibres?
23) Describe the main known dangers of microwaves, infrared, visible light, UV and X-rays.
24) Explain how X-rays can be useful in hospitals.
25) Why can't sound waves travel in space?
26) Are high frequency sound waves high pitched or low pitched?
27) If a wave source is moving towards you, will the observed frequency of its
    waves be higher or lower than their actual frequency?
28) What do red-shift observations tell us about the universe?
29) Describe the 'Big Bang' theory for the origin of the universe. What evidence is there for this theory?

Index

Index

Index and Answers

Answers

Revision Summary for Biology 1a (page 30)

2) Professional runner, mechanic, secretary

16) a) Response A b) Response B

Revision Summary for Chemistry 1a (page 63)

3) Calcium

7) a)

Could be hydrogen/oxygen/nitrogen (or any other diatomic gaseous element).

b)

Could be carbon dioxide (water molecules are bent).

8) a) $CaCO_3 + 2HCl \rightarrow CaCl_2 + H_2O + CO_2$
  b) $Ca + 2H_2O \rightarrow Ca(OH)_2 + H_2$

29) Propane — the fuel needs to be a gas at −10 °C to work in a camping stove.

Revision Summary for Chemistry 1b (page 74)

22) b) 2 cm c) 3.5 years

Efficiency of Machines Top Tip (page 83)

TV: 0.0318 or 3.18%
Loudspeaker: 0.0143 or 1.43%

Revision Summary for Physics 1a (page 88)

15) 40 years
20) 90 kJ
26) 70% or 0.7
27) a) 80 J b) 20 J c) 0.8 or 80%
29) 0.125 kWh

Wave Basics Top Tip (page 97)

2375 m/s

Revision Summary for Physics 1b (page 105)

15) 150 m/s

GCSE Edexcel
Physical Education
The Revision Guide

This book is for anyone doing **GCSE Edexcel Physical Education**.

GCSE PE is all about understanding how physical activity and your lifestyle can affect you and your body.

Happily this CGP book includes all the **PE facts** you need to learn for the exam. And in true CGP style, we've explained it all as **clearly and concisely** as possible.

It's also got some daft bits in to try and make the whole experience at least vaguely entertaining for you.

What CGP is all about

Our sole aim here at CGP is to produce the highest quality books — carefully written, immaculately presented and dangerously close to being funny.

Then we work our socks off to get them out to you — at the cheapest possible prices.

Contents

Section 1.1 — Healthy, active lifestyles

Section 1.2 — Your healthy, active body

Published by CGP

Contributors:
Charley Darbishire, Mary Falkner, David Hickinson, Sharon Keeley, Simon Little,
Andy Park, Glenn Rogers, Caley Simpson, Sarah Williams.

ISBN: 978 1 84762 308 9

With thanks to Chris Cope, Gemma Hallam, Paul Jordin for the proofreading.

Definition of Health on page 1 © WHO 2008. All rights reserved.
World Health Organisation
http://www.who.int/about/definition/en/print.html

Printed by Elanders Ltd, Newcastle upon Tyne.
Clipart from Corel®

Based on the classic CGP style created by Richard Parsons.

Healthy, Active Lifestyles

The first stop on the PE fun bus — <u>healthy</u>, <u>active lifestyles</u>. It's not just a case of cutting down on the lard sandwiches, or moving from in front of the TV once in a while (but that sure can help)...

Health <u>is a State of</u> Wellbeing

Being healthy is <u>more</u> than just having a healthy body.
Remember this definition of health — it's the one used by the World Health Organisation (WHO).

> <u>Health</u> is a state of complete <u>physical</u>, <u>mental</u> and <u>social well-being</u> and <u>not</u> merely the absence of disease or infirmity.

PHYSICAL WELLBEING:
1) Your <u>heart</u>, <u>kidneys</u>, and the rest of your body are working well.
2) You're not suffering from any <u>diseases</u> or <u>injuries</u>.
3) You're not <u>physically weak</u> (<u>infirm</u>), so you can easily do everyday activities.

MENTAL WELLBEING:
1) You don't have too much <u>stress</u> or <u>anxiety</u>.
2) You're not suffering from any <u>mental illnesses</u>.
3) You feel <u>content</u>.

SOCIAL WELLBEING:
1) You have <u>food</u>, <u>clothing</u> and <u>shelter</u>.
2) You have <u>friends</u>.
3) You believe you have some <u>worth</u> in society.

<u>Stay</u> Healthy <u>by Leading a</u> Healthy, Active Lifestyle

1) Your <u>lifestyle</u> is the <u>way</u> you live your life.
   It's <u>everything</u> you do — including your <u>work</u> and your <u>hobbies</u>.

> A <u>healthy</u>, <u>active lifestyle</u> adds to your <u>physical</u>, <u>mental</u> and <u>social wellbeing</u>. It includes <u>doing exercise</u> and <u>physical activity on a regular basis</u>.

2) For a healthy, active lifestyle — <u>exercise</u> and think **PEASED**.

P ⇒ <u>PERSONAL HYGIENE:</u> Keep yourself <u>clean</u> — it'll help you to avoid loads of diseases. It won't do your <u>social</u> life any harm, either.

E ⇒ <u>EMOTIONAL HEALTH:</u> Feeling good is important. Try to avoid too much <u>stress</u> and <u>worry</u>. This can be caused by <u>friends</u> and <u>relationships</u> as well as things like <u>work</u>.

A ⇒ <u>ALCOHOL / DRUG USE:</u> Misuse of <u>substances</u> can lead to poor health. That includes <u>alcohol</u> and <u>tobacco</u>. Even breathing in other people's smoke (<u>passive smoking</u>) can lead to health problems.

S ⇒ <u>SAFETY:</u> If you have a dangerous job or hobby, you're more likely to <u>injure</u> yourself. So use the proper <u>safety equipment</u> — and in sport, play by the rules.

E ⇒ <u>ENVIRONMENT:</u> <u>Pollution</u> can cause <u>respiratory</u> problems. Noise can cause stress and affect your <u>sleep</u>.

D ⇒ <u>DIET:</u> You need the right balance of <u>nutrients</u> so you can cope with your lifestyle.

I don't get it — I got PEASED, but I don't feel any healthier...

<u>Relax — it's part of a healthy, active lifestyle you know...</u>

<u>All</u> your <u>lifestyle choices</u> can affect your <u>health</u>. It's not just a case of doing some exercise and I'm alright (and healthy) Jack. Make sure you know the different things that make up a <u>healthy</u>, <u>active lifestyle</u>.

Healthy, Active Lifestyles

Doing exercise and physical activity is <u>good</u> for you — that's not exactly a surprise. What is surprising is just how many <u>different ways</u> it's good for you. And you get to learn them all... enjoy.

Physical Activity — *Any Form of* Exercise *or* Movement

1) <u>Physical activity</u> is just any form of <u>exercise</u> or <u>movement</u>.
   It can be <u>planned</u> and <u>structured</u> (like doing an aerobics class), or not (like dashing for the bus).
   In PE, you're normally interested in the structured and planned type.

> <u>Exercise</u> is any physical activity you do to <u>improve</u>
> or <u>maintain</u> your <u>health</u> and/or <u>fitness</u>.

It <u>doesn't</u> have to be a <u>competitive sport</u>.

2) To stay healthy, you need to be <u>physically active</u>. You can <u>increase</u> the amount of physical activity you do by just <u>changing</u> a few <u>habits</u>, like using the stairs instead of taking the lift.

Physical Activity has *Social, Physical* and *Mental Benefits*

There's almost no end of <u>good reasons</u> for taking part in regular physical activity. For your exam, you need to know whether each reason is a <u>mental</u>, <u>physical</u> or <u>social benefit</u> of doing physical activity.

Social Benefits

1) <u>FRIENDS</u> — Doing physical activity can help you <u>make friends</u> with people of different <u>ages</u> and <u>backgrounds</u>. It might also just be a way of socialising with your <u>current friends</u>.

2) <u>COOPERATION</u> and <u>TEAMWORK</u> — By taking part in <u>team activities</u> like football, you have to learn how to <u>cooperate</u> and <u>work with other people</u>.

Physical Benefits

1) <u>HEALTH</u> — You can <u>maintain</u> or <u>improve</u> your <u>health</u> with regular physical activity. You reduce your chances of getting <u>ill</u>, and can increase your <u>life expectancy</u>.

2) <u>FITNESS</u> — You can increase your <u>strength</u>, <u>endurance</u>, <u>flexibility</u> and <u>overall fitness</u> (see p11).

3) <u>PERFORMANCE</u> — The more you do an activity, the better you'll get at it.

Mental Benefits

1) <u>FEELING GOOD</u> — As you do physical activity, your body releases more of a hormone called <u>serotonin</u> into your blood stream. Serotonin is the '<u>happy hormone</u>' — the <u>higher</u> your serotonin levels, the <u>happier</u> you feel.

Stressed? Me? Don't be ridiculous.

2) <u>STRESS RELIEF</u> — Doing physical activity can help <u>relieve stress</u> and prevent <u>stress-related illnesses</u>.

I'm amazing...

3) <u>SELF-ESTEEM</u> — <u>Taking part</u> in a physical activity can increase your <u>self-esteem</u> (your opinion of yourself), <u>confidence</u>, and generally make you <u>feel better about yourself</u>.

4) <u>COMPETITION</u> and <u>PHYSICAL CHALLENGE</u> — Whether you're in a <u>competition</u>, or just trying to better your <u>last performance</u> — physical activity can <u>challenge</u> you and drive you to do <u>the best you can</u>. It can also improve how you think and act <u>under pressure</u>.

Aesthetic Appreciation — *How Good an Activity Looks*

1) If you do an activity, you get a <u>better understanding</u> of it and the <u>techniques</u> involved.

2) You also know <u>what to watch out for</u>, whether it's a <u>great pass</u> in football, or a <u>punch combination</u> in boxing. Having done the physical activity, you'll probably <u>appreciate</u> it <u>more</u> than someone who hasn't.

Phwoarr... did you see the way that frisbee glided?

<u>Social</u>, <u>physical</u> and <u>mental</u>... sounds like the Krypton Factor to me. Remember — physical activity is good for your body, mind and your ability to make friends even when sweaty. Make sure you know whether each benefit is social, mental or physical — it could be worth a tasty extra mark in the exam.

Influences on Your Lifestyle

What and how much physical activity you do is affected by many things...

Many Factors Affect the Physical Activity You Do

Your participation in and attitude towards physical activity are influenced by a whole host of things. They fit into 6 main groups. Here are the ones you need to know for the exam:

C ➤ CULTURAL — Age, gender, race, and disability can all have an affect.

H ➤ HEALTH AND WELLBEING — Any illness or health problems can affect the activity you do.

I ➤ IMAGE — Whether an activity's fashionable or gets a lot of media coverage.

P ➤ PEOPLE — Your family, peers (that's your friends) and role models (the people you look up to).

S ➤ SOCIO-ECONOMIC — Can you afford to do a particular activity? What is the social status of the activity?

R ➤ RESOURCES — Do you have enough time and access to facilities to be able to do an activity?

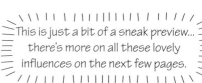

CHIPS R very influential...

This is just a bit of a sneak preview... there's more on all these lovely influences on the next few pages.

Image can Influence Which Activities You Do

MEDIA COVERAGE

You can't avoid sport — it's in the papers, on TV, on the radio, in films, on the Internet... All that media coverage will affect the activities people do.

1) The media brings sport to people who may not experience it otherwise. This can encourage participation.
2) Media companies pay for the rights to show a sport — sponsorship for a sport will also increase dramatically if it's popularised by the media. That means the opportunities to get into the sport at a high level will also go up.
3) The media helps make sporting role models (e.g. Roger Federer) for people to aspire to. This encourages more people to do a particular physical activity.
4) Sports stars are also hounded by the media, who are quick to pounce if a sports superstar's halo slips — which can then have a negative affect on their sport.

FASHION

1) Sports or leisure activities can go in or out of fashion. In the 90s, aerobics became very fashionable with endless tedious celebrity fitness videos being released.
2) Sports clothing has also become a lot more fashionable. If the clothing or equipment for a physical activity is fashionable, people are more likely to do the activity.
3) Going to the gym is very fashionable at the moment — which has meant more gyms have opened — so people now have more opportunity to go to them.

The only sport on the Net I ever hear about is surfing...

Who knew there were so many things that could influence the physical activities you do? And this my friends is just the tip of the iceberg, there are 3 more pages of influencing fun to come. Make sure you've got the influences of image sorted before turning to the influential world of people and culture (darling).

Influences on Your Lifestyle

Round Two — the people and cultural influences that affect the physical activity you do. Family, friends, religion gender, race... it all has an effect. It's amazing we think we've got free will at all really...

People Influence the Physical Activity You Do

Your family and friends can have a big influence on whether you do sport, and which sports you choose.

SUPPORT FROM YOUR FAMILY

1) Parents can encourage their children to exercise and take up sports.
2) Some activities need special clothing or equipment e.g. fencing. It's usually parents who fork out the cash.
3) Many children can't easily get to and from sporting activities. They often rely on their parents to get them there.

PEER PRESSURE

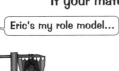

1) Most people have a group of friends they spend most of their free time with. This group of friends is their peer group.
2) The attitudes of your friends will probably influence whether you like sport, and the sports you play. If all your mates play and like football, you'll probably play and like football. If your mates think that sport is rubbish and don't play it, you'll probably do less sport.

Eric's my role model...

ROLE MODELS

People who excel in their sport can become role models and inspire people to be like them. This encourages more people to participate in their sport.

Your Gender May Influence the Activity You Do

It was tough, but I found a ballet class that'd have me eventually...

1) Many physical activities are still considered 'male only', such as rugby — so there are often fewer opportunities for women to do these activities.
2) It can work the other way round to. Some activities like netball are seen as women's activities.
3) It also doesn't help when women are often not allowed to compete with men.
4) Women's sporting events usually have a lower profile than men's events and don't get as much media coverage (see p3). That means there are often fewer role models for women than men.
5) There's usually less sponsorship available for women's sport too (because of its lower profile), which also means fewer opportunities for women to do sport at a high level.

Race, Religion and Culture can Affect Your Choices Too

1) Sometimes your religious beliefs or cultural background can influence the physical activity you may do.

E.g. Many Muslim women have to keep their bodies covered up. This may mean they're less likely to participate in activities such as swimming because of the clothing that's expected to be worn.

2) Racism and racial abuse used to be a huge problem in sport. Campaigns against racism, such as the Show Racism the Red Card campaign, have helped to bring the problem of racism into the media. Unfortunately, incidents of racial abuse still go on e.g. racist chanting at football matches.
3) A lot of work has been done to try and make sure that people of all races have equal opportunities in sport and physical activity. However, some studies show that UK ethnic minorities are still less likely to participate in physical activity at all levels than white people.

We're all under the influence...

I tried getting out of netball on religious grounds once. My teacher said if I was a actually a Jedi, I could use the force to throw the ball, but I was playing none the less. Anyway, lots of lovely influences to learn here — make sure you know them all before heading on over to the influences of age and disability.

Influences on Your Lifestyle

What your <u>body can do</u> can limit the physical activities you can do (that's not exactly the shock of the century). Whether it's your <u>age</u>, your <u>health</u> or a <u>disability</u>, it all has an effect...

Age — Your Body can Limit the Activities You Can Do

1) Some sports are more <u>popular</u> than others with different age groups.
2) Most people aged 16-30 have <u>loads of choice</u> for physical activity, but more will choose to play tennis, say, rather than something like bowls.
3) People over 50 are more <u>physically limited</u> in the sports they can choose. They tend to do <u>less strenuous</u> activities like walking or swimming.
4) Some sports, such as <u>weightlifting</u> and <u>long distance running</u>, can potentially <u>damage</u> a <u>young person's</u> body.
5) Competitions in high endurance activities often have a <u>minimum age restriction</u>.

Poor Health May Limit the Activities You Can Do...

1) Becoming <u>temporarily</u> or <u>permanently ill</u> can <u>stop</u> you from being able to do some physical activities.
2) Some physical activities can actually <u>help</u> with particular medical conditions e.g. <u>swimming</u>.

1) Swimming is thought to be one of the best forms of exercise for <u>asthma sufferers</u>.
Some <u>asthma attacks</u> are brought on by breathing in <u>cold</u>, <u>dry air</u> during physical activity. The atmosphere at a swimming pool is usually <u>warm and damp</u>, so they're less likely to have an attack while exercising.
2) Swimming's also a great way of exercising for people who have <u>joint problems</u> — the water helps <u>support</u> the body, which puts <u>less pressure</u> on the joints.

Disability will Influence You Too...

1) Having a <u>disability</u> can limit the physical activities you can do.
2) The <u>opportunities</u> in sport and <u>access to sporting facilities</u> for disabled people used to be few and far between.
3) Nowadays, there are many <u>schemes</u> set up to give disabled people <u>more opportunity</u> to exercise and take part in activities within their physical limits.
4) Disabled sporting events are now given a lot more <u>media coverage</u> than they once were. The Paralympics are now given extensive <u>media coverage</u>, like the Olympics.
5) This media coverage is helping to <u>change people's attitudes</u> towards disability and sport.
6) It's also helping create many more <u>disabled role models</u> (like <u>Dame Tanni Grey-Thompson</u> and <u>Ellie Simmonds</u>), which encourages more disabled people to get active.

I hope I'm still break dancing at 60...

Age wise it's not like you get to 50 and that's the end of the road. The oldest Olympic medallist was a Swedish chap, who won a silver for shooting at the age of 72. OK, so shooting isn't the most physical of activities... but still pretty darn impressive. Almost as impressive as the number of these influences...

Time and Resources

You'd have thought after all that there couldn't be anything else that could possibly affect the physical activities you choose to do. And that's where you'd be wrong....

People Have More Free Time to Exercise

Most of our time is taken up by things that <u>need to be done</u>:

1) <u>Social</u> duties — going to school or work, and doing chores and things.

2) <u>Bodily</u> needs — mainly eating and sleeping.

In the time that's left, we can choose what we want to do.

The <u>more free time</u> you have, the more time you have to <u>exercise</u>.

Where You Live Affects the Activities You Can Do

Your <u>location</u> will affect the physical activities you choose to do.

1) You might not need <u>good facilities</u> for many physical activities — but it definitely makes playing them <u>easier</u>. There are two sorts of facilities:

- <u>Outdoor Facilities</u> — including <u>pitches</u> (e.g. for cricket), <u>tracks</u> (e.g. athletics) and <u>facilities for water sports</u>.
- <u>Indoor Facilities</u> — usually <u>purpose-built buildings</u> such as <u>swimming pools</u> and <u>sports halls</u> (used for loads of sports, like tennis, basketball, badminton and football).

2) It's no good having great exercise facilities if you can't get anywhere <u>near</u> them. Having <u>easy access</u> to sporting facilities means you're <u>more likely</u> to use them. If the facilities aren't near by, you'll need access to <u>transport</u> to get there — having a <u>car</u>, or <u>good bus links</u> to the facilities can really help.

3) If you live somewhere like the Lake District, there's a huge amount of <u>opportunity</u> to do <u>outdoor activities</u> like hillwalking, rock-climbing or windsurfing. Because there's more opportunity, you're <u>more likely</u> to do these activities than someone who lives in the sprawling metropolis of Manchester.

Money Always Helps...

1) Some activities <u>cost</u> a lot of money to do:

- For some sports you may need <u>expensive equipment</u> e.g. rock climbing.
- For some sports, you might need to be a <u>member of a club</u> to play. That usually means paying <u>membership fees</u> to join, e.g. many golf clubs charge fees to use their facilities.
- You may have to <u>travel</u> to be able to do an activity, e.g. to <u>ski</u> you need to have access to a ski slope. This travel can be <u>expensive</u>.

2) Being unable to afford equipment or access to facilities can <u>limit</u> the activities you're able to do.

Activities can be Status Symbols

1) Some activities are seen as <u>more appropriate</u> than others for certain groups — they have a certain <u>status</u>.

2) <u>Expensive</u> activities, like polo, are often associated with the <u>wealthy</u> and 'upper class'. This image makes some expensive activities become <u>status symbols</u>.

3) Similarly, some <u>cheaper</u> activities like football tend to be associated with being 'working class'.

What ho, Geraldine — going out on the piste?

That's a lot of influences to learn — but learn them you must, I'm afraid. The best way to do it is to close your revision guide and see how many influences you can <u>scribble down</u>. Have a look and see how many you got right. It'll take a couple of goes, just keep going 'til you can remember them all.

Roles in Sport

There's more to sport than just playing it. To play a match, you usually need some <u>volunteers</u> and an <u>official</u>. To <u>do well</u> in an activity, you need <u>team captains</u> and <u>coaches</u> to be able to <u>lead</u> and inspire you.

Coaches and Team Captains Need to be Leaders

To be a good <u>team captain</u> or <u>coach</u>, you need to be able to <u>lead</u>. For both roles, you need to be <u>enthusiastic</u> about your sport and able to <u>motivate</u> yourself and your team.

Lets go team...   Aye aye Capt'n

CAPTAIN — a player that leads their team during a game

1) They should be <u>highly skilled</u> in their sport, and be able to <u>perform reliably under pressure</u>. That way they can act as <u>role models</u> for the other members of their team.

2) They also need to be <u>organised</u>. They need to be able to organise players during a game, and are often responsible for arranging practice sessions and matches.

3) They need to be <u>decisive</u> e.g. cricket team captains have to decide how to arrange the fielders and work out bowling tactics to try and beat the opposing team.

COACH — a non-player that's in charge of training the team

1) <u>Coaches</u> need to really <u>know</u> their sport well so they can come up with <u>training ideas</u> and game-winning <u>tactics</u>. They're often <u>ex-players</u> who want to stay involved in their sport.

2) Coaches also need to help players <u>improve</u> their <u>performance</u>, both <u>individually</u> and as a <u>team</u>. To do this they need to be able to <u>analyse</u> player performance and <u>communicate</u> their advice <u>clearly</u>.

All Sports need Officials

Playing any sport competitively is tricky if you don't have a <u>referee</u> or <u>umpire</u> to make sure that <u>everyone</u> follows the <u>rules</u>:

1) <u>Referees</u> and <u>officials</u> need to <u>know the rules</u> of their sport inside out.

2) They must be <u>observant</u> and <u>decisive</u> as they often need to make decisions <u>quickly</u>.

3) They need to be <u>authoritative</u> and <u>confident</u> so they can keep <u>control</u> of the game. Once they've made a decision they need to be confident enough to <u>enforce</u> it, even if players try and argue.

Volunteering — More Than a Nice Thing to Do

1) Being a <u>volunteer</u> means giving up your free time to do something <u>without being paid</u>. Sports volunteers can do anything from coaching, to driving the team minibus to matches, to washing the netball bibs.

2) Volunteers are <u>really important</u> in sport. Many sports clubs and initiatives are run by <u>volunteers alone</u>.

3) Volunteers need to be <u>enthusiastic</u> and able to work well as part of a <u>team</u>. Having <u>leadership</u> and <u>problem-solving skills</u> are always a bonus.

4) Yes, you have to work for free — but people usually get a lot <u>back</u> from volunteering. Helping people get into sport can be really satisfying. You can also make <u>new friends</u>, and improve your <u>teamwork</u> and <u>leadership</u> skills which are useful <u>outside</u> of sport.

5) It can also give you <u>contacts</u> which are really useful for getting more involved in sport. And the experience can make you generally more <u>employable</u> too.

There's no I in team... or referee... or sausage...

My particular talent has always been making incredibly weak orange squash after a match. I always wondered why I was never made team captain, but now it all becomes clear. Make sure you know the <u>qualities</u> you need to be good in each role. Close the book and see how many you can scribble down.

Levels of Participation in Sport

You can use a pyramid to show <u>four</u> levels of participation in sport — imaginatively named the <u>sports participation pyramid</u>. It's a tough climb to the top to become one of the <u>elite</u>, there's no lift or anything...

The *Sports Participation Pyramid (of joy)...*

Not every footballer in the world is making their millions playing in the Premiership (I wish...) — there are <u>different levels</u> of participation and performance within a sport...

...from being forced to do PE at school kicking and screaming... to <u>dedicating your life</u> to sport and winning an Olympic gold medal.

You can split people's level of participation in sport into <u>four</u> main stages.

The <u>number</u> of people participating get <u>smaller</u> at each increasing level, which you can handily show using a fetching <u>pyramid</u> shape.

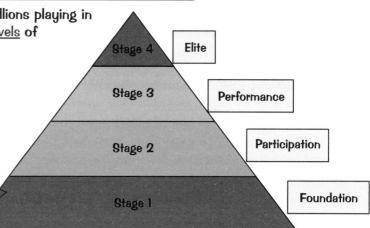

There are *Four Stages* you Need to Know

For the last time... the BALL goes through the hoop.

STAGE 1 — FOUNDATION

1) You may <u>not even understand</u> all the <u>rules</u> at this stage. You'll be developing <u>basic skills</u> and <u>movements</u> needed when participating in a sport.
2) Most people are normally at this level while at <u>school</u> — <u>PE lessons</u> are often the first place you get introduced to a sport.

STAGE 2 — PARTICIPATION

1) This is when you <u>choose</u> to do a sport <u>regularly</u>.
2) You're <u>competent</u> at your chosen activity.

> Being <u>competent</u> means <u>having</u> and <u>using</u> the <u>skills</u> needed for your sport, in combination with game <u>tactics</u> and <u>strategies</u>, so that you're able to <u>perform effectively</u>.

3) The reasons for regularly doing sport could be anything from <u>socialising</u>, <u>health and fitness</u>, or (heaven forbid) <u>fun</u>.
4) You could decide to join a <u>sports club</u> or do <u>extra curricular activities</u> to <u>develop</u> your skills further.

Your <u>performance</u> is <u>how well</u> you manage to complete a task.

STAGE 3 — PERFORMANCE

1) This is when you're <u>training seriously</u> and are <u>committed to improving</u> your <u>sport-related skills</u> — you're not just doing sport for a bit of fun or to stay fit.
2) This might mean playing for a team or club where you receive some <u>coaching</u>.
3) You're able to <u>perform</u> and <u>compete</u> at a club or <u>regional level</u>.

STAGE 4 — ELITE

1) Right at the top of the pyramid are the <u>highly-skilled</u> elites who have reached a level of <u>excellence</u> in their chosen sport.
2) At this level you're competing at <u>national</u> and <u>international</u> level competitions, and can be an <u>amateur</u> or <u>professional</u> athlete.

Stage 5 — superman...

Make sure you know the <u>four stages</u> and where they fit on the pyramid. The <u>elite stage</u> always goes at the <u>top</u> (just remember there are fewer Olympic athletes than beginners, so it can't go the other way around).

Schools and Physical Activity

If young people take part in sport at school and enjoy it, they're more likely to stay active once they've left. They need opportunities to suit them though and that's where the stuff on this page comes in...

There are Schemes to get You Involved in Physical Activity

There are lots of initiatives led by the Government or by charities that give people the opportunity to get involved in sports. These schemes are designed to:

1) Improve people's health and help them to maintain a healthy lifestyle.
   Schemes often focus on priority groups — groups of people who are less likely to do physical activity, e.g. girls, disabled people or people from lower income families.

2) Keep people involved in sport by providing sports facilities and equipment, clubs for people to join, coaches and volunteers to run activities, and exciting competitions.

3) Identify talented people and create opportunities for them to achieve success.

The Government wants a healthy population of young people, so it wants all schools to achieve 'Healthy School Status', and providing opportunities for physical activities is a big part of this.

The Youth Sport Trust Works to get Children Active

How can you say I'm not physically active?

1) The Youth Sport Trust is a charity that aims to provide PE and sport opportunities for young people. They believe that sport helps young people to succeed in all aspects of later life, e.g. by providing them with leadership and teamwork skills.

2) They work to give children with disabilities the chance to take part in sport and even compete alongside non-disabled children.

3) They have a range of programmes designed to encourage young people to get into sport. These include:

> Sainsbury's School Games — This aims to get young people involved in competitive sport in school. It involves competitions at four different levels — within schools, between nearby schools, between schools in the same county or area, and at a national level.

> Change4Life Sports Clubs — These aim to get less active children interested and involved in sport. At secondary school level they feature non-traditional sports such as fencing and handball.

The Government Wants Everyone to be Physically Active

1) Sport England is a government organisation that tries to get people of all ages doing sport regularly. They also help create 'England Talent Pathways' to make sure that talented individuals develop and get to compete at high levels (e.g. the Olympics).

2) It uses National Lottery and Government money to provide opportunities for people (particularly 14-25 year olds and those who are disabled) to become involved in sport. It even aims to offer every secondary school a sports club on its site within the next few years. It believes this will bridge the gap between school and community sport and help people stay involved after they've left school.

3) Sport England also supports national governing bodies (NGBs) of sport by providing funding and advice. An NGB manages an individual sport across the country, e.g. the All England Netball Association and Badminton England. Their role is to encourage people to get involved in that sport, train coaches and officials, organise competitions and develop talented athletes.

Change for life — it'd be handy for the parking meter...

So, there are loads of schemes out there trying to get you to lead a healthier, more active lifestyle. Make sure you know which scheme's trying to do what for your exam.

Revision Summary — Section One

Well done, you made it — that's your first section out of the way. Who knew there was so much out there that could influence you? There's a lot to take in, but fret not, for here are some handy questions to check you know it all before you skip onto Section Two. Keep revising 'til you can answer them all without cheating.

1) What is the definition of health?

2) Describe what makes up a healthy, active lifestyle. What does the word PEASED have to do with it?

3) Write down two physical, two mental and two social benefits of a healthy, active lifestyle.

4) Describe how the media can have a positive influence on the physical activities you choose to do.

5) How can fashion affect the physical activities you choose to do?

6) What is peer pressure? How can it influence somebody's participation in sport?

7) Describe how role models can affect the amount of physical activity people do.

8) Explain how your gender can affect the types of activity available for you to do.

9) Give one example of how religion could limit the range of physical activities you choose to do.

10) Give one way in which the physical activities you choose to participate in may be affected by:
    a) being young,
    b) being old.

11) Give one example where a physical activity can be beneficial for someone with a medical condition.

12) Explain how disability can affect the amount of physical activity someone participates in.

13) How will the amount of free time you have affect the amount of physical activity you do?

14) What effect will someone's location have on the physical activities they choose?

15) Give an example of a physical activity that may be too expensive for someone to participate in. Explain what makes this activity expensive to do.

16) How can the status of an activity affect participation?

17) Outline the characteristics you need to be:
    a) a good team captain,
    b) a good coach.

18) What are the qualities found in a good official?

19) Why are volunteers so important for getting people into physical activity and sport?

20) Give two examples of what a sport volunteer could get out of their experience.

21) Draw the sports pyramid of participation. Which stage on the pyramid would include:
    a) Olympic athletes,
    b) someone who takes part in a sport or physical activity on a regular basis?

22) Name three things that Government or charity sports schemes often want to achieve.

23) What are priority groups? Give two examples.

24) What is the Youth Sports Trust? Describe two of its programmes.

25) What does Sport England aim to do and where does it get its money from?

26) What does NGB stand for? What do these do?

Fitness

There are <u>two</u> different kinds of fitness — you need one sort so can make it up the stairs without passing out, and the other to be good at a particular activity. You need to know about both...

Fitness can be Health-Related or Skill-Related

Fitness means being physically able to meet the <u>demands of your environment</u>.

Trevor definitely felt he was meeting the demands of his environment.

1) So fitness just means that you're <u>able</u> to do whatever you <u>want</u> or <u>need</u> to do, without getting tired quickly.

2) There are two basic kinds of fitness — <u>health-related fitness</u> and <u>skill-related fitness</u>:

HEALTH-RELATED FITNESS:

This means you're <u>healthy</u>, and can do <u>everyday activities</u> without feeling <u>too tired</u>. It includes:

1) <u>Cardiovascular fitness</u> — your muscles can get enough oxygen to work properly.
2) <u>Muscular strength</u> — you're strong enough to lift, push, pull, etc.
3) <u>Muscular endurance</u> — your muscles don't get tired too quickly.
4) <u>Flexibility</u> — how far you can move different parts of your body.
5) <u>Body composition</u> — you shouldn't be too fat or too thin.

SKILL-RELATED FITNESS:

This is fitness to play a sport at a <u>high level</u>. You need a <u>high level</u> of <u>health-related fitness</u>, as well as some or all of these:

1) <u>Agility</u> — to change direction quickly.
2) <u>Balance</u> — to remain stable.
3) <u>Coordination</u> — to move accurately and smoothly.
4) Fast <u>reactions</u> — to respond quickly.
5) <u>Speed</u> — how fast you can move.
6) <u>Power</u> — brute strength combined with speed.

Make sure you know whether each component is health-related or skill-related. More on these components coming up...

You can be Fit Without Being Healthy

1) Health-related <u>fitness</u> is an important part of a <u>healthy, active lifestyle</u>.
2) By exercising and having a good level of fitness, you can look after your <u>physical health</u>.
3) You can have a high level of <u>fitness</u> without necessarily being <u>physically healthy</u>.

E.g. if your body doesn't get the <u>right nutrients</u> through eating a <u>balanced diet</u>, you won't be <u>healthy</u> (see p28), even if you're fit through doing exercise.

<u>Drug</u> use is <u>banned</u> in most sports, but some incredibly fit athletes still decide to use them to improve their performance (see p34). This can have a huge impact on their health.

My diet's healthy — I only eat one donut a day...

4) <u>Physical</u> health and fitness are only <u>one</u> part of <u>health</u>.
5) Health includes your <u>social</u> and <u>mental wellbeing</u>. It doesn't matter how physically fit you are — if you're permanently <u>unhappy</u>, you're <u>not</u> healthy.

All these fitness definitions are wearing me out...

So, being fit doesn't mean you're healthy, but it can jolly well help. Make sure you know the <u>definition</u> of 'fitness' — they like to ask multiple choice questions on what key words like <u>fitness</u>, <u>health</u> and <u>exercise</u> mean in the exam. Hang on to your PE kits — there's more fitness fun round the corner...

Health-Related Fitness

There are <u>five</u> components (or bits) that make up <u>health-related fitness</u>. You need to know the ins and outs of each one, <u>and</u> be able to say how <u>important</u> they are in a particular activity. Fun fun fun...

1) Cardiovascular Fitness — the Muscles' Oxygen Supply

1) Your <u>heart</u> and <u>lungs</u> work together to keep your muscles <u>supplied with oxygen</u>. The <u>harder</u> you work your muscles, the <u>more oxygen</u> they need.

> <u>CARDIOVASCULAR FITNESS</u> is the ability to exercise your <u>whole body</u> for a <u>long</u> time.

2) So if you have a <u>high level</u> of cardiovascular fitness, your body is able to supply the oxygen your muscles need during <u>whole body exercise</u> (e.g. star jumps) for a <u>long time</u>.

3) Obviously no one spends all day doing star jumps, but good cardiovascular fitness makes <u>everyday activities</u> like <u>walking up flights of stairs</u> a whole lot <u>easier</u>.

See p38 for more on cardiovascular fitness.

4) You use your muscles in <u>all</u> physical activities — which is why cardiovascular fitness is usually one of the <u>most important</u> components of a health-related exercise.

2) Muscular Strength — the Force a Muscle can Exert

1) <u>Muscular strength</u> is just how <u>strong</u> your muscles are (unsurprisingly).

> <u>MUSCULAR STRENGTH</u> is the amount of <u>force</u> that a muscle can apply.

2) It's very important in sports where you need to push or pull things using a lot of <u>force</u>, like <u>weight lifting</u> and <u>judo</u>.

3) In everyday life, muscle strength means you have the strength to <u>lift shopping bags</u>, <u>open doors</u>, <u>stand up</u> from sitting down — all very useful stuff.

4) If your muscles are strong you're also <u>less</u> likely to <u>injure</u> yourself by picking something up that's <u>heavy</u>.

3) Muscular Endurance — How Long 'til You get Tired

1) There are two main types of muscle — <u>involuntary</u> and <u>voluntary</u> muscles.

> <u>Involuntary muscles</u> (e.g. the heart) work <u>without</u> any <u>conscious effort</u> from you.
> <u>Voluntary muscles</u> are attached to the skeleton. They're under <u>your control</u>.

2) When your voluntary muscles have been overworked, they get tired and start to feel <u>heavy</u> or <u>weak</u>.

> <u>MUSCULAR ENDURANCE</u> is the ability to <u>repeatedly</u> use your <u>voluntary</u> muscles <u>over a long time</u>, without getting <u>tired</u>.

3) Muscular endurance is really important in any physical activity where you're using the <u>same muscles repeatedly</u> — e.g. in <u>racquet sports</u> like <u>squash</u> where you have to <u>repeatedly</u> swing your arm.

Dave's muscular endurance was low, his arm felt heavy after 3 swigs of tea.

My muscles don't feel like they volunteer for anything...

Make sure you get muscular <u>endurance</u> and muscular <u>strength</u> the right way round — it's easy to get them mixed up. Muscular endurance is the <u>number of reps</u> you can do, strength is the <u>force</u> you use.

Health-Related Fitness

Three down, only <u>flexibility</u> and <u>body composition</u> to go.

4) Flexibility — Range of Movement

He'll bend over backwards to help you, you know.

So I've heard.

1) <u>Flexibility</u> is to do with <u>how far</u> your joints move. This depends on the <u>type of joint</u> and the '<u>stretchiness</u>' of the <u>muscles</u> around it.

> **FLEXIBILITY** is the <u>amount of movement</u> possible at a <u>joint</u>.

2) It's often forgotten about, but <u>flexibility</u> is dead useful for <u>any</u> physical activity. Here's why...

FEWER INJURIES:

If you're <u>flexible</u>, you're <u>less likely</u> to <u>pull</u> or <u>strain</u> a muscle or stretch too far and injure yourself.

BETTER PERFORMANCE:

You can't do some sports <u>without</u> being flexible — e.g. gymnastics and dance.

Flexibility makes you <u>more efficient</u> in other sports like swimming or hurdling — so you use less <u>energy</u>.

BETTER POSTURE:

More flexibility means a <u>better posture</u> and <u>fewer aches and pains</u>.

Bad posture can lead to permanent <u>deformity</u> of the spine, as well as straining your <u>back</u>.

It can also <u>impair breathing</u> — another way that flexibility affects performance.

It took me years to get this flexible.

5) Body Composition — % of Fat, Muscle and Bone

> **BODY COMPOSITION** is the <u>percentage</u> of your body weight made up by <u>fat, muscle and bone</u>.

1) If you're healthy, your body will normally be made up of between <u>15%</u> and <u>25% body fat</u>.

2) Having too much body fat can put <u>strain</u> on your <u>muscles</u> and <u>joints</u> during physical activity.

3) Many physical activities become <u>harder</u> to do, and the increased strain on your body means you have a <u>higher risk</u> of <u>injuring</u> yourself.

> Having a high percentage of body fat is often due to a poor diet. It can lead to other health problems, e.g. heart trouble.

Some Components are More Important than Others

1) To be good at <u>any</u> physical activity, you need have <u>all</u> of the components of health-related fitness.

2) For a particular activity, there will always be some components of fitness which are <u>more important</u> than others.

> For example in <u>weight lifting</u>, your <u>muscular strength</u> is more important than your <u>cardiovascular fitness</u>.

I like to think my body composition is 20% fat, 80% hero...

Health-related fitness. Done. Well... almost. Make sure you know <u>all five</u> components by covering the page and writing down what you can remember. Next stop on the fitness train — <u>skill-related fitness</u>...

Skill-Related Fitness

There are <u>six</u> components of <u>skill-related fitness</u> you need to know. Just like the health-related ones, you need to be able to rank their <u>importance</u> in activities too. First up — <u>agility</u>, <u>balance</u> and <u>coordination</u>.

1) Agility — Control Over Your Body's Movement

<u>AGILITY</u> is the ability to control the <u>movement</u> of your <u>entire body</u>, and to be able to <u>change</u> your body's <u>position quickly</u>.

Agility is important in any activity where you've got to run about, <u>changing direction</u> all the time, like <u>football</u> or <u>hockey</u>.

2) Balance — More Than Not Wobbling

Having a good sense of <u>balance</u> means you <u>don't wobble</u> or <u>fall over</u> easily. Great. Unfortunately you have to know a slightly fancier definition of balance for your exam.

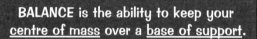

BALANCE is the ability to keep your <u>centre of mass</u> over a <u>base of support</u>.

1) You can think of the <u>mass</u> of any object as being <u>concentrated</u> at just <u>one point</u>. This point is called the <u>centre of mass</u> (or <u>centre of gravity</u>).

2) If you <u>support</u> an object at its centre of mass (e.g. <u>by hanging</u> it by that point), the object will be perfectly <u>balanced</u>.

3) <u>Everything</u> has a centre of mass — and that includes <u>us</u>.

4) As you change body position, the <u>location</u> of your centre of mass will change too.

5) Whatever activity you're doing, you need to have your centre of mass <u>over</u> whatever is <u>supporting</u> you (your <u>base of support</u>) to <u>balance</u>. If you don't, you'll <u>fall over</u>.

This is true whether you're <u>moving</u> (<u>dynamic balance</u>)...

centre of mass

Base support: Geoff

...changing <u>orientation</u> and <u>shape</u> (like in dance and gymnastics)...

Base support: arms

...or just staying still (<u>stationary</u> or <u>static balance</u>).

Show off...

Base support: legs

3) Coordination — Using Body Parts Together

<u>COORDINATION</u> is the ability to use <u>two or more</u> parts of your body <u>together</u>.

1) <u>Hand-eye coordination</u> is important in loads of sports. E.g. being able to hit a ball in <u>tennis</u>, or shoot a bullseye in <u>archery</u>.

2) <u>Limb coordination</u> allows you to be able to <u>walk</u>, <u>run</u>, <u>dance</u>...

3) Coordinated movements are smooth and <u>efficient</u>. E.g. a <u>runner</u> with well coordinated arms and legs will be able to run <u>faster</u> than someone who is less coordinated.

4) Limb coordination is really important in activities like <u>gymnastics</u>, where your performance is judged on your coordination.

Learn your ABCs — Agility, Balance and Coordination...

<u>Agility</u>, <u>balance</u> and <u>coordination</u> all go together really. Without being able to coordinate your limbs, you're almost bound to be unbalanced and fall flat on your face. Make sure you know the definitions of each component and what type of activities they're important in.

Skill-Related Fitness

So you have the <u>agility</u>, <u>balance</u> and <u>coordination</u> of a ninja — what more could you want?
Well... <u>speed</u>, <u>good reactions</u> and ultimate cosmic <u>power</u>(s) would be pretty good too...

4) Speed — How Quickly

1) <u>Speed</u> is a measure of how <u>quickly</u> you can do something.

2) This might be a measure of how quickly you <u>cover a distance</u>. It could also
be how quickly you can <u>carry out a movement</u> e.g. how quickly you can throw a punch.

3) To work out speed, you just <u>divide</u> the <u>distance</u> covered by the <u>time</u> taken to do it.
A fancy way of saying this is '<u>differential rate</u>'.

4) Speed is important in lots of activities, from the
obvious like a <u>100 m sprint</u>, to the less obvious
(like the speed a hockey player can <u>swing their arm</u>
to whack a ball across the pitch).

> SPEED is the <u>rate</u> at which someone
> is able to <u>move</u>, or cover a <u>distance</u>
> in a given amount of <u>time</u>.

5) Reaction Time — The Time it Takes You to React

> REACTION TIME is the <u>time</u> it takes you to <u>move in response</u> to something (a '<u>stimulus</u>').

1) In many sports and activities, you need to have <u>fast reactions</u> as well as <u>speed</u>.

2) The <u>stimulus</u> you respond to could be a <u>starter gun</u>, or a <u>pass</u> in football...

3) You need fast reactions to be able to <u>hit a ball</u> or <u>dodge a punch</u>.
It doesn't matter how fast you can move, if you don't react in time you'll miss or get hit.

4) Having fast reactions can effectively give you a <u>head start</u>.

Getting away quickly at
the start of a <u>sprint</u> can
be the difference
between winning and
losing.

Having faster reactions in team
sports can help you get away from
your opponents, so you can get
into better playing positions.

6) Power Means Speed and Strength Together

<u>Power</u> is a combination of <u>speed</u> and <u>strength</u>.

> POWER is ability to do <u>strength</u> movements or actions <u>quickly</u>.

> <u>power</u> = <u>strength</u> × <u>speed</u>

Most sports need power for some things — even ones like <u>golf</u>, where it's not obvious.

I have the power.

SPORT	YOU NEED POWER TO...
Football	...shoot
Golf	...drive
Table tennis	...smash
Tennis	...serve and smash
Cricket	...bowl fast and bat

<u>Coordination</u> and <u>balance</u> also
help make the most of power
— it's <u>not</u> just strength and
speed you need.

Strong, powerful, handsome — but enough about me...

Another page with lots on it. The <u>names</u> of the different kinds of strength give you clues about the
differences between them. <u>Power's</u> just a combination of two other skills, so there's not really anything
new in the last bit. Make sure all this stuff is in your <u>head</u>.

Revision Summary — Section Two

That's it then — the end of another section. There's lots in it, but it's all stuff you need to know for the exam. But don't panic — all you need to do is learn the facts, and then the exam will be easy. To test how much you know, and how much you still need to revise, try these questions — keep revising until you know all the answers.

1) What is the definition of fitness?
2) Name the two types of fitness.
3) List the components of health-related fitness.
4) Describe what is meant by cardiovascular fitness.
5) Explain why having a good level of cardiovascular fitness is important in most physical activities.
6) What is muscular strength?
7) Describe the difference between involuntary and voluntary muscles.
8) What is muscular endurance?
9) Write down two benefits of being flexible.
10) What is meant by 'body composition'?
11) Define agility. Give one example of a sport in which being agile is important.
12) What point has to be in line with your base support for you to be balanced?
    Is this point always in the same place?
13) Describe the difference between 'dynamic' and 'static' balance.
14) What is coordination?
15) Write down the definition of speed.
16) How is reaction time different to speed?
17) Describe how having fast reactions can give you an advantage over the other competitors in a 100 m sprint.
18) Write down the definition of power.
    How is power a useful component of fitness in golf?

And now for a picture round...
Decide which of the components of fitness listed is the most important in each activity.

19)

100 m sprint
a) agility
b) speed
c) flexibility

20)

Boxing
a) flexibility
b) cardiovascular
   fitness
c) power

21)

Archery
a) speed
b) coordination
c) cardiovascular fitness

Fitness Testing

So now you know what health-related fitness is, you need to know how to <u>measure it</u>.

PAR-Q — *Physical Activity Readiness Questionnaire*

1) <u>Increasing</u> the amount of physical activity you do is normally a safe thing to do — but if you have an <u>injury</u> or <u>physical problem</u> it could damage your health.

2) <u>PAR-Qs</u> are questionnaires made up of 'yes or no' questions, designed to <u>assess</u> your <u>personal readiness</u> (whether it's <u>safe</u> for you) to increase your physical activity.

3) If you answer <u>no</u> to all of the questions, you can be <u>fairly</u> sure it's safe for you to increase your physical activity.

4) If you answer <u>yes</u> to any of the questions, you need to visit your <u>doctor</u> to make sure it's safe first.

	PAR-Q	Yes	No
1)	Have you ever experienced any chest pain while doing physical activity?	☐	☐
2)	Have you ever been diagnosed with a heart problem?	☐	☐
3)	Are you currently being prescribed any medication?	☐	☐
4)	Do you have a joint problem that may be made worse by physical activity?	☐	☐

You Need to Know *Five Tests* for *Health-Related Fitness...*

CARDIOVASCULAR FITNESS — COOPER'S 12-MINUTE RUN TEST

1) <u>Jog</u> to warm up.

2) When a whistle sounds, <u>run</u> round a track as many times as you can in 12 minutes.

3) The <u>distance</u> you run is recorded. The further you can run, the fitter you are.

CARDIOVASCULAR FITNESS — TREADMILL TEST

1) Treadmill tests usually test <u>how long</u> you can run for. Your time is used to work out the maximum amount of <u>oxygen</u> you use in one minute.

2) Start walking with the treadmill on a slow/flat setting, then gradually increase the <u>slope</u> and/or the <u>speed</u> of the treadmill.

3) The <u>longer</u> you can run for, the more oxygen you use, and the <u>fitter</u> you are.

STRENGTH — HAND GRIP TEST

A <u>dynamometer</u> is a device used to measure <u>power</u>. This kind of <u>dynamometer</u> measures <u>hand</u> and <u>forearm strength</u>. Just grip as hard as you can...

Any test longer than <u>30 seconds</u> isn't a good strength test — it's better for testing <u>muscular endurance</u>.

FLEXIBILITY — SIT AND REACH TEST

This measures <u>flexibility</u> in the <u>back</u> and <u>lower hamstrings</u>.

1) Sit on the floor with your legs pointing <u>straight</u> out in front of you.

2) Push a ruler, placed on a box, as far <u>forwards</u> as you can with your fingers — keeping your legs <u>straight</u> all the time.

Ruler

CARDIOVASCULAR FITNESS — HARVARD STEP TEST

This new Harvard Step Test is just step-tastic

1) Using a 45 cm step, do <u>30 step-ups a minute</u> for 5 minutes. (Or if you have to go slower, keep going for <u>20 seconds</u> after you <u>begin</u> to slow down, then stop.)

2) <u>Rest</u> for 1 minute, then take your pulse for 15 seconds — multiply this by 4 to get your heart rate.

3) Use this <u>formula</u> to work out your score — the higher your score, the fitter you are.

$$\frac{\text{length of exercise in seconds} \times 100}{5.5 \times \text{pulse count}}$$

4) There are different versions of the Harvard step test so check the details (height of the step, rest time etc.) before comparing results.

PAR-Q and Ride...

Being fit is really important, but there's no point trying to improve your fitness if you're just going to do yourself a mischief. By filling out a <u>PAR-Q</u> and testing fitness before you start, you lower your chances of getting injured. Make sure you know the tests for <u>health-related</u> fitness, and which components they test.

Skill-Related Fitness Testing

Aerobic fitness isn't the only thing you'll need to know how to test. You've also got to know about testing all those lovely components of <u>skill-related fitness</u> too. Here's the info — get learning.

You can *Test* Your *Agility, Balance* and *Coordination...*

AGILITY — ILLINOIS AGILITY RUN TEST

1) Set out a course using cones like this:

2) Start <u>lying face down</u> at the start cone. When a start whistle blows, run around the circuit as fast as you can.

3) The course is set up so you have to constantly <u>change direction</u>.

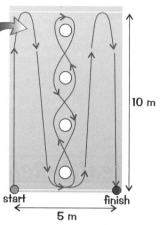

10 m

start   finish

5 m

4) The <u>more agile</u> you are, the <u>quicker</u> you'll be able to complete the course.

COORDINATION — 3-BALL JUGGLE

To be able to juggle, you need to be <u>coordinated</u>. The better your coordination — the <u>longer</u> you should be able to juggle for.

BALANCE — THE STANDING STORK TEST

Stand on your best leg with your other foot touching your knee, and your hands on your hips.

Time how long you can stand there. <u>Wobbling</u>'s allowed, but no moving your feet or hands.

Do the test <u>three times</u>, and record your <u>best time</u>.

Cheat!

...as well as Your *Speed, Reactions* and *Power*

POWER — STANDING BROAD JUMP TEST

It's just like doing the long jump, but from a <u>standing start</u>.

1) Stand behind a line with both your feet next to each other.

2) <u>Jump</u> as far <u>forward</u> as you can (you can swing your arms to help you jump further), <u>landing on both feet</u>.

3) How far you jump depends on the <u>power</u> your leg muscles can produce.

The <u>greater</u> the power, the <u>further</u> you jump.

SPEED — 30-METRE SPRINT TEST

Simply time how long it takes you to <u>run 30 m</u>.

REACTIONS — THE RULER DROP TEST

1) Get a friend to hold a ruler <u>vertically</u> between your thumb and first finger. The <u>0 cm</u> mark on the ruler should be <u>in line</u> with the <u>top of your thumb</u>.

2) Your friend drops the ruler — you have to try and catch it <u>as soon as you see it drop</u>.

3) Read off the distance the ruler fell before you managed to catch it.
The <u>slower</u> your reactions, the <u>longer</u> it takes you to catch the ruler, so the further up the ruler you'll catch it.

You might also see this called the Sergeant jump test.

POWER — SARGENT JUMP TEST

1) Put chalk on your finger tips, and stand <u>side-on</u> to a wall.

2) Raise the arm that's nearest the wall and mark the <u>highest point</u> you can reach.

3) Still standing side-on to the wall, <u>jump and mark the wall</u> as high up as you can.

4) The more <u>powerful</u> your leg muscles are, the larger the <u>distance</u> will be <u>between</u> your first mark and second mark.

Learn this page — and give your brain a stretch...

Just like you get tested on how much you know about PE, athletes get tested on things like <u>muscle strength</u>, <u>endurance</u> and their <u>flexibility</u> — so you've got to know how to test them. Make sure you know all the tests on these two pages, and which component of health or skill related-fitness they test.

Training Sessions

Training's not about running for as long as possible, or lifting the heaviest weights you can.
There's much more to it than that — and you'll be asked about it in the exam, so get reading.

Train to Improve Your Health, Fitness or Performance

1) To improve your health, fitness or performance, you should follow a Personal Exercise Programme (PEP).

2) A PEP is a training programme designed to improve whatever you want it to improve — it could be your general health and fitness, or a particular skill.

> TRAINING — a programme designed to improve your performance, physical fitness, or skills (including motor skills).

> A motor skill is a learned set of movements that make up a smooth, efficient action e.g. walking, or a tennis serve.

3) A PEP needs to be interesting and must suit the person it's for — so you've got to find out about them. Some good questions to ask are:

| What exercise do you like/dislike? | How fit are you now? | What sports do you play? | How old are you? | Do you have any injuries or health problems? |

| Do you live near any sports facilities? | Why do you want to get fitter? |

I'm begging you — no more questions.

RIPS — The Four Principles of Training

R ➡ REST and RECOVERY: Recovery is the time needed for you to repair any damage caused by physical activity. Rest is the amount of time you allow your body to recover.

1) You need to allow time for your body to repair and recover after vigorous exercise.

2) You need to rest until your body has fully recovered, or you'll just end up injuring yourself. E.g. If you're training hard for a marathon, you need to have rest days in your training programme to allow your muscles to recover.

I ➡ INDIVIDUAL DIFFERENCES/NEEDS — making training match the needs of an individual.

Every person will need a different training programme — we're all different and we all do different things. Training needs to be done at the right level — if someone's dead unfit, don't start them with a 5-mile swim.

P ➡ PROGRESSIVE OVERLOAD — to gradually increase the amount of overload you do to increase your fitness without the injury risk.

1) The only way to get fitter is to work your body harder than it normally would — this is called overload.

2) You can overload by increasing the frequency, intensity or duration of training (see next page).

S ➡ SPECIFICITY — matching training to the skills/fitness components for an activity.

1) You need to train the right parts of the body.

2) There's no point making a weightlifter run 10 miles a day — it won't improve their weightlifting.

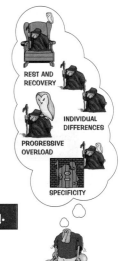

REST AND RECOVERY

INDIVIDUAL DIFFERENCES

PROGRESSIVE OVERLOAD

SPECIFICITY

Get Ripped with a PEP and RIPS...

Those principles of training are a bit tricky, but once you know them that's it, you'll be able to make a training programme fit for a king, or queen, or jester... well, anyone really. Make sure you know how each principle helps to improve fitness. Just remember that the first letter of each principle spells out RIPS.

Training Sessions

The best training programmes aren't just thrown together at the last moment — they have to be <u>carefully</u> planned. All the stuff you need to know is here — get it all in your head.

Training Programmes can be Planned using FITT

Frequency, intensity and time are all part of making sure you <u>overload</u> while you're training.

<u>F</u> = <u>FREQUENCY</u> of activity — how <u>often</u> you should exercise.

E.g. if you just want to stay healthy you should exercise for at least 20 minutes three to five times a week. If you do a hard workout you should give your body at least <u>24 hours rest</u> before you exercise again.

Remember to give yourself 24 hours rest after every hard exercise session.

I think I might have overdone it.

<u>I</u> = <u>INTENSITY</u> of activity — how <u>hard</u> you should exercise.

E.g. if you wanted to <u>lose weight</u> you should raise your heart rate to about 75% of your maximum safe heart rate for 20 minutes or more (see p26).

<u>T</u> = <u>TIME</u> spent on activity — how <u>long</u> you should exercise.

Training sessions to improve <u>cardiovascular fitness</u> tend to last for <u>20 minutes</u> or longer. <u>Strength</u> training sessions are generally shorter and less sustained.

I've been hula-hooping for fifty years.

Maybe the desert wasn't the best place to go snorkelling...

<u>T</u> = <u>TYPE</u> of activity — <u>what exercises</u> you should use.

It can be good to <u>vary</u> training sessions to stop you tiring and getting bored of the same old workout. In aerobic training this is called <u>cross-training</u> — a different exercise (e.g. cycling instead of running) is used to <u>increase fitness</u>, but <u>without over-stressing</u> the tissues and joints used in your main activity.

Eventually your body will <u>adapt</u> to the training and you'll get fitter, and your performance and competence will improve. All training programmes need to be <u>constantly monitored</u> to make sure that the activities are still producing <u>overload</u>. As you get fitter your PEP will need to <u>change</u> to <u>keep</u> improving your fitness.

Reversibility — Keep Training or Your Fitness will Drop

1) You can't train really hard for 4 weeks and get hyper fit, then sit around eating cake forever more.

2) If you stop training, eventually you'll lose all the fitness you gained — it will <u>reverse</u>. This is imaginatively called <u>reversibility</u>.

> REVERSIBILITY — any fitness improvement or body adaptation caused by training will gradually <u>reverse</u> and be lost when you stop training.

Charity Fun Run
I just don't understand it. I played tennis back in 1958.

3) It takes much longer to <u>gain fitness</u> than to <u>lose fitness</u>, which isn't ideal.

4) When you're training, you need to <u>balance</u> your <u>recovery time</u> with the effects of reversibility.

5) If you rest for <u>too long</u> you'll <u>lose</u> all the <u>benefits</u> of having done the training in the first place. If you don't rest enough you could <u>injure</u> yourself.

6) If you get <u>injured</u>, not only have you got to wait for your injury to <u>heal</u>, but thanks to reversibility your <u>fitness</u> will start to decrease while you do.

Flip Reverse it...

Use <u>FITT</u> to get fit — <u>F</u>requency, <u>I</u>ntensity, <u>T</u>ime and <u>T</u>ype. Remember that the training has got to be suited to the <u>individual</u> — it's no good making an unfit businessman run 10 miles a day in his first week of training. And make sure that the training's not too <u>boring</u>, or you'll never do any...

SMART Targets

Setting goals and targets can often seem a bit of a hassle. But if you put the effort in and set them properly, not only do you have something to aim for, but reaching your targets can make you feel ace.

Goal Setting can Help you Train

Geoff's Goals:
Long term — become an Olympic diver
Short term — get over his fear of heights

1) Goal setting means setting targets that you want to reach.
2) Short-term goals that you can reach quite quickly are steps on the way to a long-term one — like winning an Olympic medal.

> Goal setting helps training because:
>
> 1) It gives you something to aim for and motivates you to work hard.
> 2) Reaching a goal can boost your confidence and can give you a sense of achievement.

Goal Setting Should be SMART

When you're setting targets make sure they're SMART.

S ➡ SPECIFIC: Say exactly what you want to achieve.
  1) Saying 'My goal is to be dead good at swimming' isn't very useful. It could mean anything — being able to swim very fast, for long distances, without your arm bands...
  2) You need to be specific and outline exactly what you need to do to reach your target.
     E.g. 'My goal is to swim 1000 m continuously'.

M ➡ MEASURABLE: Goals need to be measurable so you can know when you've achieved them.
  E.g.   Good target — 'My goal is to run 100 m in under 12 seconds'.
         Bad target — 'My goal is to run the 100 m faster than I do now'.

A ➡ ACHIEVABLE: You need to make sure your targets are set at the right level of difficulty. If a target's too easy, it won't motivate you. If it's too difficult, you might just give up.

R ➡ REALISTIC: Set targets you can realistically reach.
  1) This means making sure you have everything you need to be able to fulfil your target.
  2) That could mean being physically able to so something.
  3) It could be that you have enough resources (time, money, facilities...) to be able to reach your target.

T ➡ TIME-BOUND: Gives you a deadline for reaching your goal.
  1) You need a time limit to make sure your target is measurable.
  2) By meeting short-term target deadlines, you make sure you reach your long-term goals in time.

You should try and make your goals exciting (boring goals won't motivate you). Record your goals so you can check your progress.

Goal setting — jumpers for goal posts...

This SMART rule to goal setting isn't just used in PE — it crops up everywhere, so it's worth while knowing about it. Make sure you know what SMART stands for, and you can use it when you're setting targets. After all, you don't want to accidentally set yourself numpty targets.... that would just be embarrassing.

Aerobic and Anaerobic Training

Brace yourselves — it's all about to go a bit biology. There are two different types of activity — <u>aerobic</u> and <u>anaerobic</u>. Whether an activity is one or the other depends on <u>how</u> your muscles get their <u>energy</u>.

Aerobic Activity — With Oxygen

1) <u>All</u> the living cells in your body need <u>energy</u>. Normally the body converts <u>glucose</u> (a <u>sugar</u> found in food) into <u>energy</u> using <u>oxygen</u>. This process is called <u>aerobic respiration</u>.

2) <u>Oxygen</u> is taken into your body by the <u>lungs</u> and carried around the body by <u>blood</u>.

3) During physical activity, your <u>muscles</u> are <u>working harder</u> and so need <u>more energy</u> than normal. That means they need to be supplied with <u>more blood</u> and <u>oxygen</u> to release the energy.

4) Activities where your body can keep up with oxygen demand are called <u>aerobic activities</u>.

> **AEROBIC ACTIVITY:** Any exercise done at a <u>steady rate</u>, and <u>slow</u> enough so that your heart can keep your muscles supplied with the oxygen they need.

5) As long as your muscles are <u>supplied with enough oxygen</u>, you can do aerobic exercise — this is needed for <u>long periods</u> of exercise. It's how <u>marathon runners</u> get their energy.

Your Body Moves Up a Gear When You Exercise

To keep your muscles supplied with <u>oxygen</u>, these changes 'kick in' when you start to exercise.

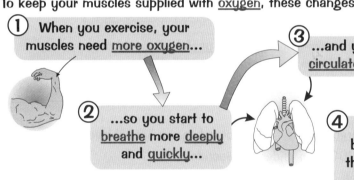

① When you exercise, your muscles need <u>more oxygen</u>...

② ...so you start to <u>breathe</u> more <u>deeply</u> and <u>quickly</u>...

③ ...and your heart beats <u>faster</u> to <u>circulate</u> more oxygenated blood.

Muscles

Gut, Liver, Stomach...

④ To make the most of your <u>blood supply</u>, blood that would usually go to organs like the <u>gut</u> and <u>liver</u> is <u>diverted</u> to the <u>muscles</u>. This is called <u>blood shunting</u>.

Anaerobic Activity — Without Oxygen

1) If your body can't supply the oxygen needed, your muscles release energy <u>without</u> using oxygen.

2) Activities where your body has to do this are called <u>anaerobic activities</u>.

> **ANAEROBIC ACTIVITY:** Any exercise done in <u>short, fast bursts</u> — where your heart can't keep up with your muscles' need for blood and oxygen.

3) Anaerobic respiration releases energy, but also produces a <u>mild poison</u> called <u>lactic acid</u>.

4) <u>Lactic acid build-up</u> soon makes your muscles feel <u>tired</u> — so this is used for <u>short</u>, <u>strenuous</u> activities. This is how <u>sprinters</u> get their energy.

5) You need <u>oxygen</u> to get rid of this lactic acid once you've stopped exercising.

Lactic acid build up — sounds nasty...

The <u>aerobic</u> system is much more <u>efficient</u>, so the body uses it whenever it can. The trouble is, it's not that fast. If the body can't get enough <u>oxygen</u> to the muscles, it has to use the <u>anaerobic</u> system. Make sure you know the difference between <u>anaerobic</u> and <u>aerobic activity</u>, and why <u>blood shunting</u> happens.

Training Methods

Training should make you <u>better</u> at whatever it is you're training for. For this to work, you need to match the type of training to what you want to achieve. There are <u>six</u> main training methods you need to know.

Your Training Should Suit the Activity

1) Your training should <u>match</u> the type of activity or component of fitness you want to improve.

2) If you want to be good at an <u>aerobic activity</u> like <u>long distance running</u> — you should do a lot of aerobic activity as part of your training.

3) The more <u>anaerobic training</u> you do, the longer your muscles are able to <u>put up with</u> lactic acid. They also <u>get better</u> at <u>getting rid</u> of it. For <u>anaerobic activity</u> like <u>sprinting</u>, you need to do <u>anaerobic training</u>.

4) Lots of activities are a <u>mixture</u> of aerobic and anaerobic activity.

> In many <u>team sports</u> like lacrosse, you need to be able to move about <u>continuously</u> (aerobic), as well as needing to have <u>spurts</u> of <u>fast movement</u> (anaerobic). You should have a <u>mix</u> of aerobic and anaerobic activities in your training for these.

Always Warm-Up First and Cool-Down Afterwards

<u>All</u> exercise and training sessions should be made up of a <u>warm-up</u>, a <u>main activity</u>, and a <u>cool-down</u>.

<u>WARM-UP</u> — gets your body ready for exercise.

1) Increases <u>blood flow</u> to the muscles — so they can do the work later on in the training.

2) Stretches the <u>muscles</u>, moves the <u>joints</u> and increases the <u>range</u> of movement — so you're ready for the work and less likely to <u>injure</u> yourself.

3) Concentrates the <u>mind</u> on the training.

<u>COOL-DOWN</u> — gets your body back to normal.

1) Helps replace the <u>oxygen</u> in your muscles and so gets rid of any <u>lactic acid</u>.

2) Helps reduce <u>muscle tightening</u> and <u>stiffness</u> later.

3) Gets rid of the <u>extra blood</u> in your muscles, and so stops it <u>pooling</u> in your veins. Blood pooling can make you feel dizzy and weak if you stop exercising suddenly.

1) Weight Training Improves Muscular Strength

When you weight train, you <u>contract</u> your muscles.
There are two types of muscle contraction you can do in weight training.

1) You can train by <u>increasing the tension</u> in a muscle, <u>without</u> changing the muscle's <u>length</u> (so there's <u>no movement</u>). You can do this by pressing against stationary objects.

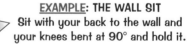

EXAMPLE: THE WALL SIT
Sit with your back to the wall and your knees bent at 90° and hold it.

2) You can also train by contracting your muscles to make your limbs <u>move</u>.

EXAMPLE: PULL-UPS
Hang from a bar and then pull yourself up until your head is over it.

3) Both types of weight training can be used to develop <u>muscular strength</u> and <u>muscular endurance</u>.

4) For the training to improve your fitness, you need to <u>overload</u> (see p19).

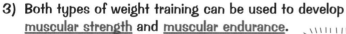
OVERLOAD is achieved by lifting the weights more times, or using heavier weights.

5) Weight training is a type of <u>anaerobic training</u>. It's good for improving performance in anaerobic activities such as <u>sprinting</u>. It can also just be a great way to improve your <u>health-related fitness</u>.

Weight Training — teaching a kilogram to "sit"...

So you want muscles like Arnie...? Well, this is the topic that'll tell you how to do it — kind of.
But never mind what <u>you</u> want, the <u>examiners</u> will want you to be able to churn out all the major points on each training method. You know the drill — cover up the page and get <u>scribbling</u>...

Training Methods

All the training methods on this page are great at improving your cardiovascular fitness and muscular endurance. You need to make sure you know the ins and outs of each method...

2) Interval Training uses Fixed Patterns of Exercise

1) Fixed patterns of high intensity and low intensity exercise intervals are used in interval training.

2) For example, you might alternate sprinting 200 m with jogging 100 m, or in swimming, maybe alternate sprinting a set number of lengths with resting for a fixed length of time.

3) By doing aerobic exercise while recovering from anaerobic exercise, you push your heart and lungs more and improve your cardiovascular fitness loads — so it's good training for team sports like rugby.

4) But you need to overload to improve your fitness.

5) The downside is it's very exhausting.

> OVERLOAD is achieved by increasing the proportion of time spent on the high intensity exercise, or by increasing the intensity (e.g. running faster).

3) Continuous Training Means No Resting

1) Continuous training involves exercising at a constant rate doing activities like running or cycling.

After six years of continuous training surely I deserve a rest...

2) It usually means exercising so that your heart rate is between 60% and 80% of its maximum (see p26).

3) Of course, you need to overload during training to get fitter:

> OVERLOAD is achieved by increasing the duration, distance, speed, or frequency of the training.

4) As well as improving your cardiovascular fitness and muscular endurance, it's also good for using up body fat and improving your body composition.

5) Continuous training is only made up of aerobic activity — so it's good training for activities like marathon running.

4) Fartlek Training is All About Changes of Speed

1) Fartlek training can be made easy or hard to suit your fitness and can be adapted to fit any continuous exercise (e.g. running, cycling, swimming, rowing).

2) It involves changes in intensity and type of exercise without stopping.

> For example, part of a fartlek run could be to sprint for 10 seconds, then jog for 20 seconds (repeated for 4 minutes) — followed by long-stride running for 2 minutes.

> OVERLOAD is achieved by increasing the times or speeds of each bit, or the terrain difficulty (e.g. running uphill).

3) It's a mix of aerobic and anaerobic activity, so it's good training for activities that need different paces, like football and basketball.

4) The really good thing about Fartlek training is that it can be easily changed to suit an individual or activity.

Nige's fartlek training:
Run for 1 minute
Bathe for 30 minutes

Fartlek training .... (Add your own joke.)

This section on training methods doesn't mess around — everything does exactly what it says in the heading. So it's not difficult — but it's loads more boring lists to learn. Oh, and in case you were wondering, fartlek actually means 'speed play' in Swedish. How disappointing...

Training Methods

Circuit training's great for improving cardiovascular fitness too, but it can also improve strength. There's no single exercise you can do to improve all the components of fitness — you've got to cross train...

5) Circuit Training Uses Loads of Different Exercises

1) Each circuit usually has between 6 and 10 stations in it.

2) At each station you do a specific exercise for a set amount of time before moving onto the next station. You're allowed a short rest between stations.

3) All the exercises are different, which makes circuit training a lot more interesting than some other training methods.

OVERLOAD is achieved by doing more repetitions at each station, completing the circuit more quickly, resting less between stations, or by repeating the circuit.

4) Circuit training can be easily adapted to suit your needs.

A circuit's 'stations' might include weight training, or aerobic exercises...

Because you design the circuit, you can use circuit training to improve muscular endurance, strength, cardiovascular fitness... anything you want really.

6) Cross Training Improves Overall Performance

1) No single exercise will improve all components of health-related and skill-related fitness equally well.

2) By picking activities that use different muscle groups or focus on different components of fitness, you can improve your general overall fitness — this is cross training.

3) In cross training, you can do activities that focus on one muscle group while waiting for another set of muscles to recover. This means you can train more, but without the risk of getting injured.

EXAMPLE: A swimmer might decide to take up squash and cycling. These activities still help improve cardiovascular fitness but use different muscles to swimming.

4) Because you're doing different activities, it can be a lot more interesting than some of the other training methods.

5) Whatever activities you do as part of cross training, you still need to overload to improve your fitness.

6) As with circuit training, you can adapt cross training to improve whichever skill or component of fitness you want to.

Training Helps Improve your Mental Capacity

1) Training can not only help you to improve physically, but mentally too.

2) For a lot of sports and physical activities, there comes a point where you 'hit a wall'. You're tired, and voices inside your head start shouting at you to stop and rest.

3) By training, you can increase your ability to keep going even when you're tired.

4) You can also put pressure on yourself during training. This will help you be able to cope with competition pressure, which improves your competence and performance.

What happens if the voices start shouting 'kill'?

Hurray — that's the end of the training methods you need to know. Make sure you know which training method you'd use for what, and the good points and bad points of each.

Target Zones and Recovery Rates

As you exercise, your muscles need <u>more oxygen</u> so your heart beats <u>faster</u> to get it to them.
Simple enough, but you have to be able to draw <u>pretty graphs</u> like the ones on this page to show it.

Heart Rate — Heartbeats *per* Minute

1) Your <u>resting heart rate</u> is the <u>number of times your heart beats per minute</u> when at <u>rest</u> (i.e. when you're <u>not</u> doing any physical activity).

2) An adult's resting heart rate is normally between 60 and 80 beats per minute (bpm).

3) When you exercise, your <u>heart rate increases</u> to increase the <u>blood</u> and <u>oxygen supply</u> to your muscles.

4) The <u>more efficient</u> your cardiovascular system, the <u>slower</u> your pulse rate will be (either resting or exercising), and the <u>quicker</u> it will <u>return to normal</u> after you've been exercising.

5) You can find your theoretical <u>maximum heart rate</u> by subtracting your age from <u>220</u>.

6) The <u>difference</u> between your maximum heart rate and your resting heart rate is called your <u>working heart rate</u>.

> Working **Heart Rate** = Maximum − Resting

Aerobic Training — *get Your* Pulse *in the* Target Zone

1) To <u>improve</u> your cardiovascular fitness and do <u>aerobic</u> training, you have to <u>work</u> your <u>heart and lungs</u> hard for <u>at least 15 minutes</u>.

2) To aerobically train, you need to <u>overload</u> by making sure your heart rate is in the <u>target zone</u>.

> **TARGET ZONE** — between <u>60%</u> and <u>80%</u> of your <u>maximum heart rate</u>. The <u>boundaries</u> of the target zone are called <u>training thresholds</u>.

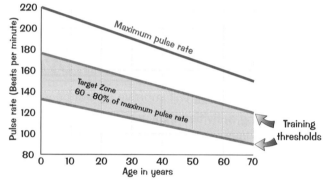

3) If you're just <u>starting</u> a training programme, you should be training with your heart rate near to the <u>60%</u> training threshold. <u>Professional athletes</u> will train <u>above</u> the <u>80%</u> threshold.

Recovery Rate *Depends on* Fitness

1) It takes a while for your heart rate to return to <u>normal</u> when you stop exercising.

2) The length of <u>time</u> it takes for your heart rate to return to normal (your resting heart rate) is your <u>recovery rate</u>. The <u>fitter</u> you are, the <u>faster</u> your heart rate falls.

3) You can look at comparative fitness by using lovely <u>graphs</u> like these.

4) The fitter you are, the better your body will be at supplying your muscles with oxygen, so the <u>longer</u> it will take for your heart rate to go up.

5) Your recovery time not only depends on your fitness, but how <u>strenuous</u> the activity was too.

6) The more strenuous the activity, the more <u>anaerobic activity</u> your body will have been doing. You'll still need lots of oxygen when you <u>stop</u> exercising to get rid of the <u>lactic acid</u> build up.

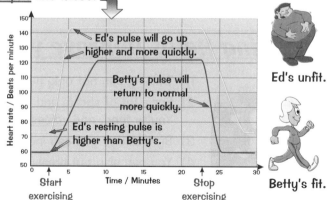

Johnny Depp gets my heart in the target zone...

So the <u>fitter</u> you are, the <u>slower</u> your heart rate goes up, the <u>faster</u> it comes back down again. Got it? Good. Oh, make sure you know all the heart rate, target zone shenanigans too... it's all important stuff.

Revision Summary — Section Three

Woo... Section Three is over. It's no walk in the PAR-Q, but it's all stuff you need to know for the exam.
You'll need to learn all the info about fitness testing, training methods and the beatings of your heart.
But don't panic — all you need to do is learn the facts, and then the exam will be easy. To test how much
you know, and how much you still need to revise, try these questions — and keep revising until you know
all the answers.

1) What does PAR-Q stand for?
2) Explain why a PAR-Q test should be taken before taking part in physical activity.
3) Describe how you can test these health-related components of fitness:
   a) cardiovascular fitness, b) muscular strength, c) flexibility.
4) Describe the Illinois Agility Run test.
5) How could you test a) coordination, b) balance?
6) Describe the ruler drop test. What component of fitness does it test?
7) Describe how you could measure these components of skill-related fitness: a) speed, b) power.
8) What is a PEP?
9) Name the four principles of training, and explain briefly what each one means.
10) Name the four 'FITT' factors that must be decided when designing a training programme.
11) What is meant by 'reversibility'?
12) Describe what each letter in 'SMART' stands for in goal setting.
13) What is aerobic activity? Give an example of an aerobic activity.
14) Describe what is meant by 'blood shunting'. Why does blood shunting occur?
15) Describe what is meant by anaerobic activity.
16) Should a marathon runner mostly focus on aerobic or anaerobic training? Explain your answer.
17) Name one component of fitness that can be improved using weight training.
18) Describe each of the following training methods:
    a) weight training,
    b) interval training,
    c) continuous training,
    d) fartlek training,
    e) circuit training,
    f) cross training.
19) How can training help improve your mental capacity?
20) What is meant by 'resting heart rate'?
21) Describe how to calculate:
    a) your maximum heart rate,
    b) your working heart rate.
22) What is meant by the 'target zone'?
23) What are training thresholds?
24) How does recovery rate vary with fitness?
25) Explain why your heart rate doesn't return to normal as soon as you stop exercising.

Diet and Nutrition

"You are what you eat," people sometimes say — that's how <u>vital</u> this subject is. It's very important to know about different foods, <u>what</u> they contain, and <u>why</u> we need to eat them.

You Need to Eat a <u>Balanced Diet</u> to be <u>Healthy</u>

1) Eating a balanced diet is an <u>important</u> part of a healthy, active lifestyle.
2) What makes up a balanced diet is slightly <u>different</u> for everyone. E.g. if you exercise loads, you'll need to eat more high energy foods than someone who doesn't (see p30).

> A balanced diet contains the <u>best ratio</u> of nutrients to match your lifestyle.

3) If you <u>don't</u> eat a balanced diet, not only could you be <u>physically unable</u> to do the activities you want to, but you might actually be <u>damaging</u> your body.

You Need <u>More of Some</u> Nutrients <u>Than Others</u>

There are <u>two</u> main groups of nutrients your body needs:

<u>Macro nutrients</u> — nutrients your body needs in <u>large</u> amounts.

<u>Micro nutrients</u> — nutrients your body still needs, but in <u>smaller</u> amounts.

MACRO NUTRIENTS:
1) Proteins
2) Carbohydrates
3) Fats

MICRO NUTRIENTS:
1) Vitamins
2) Minerals

WATER AND DIETARY FIBRE

On top of these, you also need plenty of <u>water</u> and <u>dietary fibre</u> in your diet to be healthy. The best way to get all of these nutrients is to eat a <u>varied</u> diet with plenty of <u>fruit</u> and <u>vegetables</u>, but not too much <u>fat</u>.

Carbohydrates, Fats <u>and</u> Proteins <u>Give You Energy</u>

Carbohydrates, fats and proteins are <u>macro nutrients</u> — they make up the bulk of your food. They provide you with <u>energy</u> and help you <u>grow</u>.

CARBOHYDRATES

1) Carbohydrates are the main source of <u>energy</u> for the body.
2) You can get <u>simple</u> ones e.g. sugar, and <u>complex</u> ones e.g. starch.
3) Whenever you eat carbohydrates, some will get <u>used</u> by the body <u>straight away</u>.
4) The rest gets <u>stored</u> in the liver and muscles ready for when it's needed.

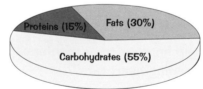

This pie chart (mmm, pie) shows about how much of each nutrient you should eat.

PROTEINS

1) Proteins help the body <u>grow</u> and <u>repair itself</u>.
2) They're made from molecules called <u>amino acids</u> — your body can make new amino acids from the ones you get from food.

FATS

1) Fats are made from molecules called <u>fatty acids</u>.
2) They provide <u>energy</u> for the body but they're also really important for helping keep the <u>body warm</u> and <u>protecting organs</u>. There are also some <u>vitamins</u> that the body can <u>only</u> absorb using fats.

Energy value is measured in <u>kilojoules (kJ)</u> or <u>kilocalories (kcal)</u> — but people usually say <u>calories</u> instead of kilocalories.

If you are what you eat, would French fries turn you French?

...and would sweetcorn make you sweet? Or does it just make that joke 'corny'?. Hmmmm... I need to get out more. Anyway, this page might look pretty full, but really it's just a <u>definition</u>, <u>three blue boxes</u> and a <u>pie</u> made from 15% protein, 30% fat and 55% sweet, sweet, sugar... err I mean carbohydrate.

Diet and Nutrition

Micro nutrients are just as important as macro nutrients — you just need smaller amounts of them.

You need Small Amounts of Vitamins and Minerals

VITAMINS

1) Vitamins help your bones, teeth, and skin to grow.
2) They're also needed for many of the body's chemical reactions.
3) Vitamins can come in two forms:

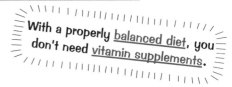
With a properly balanced diet, you don't need vitamin supplements.

FAT-SOLUBLE VITAMINS — which can be stored in the body.

E.g. Vitamin A — needed for your growth and vision, and can be found in vegetables, eggs and liver.

Vitamin D — needed for strong bones, so you don't get bone softening diseases like osteoporosis (see p43). Vitamin D can be made by the skin in sunshine, but it's also found in milk, fish, liver and eggs.

WATER-SOLUBLE VITAMINS — which can't be stored, so you need to eat them regularly.

E.g. Vitamin C is good for your skin and the stuff that holds your body tissues together. Without it, your body tissues can't form properly and you get a nasty disease called scurvy. Vitamin C is found in fruit and veg — especially citrus fruit like oranges and lemons.

MINERALS

1) Needed for healthy bones and teeth, and to build other tissues.
2) Trace elements are minerals you only need a very little bit of.
3) Minerals help in various chemical reactions in the body.

E.g. Calcium — needed for strong bones and teeth, but also for muscle contraction (see p44). Lots in green vegetables, milk, cheese and some fish.

Iron — handy for making red blood cells. Without it your blood can't carry much oxygen. There's tons in liver, beans and green vegetables.

Earl   Mini-earl

Water and Dietary Fibre are Just as Important

Water and dietary fibre are pretty important too...

WATER

1) Water's needed in loads of chemical reactions in the body. It's also lost in your breath, sweat, urine and faeces.
2) If you don't drink enough to replace what your body uses or loses you'll become dehydrated, and you won't perform as well.
3) If you drink too much, your kidneys will produce more urine to get rid of the excess.

Not the best way to increase your fibre intake

DIETARY FIBRE

1) You need fibre to keep your digestive system working properly.
2) There's lots of fibre in fruit and vegetables — another good reason to eat loads of them.

A balanced diet — an apple in each hand...

You would think that I could come up with a joke about dietary fibre but they all seem a bit...... rubbish. Anyway, there's lots more stuff to learn on this page. Each point's a doddle by itself, so just take it a bit at a time — soon you'll be reeling those facts off faster than a puppy can pull on toilet paper.

Section Four — Personal Health and Wellbeing

Diet and Exercise

It's really important to have a balanced diet. But that's not all you have to think about — you need to know <u>when</u> you should eat if you're exercising too.

Different People Need Different Amounts of Food

How much food and nutrients you need depends on a few different things.

1) <u>LIFESTYLE</u> —

The <u>amount of activity</u> you do affects how much you should eat.

E.g. an office worker who sits at a desk all day needs less food than a builder. The builder will need <u>more carbohydrates</u> and <u>fats</u> because he's more active.

2) <u>AGE</u> —

When you're <u>young</u>, you're <u>growing</u> and <u>active</u>, so you need to eat a lot.

Adults have stopped growing and are generally less active, so they need less food.

3) <u>SIZE & SEX</u> —

The <u>bigger</u> you are, the <u>more food</u> your body needs.

Men are usually bigger and have <u>more muscle</u> than women, so they need to eat more.

Organise Your Meals Around Activities

It's important to eat at the <u>right times</u> if you want to perform well at sport. Otherwise <u>blood shunting</u> might slow you down.

BEFORE

1) Top athletes <u>increase</u> their <u>carbohydrate</u> intake a few days before an event.
2) This increases the amount of <u>energy</u> the athlete has <u>stored</u> in their muscles, giving them plenty of energy for the event.

DURING

1) You should drink to <u>replace lost fluid</u> both <u>during</u> and <u>after</u> an activity.
2) You <u>shouldn't eat</u> for a couple of hours <u>before</u> or <u>during</u> exercise — your digestive system may <u>not</u> be able to cope because of <u>blood shunting</u>.

Blood Shunting

1) When you exercise, blood is <u>redistributed</u> around the body to <u>increase</u> the supply of <u>oxygen</u> to your <u>muscles</u> — this known as <u>blood shunting</u> (see p22).
2) Blood is diverted <u>away</u> from some organs, including your <u>digestive system</u>.
3) Your digestive system <u>can't work</u> properly with a limited blood supply.
4) This means if you've eaten just <u>before</u> or <u>during exercise</u>, you're more likely to get <u>indigestion</u> or <u>feel sick</u>.

AFTER

Within an <u>hour or two</u>, you should <u>start eating</u> to replace used energy.

Food for sport — runner beans...

So the more active you are, the more cake you can eat (as part of a balanced diet obviously). But remember — don't eat your cake just before exercise, or <u>blood shunting</u> might mean you see it again...

Revision Summary — Section Four

Well, that was a nice short section. I bet you're thinking I won't be able to come up with many questions on it. But haha — that's where you're wrong. There's a lot to learn in these few pages. Make sure you know the answers to these questions before you move onto the next section. Or else...

1) Give the definition of a balanced diet.

2) What are the three types of macro nutrients?

3) What are the two types of micro nutrients?

4) Macro and micro nutrients form part of a balanced diet.
   Name two other things that you need for a balanced diet.

5) Which of the following pictures (A, B, C or D) show the percentage of your diet
   that should be made up of:
   a) carbohydrates,   b) proteins,   c) fats?

15%   30%   55%   18%

A   B   C   D

6) What do we need carbohydrates for?

7) Give two ways the body uses fats.

8) What does the body use proteins for?

9) Vitamins are either fat soluble or water soluble.
   Give examples of each type of vitamin and say what they are used for.

10) What is a trace element?

11) What mineral is needed to make red blood cells?

12) Give two ways that your body loses water.

13) Why do you need fibre in your diet?

14) Describe how and why the following factors will affect a person's balanced diet:
    a) gender,
    b) age,
    c) size,
    d) physical activity.

15) Why do athletes eat a lot of carbohydrate before an event?

16) Describe 'blood shunting'.

17) Why shouldn't you eat just before or during exercise?

18) Roughly how long after exercise should you wait before you eat something?

Somatotypes

Somatotype means the basic shape of your body. Your somatotype can have a big effect on your suitability for a particular sport. Being the right shape is no guarantee of success, but it helps.

Somatotypes are Body Types

There are three basic somatotypes — ectomorph, mesomorph and endomorph.
Very few people are a perfect example of one of these body types — pretty much everyone is a mixture.
You can think of these basic somatotypes as extremes — at the corners of a triangular graph.

REMEMBER
ENDOMORPH — Dumpy
MESOMORPH — Muscular
ECTOMORPH — Thin

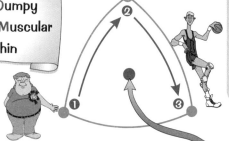

You look as thin as a rake — you must be an ectomorph. My mistake — you're a rake.
BAM

② MESOMORPH
1) Wide shoulders and relatively narrow hips.
2) Muscular body.
3) Strong arms and thighs.
4) Not much body fat.

① ENDOMORPH
1) Wide hips but relatively narrow shoulders.
2) A lot of fat on body, arms and legs.
3) Ankles and wrists are relatively slim.

Mr Average would be in the middle of the graph.

③ ECTOMORPH
1) Narrow shoulders, hips and chest.
2) Not much muscle or fat.
3) Long, thin arms and legs.
4) Thin face and high forehead.

People who play sport at a very high level tend to be closer to the mesomorph corner of the graph, since strength is often important in sport.

Different Somatotypes Suit Different Sports

Sports are usually more suited to certain body types — having the right body type can give an advantage.

ECTOMORPHS suit activities like the high jump and long distance running — where being light and tall is an advantage.
They don't usually suit activities where strength is important.

E.g. high jumpers need to be light so they have less weight to lift over the bar. The taller the jumper, the smaller the distance they (and their centre of mass) have to travel to be able to get over the bar.

Weightlifters
Sprinters
Tennis Players
Sumo Wrestlers
High Jumpers

Ideal somatotypes for different sports.

MESOMORPHS are suited to most types of activity.
1) They're able to build up muscle quickly and easily — which gives them an advantage in any activity where strength is important. E.g. sprinting, tennis, weightlifting...
2) Mesomorphs also have broad shoulders, which make it easier for them to be able to support weight using their upper body. This can be a huge advantage in activities like weightlifting and gymnastics.

Who ate all the pies? Ah, it was me.

ENDOMORPHS are usually best at activities like wrestling and shotput — where weight, and a low centre of mass (see p14) can be an advantage.

E.g. in sumo wrestling, being heavy and having a low centre of mass makes it much harder for your opponent to throw you around the wrestling ring.

"This will be the endomorph" — Not a SMart decision...

Be sure to learn the word somatotype. It's a fancy word — but all it means is somebody's shape.
Remember — nearly everybody's a mixture of the three basic body types. Learn the names well — it'd be a bad mistake to get the three basic somatotypes confused. Get your learning hat on.

Optimum Weight

Everyone's expected and optimum weight are slightly <u>different</u>, and you need to know why...

Expected and Optimum Weight Depend on Many Things...

1) A person's <u>expected weight</u> is (unsurprisingly) the weight you'd <u>expect</u> them to be.

2) Your <u>optimum weight</u> is the weight at which you <u>perform</u> at your <u>best.</u>

3) The <u>taller</u> someone is, the <u>larger their body</u> — so the <u>heavier</u> you'd <u>expect</u> them to be. Your expected and optimum weight aren't just affected by height — two people of the <u>same</u> <u>height</u> can have <u>different</u> expected and optimum weights for many reasons:

1) <u>BONE STRUCTURE</u> — some people have a <u>larger bone structure</u> than others. The <u>more bone</u> you have, the <u>higher</u> your optimum weight will be.

2) <u>MUSCLE GIRTH</u> — this is a measurement of the <u>circumference</u> (the distance around) your muscles when they're flexed. Some people naturally have <u>more muscle</u> than others — which means they'll have a <u>larger</u> muscle girth and a <u>higher</u> optimum weight.

3) <u>GENDER</u> — men and women naturally have different body compositions. Men usually have <u>larger bone structures</u> and <u>more muscle</u> than women, so men generally have <u>higher</u> optimum weights.

Being Underweight or Overweight Affects Performance...

> Being **UNDERWEIGHT** means weighing <u>less</u> than is <u>normal</u>, <u>needed</u> or <u>healthy</u>.

> Being **OVERWEIGHT** means weighing <u>more</u> than is <u>normal</u>.

1) A jockey may be <u>underweight</u> compared with his <u>expected weight</u>, but at his <u>optimum weight</u> for his sport — the less he weighs, the faster his horse will be able run and the better he'll perform.

2) A boxer may be <u>overweight</u> compared to his expected weight, but at his <u>optimum fighting weight</u>.

3) In sport, you can be classed as underweight if you weigh less than you <u>need</u> to for your activity. E.g. being underweight could mean being too light to fight in a particular <u>weight division</u>.

4) Being overweight <u>doesn't</u> necessarily mean you're <u>unhealthy</u>. E.g. you could just have more <u>muscle</u> than average. Being overweight is usually only <u>harmful</u> when it's caused by being <u>overfat</u> or <u>obese</u>.

5) Obesity usually has a <u>bad</u> effect on <u>performance</u>, but there are some sports where you need to be obese to be at your <u>optimum weight</u> (e.g. sumo wrestling).

> **OVERFAT** means having more <u>body fat</u> than you should. Being **OBESE** means being <u>very overfat</u>.

...and Your Ability to Do Sport

1) Being overweight means you're basically carrying <u>extra weight</u> around. This can mean you get <u>tired</u> more easily, so you might not be able to do <u>high endurance</u> sports e.g. tennis or long distance running.

2) Being overfat or obese can also <u>limit</u> your <u>flexibility</u> and limb movement. The <u>stress</u> the excess weight puts on the body (especially the heart) can make doing <u>vigorous exercise</u> potentially <u>harmful</u>.

3) Being <u>underweight</u> because of a <u>poor diet</u> may mean you don't have <u>enough energy</u> or the <u>muscular</u> <u>endurance</u> to do physical activities for long periods of time.

> <u>Anorexia</u> is an <u>eating disorder</u> where sufferers believe they're fat and <u>starve</u> themselves to lose weight. Without sufficient nutrients in their diet, sufferers will feel <u>extremely tired</u>, their muscles will start to <u>waste away</u> and their <u>bones weaken</u> — doing any physical activity can become extremely difficult.

'Oh Bee City' — a short poem about an insect metropolis...

Now we're getting on to the heavyweight subjects (ho ho ho...). Keep going over this page until you know what affects someone's <u>optimum weight</u>, and all the <u>underweight</u> and <u>overweight</u> stuff too.

Drugs

Doping, or taking drugs, is a big problem in sport. You need to learn what the performance-enhancing and recreational drugs on this page do, and why some people risk damaging their health by taking them.

Alcohol and Tobacco are Recreational Drugs

Although drinking alcohol and smoking tobacco are legal, they're still drugs and can seriously damage your health and ability to do physical activity. Small amounts of alcohol don't do too much harm, but every cigarette does damage.

ALCOHOL:

1) Affects your coordination, speech and judgement,
2) Slows your reactions,
3) Makes your muscles get tired more quickly,
4) Eventually damages your liver, kidneys, heart, muscles, brain, and the digestive and immune systems.

SMOKING:

1) Causes nose, throat and chest irritations,
2) Makes you short of breath,
3) Causes changes to your cardiovascular and respiratory system (see p38-40), which increases the risk of developing heart disease, lung cancer, and other diseases.

Many Drugs can Improve Performance

Some athletes use drugs to improve their performance. These drugs are usually banned in sport — and they usually have nasty side effects too. Unfortunately, some athletes still think it's worth the risk.

Here are the performance-enhancing drugs you need to know for your exam.

REMEMBER
B — Beta blockers
A — Anabolic agents
D — Diuretics
S — Stimulants
Na — Narcotic analgesics
P — Peptide hormones

BETA BLOCKERS

1) Are drugs that control heart rate.
2) They lower the heart rate, steady shaking hands, and have a calming, relaxing effect.

But...

They can cause low blood pressure, cramp and heart failure.

STIMULANTS

1) Affect the central nervous system (the bits of your brain and spine that control your reactions).
2) They can increase mental and physical alertness.

But...

1) They can lead to high blood pressure, heart and liver problems, and strokes.
2) They're addictive.

ANABOLIC STEROIDS

1) Mimic the male sex hormone testosterone.
2) Testosterone increases your bone and muscle growth (so you can get bigger and stronger). It can also make your more aggressive.

But...

1) They cause high blood pressure, heart disease, infertility and cancer.
2) Women may grow facial and body hair, and their voice may deepen.

NARCOTIC ANALGESICS

Kill pain — so injuries and fatigue don't affect performance so much.

But...

1) They're addictive, with unpleasant withdrawal symptoms.
2) Feeling less pain can make an athlete train too hard.
3) They can lead to constipation and low blood pressure.

Now, which one of you gentlemen has been taking steroids?

DIURETICS

1) Increase the amount you urinate, causing weight loss — important if you're competing in a certain weight division.
2) Can mask traces of other drugs in the body.

But...

They can cause cramp and dehydration.

PEPTIDE HORMONES

1) Cause the production of other hormones — most have a similar effect to anabolic steroids.
2) EPO (Erythropoietin) is a peptide hormone that causes red blood cells to multiply which increases aerobic capacity.

But...

They can cause strokes and abnormal growth.

Anna Bolic — don't mess with her...

Cancer? Strokes? It's a wonder any athletes think taking drugs is worth the risk, but there are idiots out there. Make sure you know each type of recreational and performance-enhancing drug and their effects.

Risks

From bowls to flaming knife juggling — there's a risk of injury whatever activity you're doing. You need to know the key things you can do to make exercising <u>as safe as possible</u>. Here's all the info...

A Lot of Injuries can be *Prevented*

There are lots of thing you can do <u>before</u> and <u>during exercise</u> to lessen your chances of getting hurt.

Before *the Activity*

PERSONAL READINESS

Before you do a new activity or exercise programme, you should fill in a <u>PAR-Q</u> (see p17). That way you can be pretty sure you're <u>fit</u> and <u>healthy</u> enough to do the new activity.

Exercise, EXERCISE

WARM UP

<u>Warm up</u> before the activity, making sure you <u>exercise the muscles</u> you're going to use.

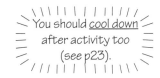

You should <u>cool down</u> after activity too (see p23).

CHECK EQUIPMENT/FACILITIES

1) Use the right <u>equipment</u> — and check it's not damaged and is in <u>good condition</u>.
2) Use the correct <u>technique</u> when <u>lifting</u>, <u>carrying</u> or <u>placing</u> equipment. These techniques help stop you putting your back out or pulling a muscle.
3) Check for <u>possible dangers</u> in the area you're going to be exercising in — e.g. glass hidden in the grass on a football pitch, or slippery patches caused by bad weather on tennis courts.

CATCH IT

During *the Activity*

BALANCED COMPETITION

Play with people of the same:
1) <u>Size</u> and <u>strength</u> — e.g. make sure you're boxing in the right <u>weight division</u>, and not against someone who's twice your size.
2) <u>Skill level</u> — don't try and play rugby against professionals on your first go.
3) <u>Gender</u> — generally men are physically stronger and faster than women, so many sports have separate women's and men's divisions.

PLAY BY THE RULES

1) Know and follow the <u>rules</u> of the game — be sporting and try not to hurt your opponents. Some rules are there to help <u>stop injuries</u> e.g. giving yellow or red cards for bad tackles in football.
2) Use the correct <u>technique</u> — e.g. safely tackling someone in rugby or hockey.
3) Use <u>officials</u> (e.g. a referee) to ensure there's <u>fair play</u> and the rules are followed.

CORRECT CLOTHING

1) Make sure you're not wearing anything that could get caught (e.g. jewellery, watches).
2) Wear suitable <u>footwear</u> — e.g. wearing studded football boots or spiked running shoes will make you less likely to slip and injure yourself.
3) Use <u>protective clothing</u>/<u>equipment</u> where appropriate e.g. mouth guards, cycling helmets.

Sport — it's a risky business...

You'd think snooker was a fairly safe sport, but no. It can be a veritable bloodbath — and I've seen it happen. The King's Head Snooker Tournament 2009 descended into chaos — 3 killed, 6 injured and 7 more still undergoing counselling. I've still got the scars from continuous prodding with a snooker cue.

Revision Summary — Section Five

Is that it? Are we done? Blimey, that was a short section. And I was just starting to get into it. Well, if this is the end of the section, you know what that means. It's time to gather round the camp fire, break out a bag of revision marshmallows and get them toasting. Flick back through somatotypes, weight, drugs and risks and then have a go at these fantabulous questions.

1) What does the term 'somatotype' mean?

2) Name the three basic somatotypes.

3) Write down the main characteristics of each somatotype.

4) What type of somatotype are most athletes? Why is this?

5) For each somatotype, write down one sport each body type would be naturally suited to. Explain why that body type has an advantage in the sports you've named.

6) List four things that can affect someone's optimum weight.

7) What does the term 'underweight' mean?

8) Give a sport where being underweight compared to your expected weight would be an advantage.

9) What does the term 'overweight' mean?

10) Give a sport where someone being overweight compared to their expected weight could be an advantage.

11) What's the difference between overweight and overfat?

12) Why might someone who is obese find it difficult to do a lot of exercise?

13) Why might someone who's underweight find high endurance exercise difficult?

14) What is anorexia? Why might someone suffering from anorexia find exercise difficult?

15) Describe how alcohol can affect your health.

16) Explain why smoking is bad for your health.

17) Name six different types of performance-enhancing drug.

18) Why might an athlete risk taking a narcotic analgesic?

19) Which performance-enhancing drug that mimics the hormone testosterone? Describe the effects this type of drug will have on the body.

20) Which performance enhancing drug helps weight loss by increasing the amount you urinate?

21) How might taking beta blockers give a snooker player an advantage?

22) Why would EPO give long distance runners an advantage?

23) Name three things you can do before a game to reduce the risk of injury.

24) Give an example of how the rules of a sport can help reduce your chances of getting injured during the game.

25) Give two examples of how wearing the correct clothing can help reduce your risk of getting injured while playing sport.

The Cardiovascular System

Your cardiovascular system's pretty funky and it's in two bits — the blood goes round one, then the other, passing through <u>each side</u> of the heart in turn. Here's all the info...

The Cardiovascular System Has a Double Circuit

1) The <u>cardiovascular system</u> is made up of three main parts — the <u>heart</u>, the <u>blood</u> and the <u>blood vessels</u>.

2) There are <u>two</u> main types of blood vessel:
   <u>Arteries</u> — which carry blood <u>away from</u> the heart.
   <u>Veins</u> — which carry blood <u>towards</u> the heart.

3) The main purpose of the cardiovascular system is to <u>transport oxygen</u> and <u>nutrients</u> around the body.

4) Each time a blood cell goes right round your body, it goes <u>through the heart twice</u> — once through each side.

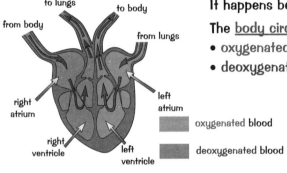

It happens because <u>there are two circuits</u>:

The <u>body circuit</u> is the main circuit. It carries:
- oxygenated blood around the body in the <u>arteries</u>.
- deoxygenated blood back to the heart along the <u>veins</u>.

The <u>other circuit</u> includes the lungs.
- It carries deoxygenated blood from the heart to the lungs to be oxygenated.
- The blood then goes <u>back to the heart</u> to be pumped around the <u>body circuit</u>.

Stroke Volume — Volume of Blood Pumped

1) Your <u>heart rate</u> is the number of times your heart beats <u>each minute</u>.

2) Your <u>stroke volume</u> is the amount of blood <u>each ventricle</u> pumps with <u>each contraction</u> (or heartbeat).

3) By <u>multiplying</u> your heart rate and stroke volume together, you can work out the volume of blood pumped by a <u>ventricle per minute</u>. This is your <u>cardiac output</u>.

HEART RATE × STROKE VOLUME = CARDIAC OUTPUT
HR   ×   SV   =   CO

The Blood is Under Pressure

1) Every time your heart contracts, it <u>forces</u> blood around your body by <u>increasing</u> your <u>blood pressure</u>.

> Blood pressure is the force caused by the blood on the walls of the blood vessels.

2) When you measure your blood pressure, you get two readings:

   <u>SYSTOLIC PRESSURE</u> — the blood pressure in the arteries when the ventricles <u>contract</u>. This is when your blood pressure is at its <u>highest</u>.

   <u>DIASTOLIC PRESSURE</u> — the blood pressure in the arteries when the ventricles <u>relax</u>. This is when your blood pressure is at its <u>lowest</u>.

The heart — it's all just pump and circumstance...

The first page of a new section and it's certainly making my blood pressure go up. There are lots of things to remember on this page. Make sure you know the definitions for <u>stroke volume</u>, <u>heart rate</u> and <u>cardiac output</u>. You need to remember the two different readings for <u>blood pressure</u> too.

The Cardiovascular System

For the exam, you need to know the <u>short-term</u> and <u>long-term</u> effects of <u>exercise</u> and your <u>lifestyle</u> on your cardiovascular system. It's enough to get your heart racing...

Exercise _is Good_ for Your Cardiovascular System

Short Term Effects

1) When you exercise, your <u>heart rate increases</u> to <u>increase</u> the blood supply to your muscles.
2) Your heart also <u>contracts more strongly</u> to pump even more blood around the body. This <u>increases</u> your <u>blood pressure</u>:

> The <u>more strongly</u> your heart <u>contracts</u>, the higher your <u>systolic</u> blood pressure will be. But your <u>diastolic</u> blood pressure usually stays the <u>same</u>.

Long Term Effects

<u>Regular</u> exercise also has all these lovely <u>long-term</u> effects on your cardiovascular system.

1) Your heart is just a <u>muscle</u> — when you exercise it <u>adapts</u> and gets <u>bigger</u> and <u>stronger</u>.
2) A bigger, stronger heart will contract more <u>strongly</u> and pump <u>more</u> blood with each beat — so your <u>stroke volume</u> and <u>cardiac output</u> will <u>increase</u>.
3) A larger <u>stroke volume</u> means your heart has to beat <u>less often</u> to beat to pump the same amount of blood around your body. This means your <u>resting heart rate decreases</u>.
4) Physical activity is really important to keep your <u>blood vessels healthy</u>. With regular exercise, your veins and arteries get <u>bigger</u> and <u>stretchier</u> — so your <u>blood pressure falls</u>. They also get <u>stronger</u>, so they're less likely to <u>burst</u> under pressure.
5) The better the blood supply to your muscles, the <u>faster</u> your body can <u>recover</u> after exercise.

> You need to <u>rest</u> after exercise — you need time to <u>recover</u> before your next exercise session. Resting also lets your body <u>adapt</u> to the <u>changes</u> that have been caused by the exercise.

Your _Lifestyle_ Affects Your Cardiovascular System

As always, it's not just exercise that affects the cardiovascular system — your whole <u>lifestyle</u> affects it too.

1) <u>DIET</u> — eating a diet that's high in saturated fat and salt can cause your <u>blood pressure</u> and <u>cholesterol</u> levels to go <u>up</u>.

> You need a certain amount of cholesterol to live (it's really important for making cell membranes). Cholesterol gets transported in your bloodstream by two different proteins — LDL and HDL.
> - <u>Low-density lipoprotein (LDL)</u> transports cholesterol to your cells. LDL cholesterol is often called the 'bad type' because having <u>too much</u> of it can <u>clog up</u> your <u>blood vessels</u>.
> - <u>High-density lipoprotein (HDL)</u> helps get rid of excess cholesterol from the body. Having a lot of HDL is a good thing, as it helps <u>stop</u> a <u>build up</u> of cholesterol. You can <u>increase</u> your levels of HDL by <u>exercising</u>.

2) <u>DRUGS</u> — unsurprisingly, drugs can also have an effect on your blood pressure. Drinking <u>alcohol</u> will <u>increase</u> your <u>blood pressure</u> — the <u>more</u> you drink, the <u>higher</u> it gets. <u>Smoking</u> and <u>nicotine</u> cause a <u>temporary rise</u> in blood pressure.

Romantic comedies — exercise for your heart...

There's <u>a lot</u> of information on this page, but once you've read it a few times it'll all start to sink in. Perhaps the worst bit is discovering that <u>fat and salt</u> cause your <u>blood pressure</u> to <u>increase</u>. So, no more 12 inch crispy base pizzas covered with loads of toppings and heaps of cheese — mmmmmm cheese...

The Respiratory System

You'll probably recognise most of stuff on this page from <u>biology</u> — but it's always good to have a quick recap before we launch into the <u>effects of exercise</u> on the next page. Enjoy...

The <u>Air</u> You Breathe Ends Up in the Alveoli

The respiratory system is <u>everything</u> we use to <u>breathe</u>.

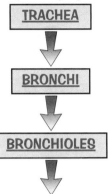

1) Air passes through the nose or mouth and then on to the <u>trachea</u>.

2) The trachea splits into two tubes called <u>bronchi</u> (each one is a 'bronchus') — one going to each lung.

3) The bronchi split into progressively smaller tubes called <u>bronchioles</u>.

4) The bronchioles finally end at small bags called <u>alveoli</u> (each one is an 'alveolus') where the <u>gas exchange</u> takes place.

The area inside the chest containing the lungs, heart and all the other bits is the <u>chest cavity</u>.

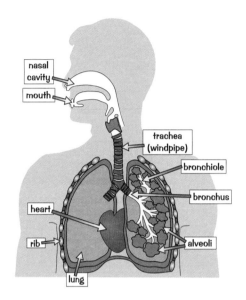

Oxygen and Carbon Dioxide are Exchanged in the Alveoli

There are millions of alveoli in your lungs. This is where the <u>gaseous exchange</u> happens.

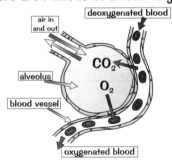

1) The blood <u>collects</u> carbon dioxide as it travels around the body and takes it to the lungs.
2) <u>Carbon dioxide</u> moves from your blood into the <u>alveoli</u>.
3) <u>Oxygen</u> from the <u>air</u> you breathe in moves across from the alveoli to the <u>red blood cells</u>.
4) The red blood cells then <u>carry</u> the oxygen around the body and <u>deliver</u> it where it's needed.

Vital Capacity — the Most Air You Can Breathe In or Out

1) When you're breathing <u>normally</u>, you only breathe a <u>small</u> amount of air in and out.
2) The <u>most</u> air you could possibly breathe in or out in one breath is called your <u>vital capacity</u>.
3) You can <u>improve</u> your vital capacity by <u>exercising</u> (see next page).

That's it Mr Wolf. We'll soon work out if your vital capacity is enough to blow down a brick wall...

Bronchosaurus — a dinosaur with big lungs...

This breathing stuff isn't so hard. I mean, just look at me — I've been doing it all my life. In through the nose and out through the mouth. Regular as clockwork. I have such control I can even stop for short periods of time. Anyway, next up the <u>effects of exercise</u> on the <u>respiratory system</u>. Onwards...

The Respiratory System

Just like the cardiovascular system, you need to know the <u>effects of exercise</u> on the respiratory system too.

Exercise has <u>Short-Term</u> Effects...

Your <u>respiratory system</u> lovingly provides the <u>extra oxygen</u> your body needs when you <u>exercise</u>.

To increase the oxygen supply:

1) You breathe more <u>quickly</u>.

2) You also breathe more <u>deeply</u>, so you take in a <u>larger volume</u> of air with each breath.

3) If you're doing <u>anaerobic activity</u>, your muscles will build up <u>lactic acid</u> (see p22).

4) The amount of oxygen needed to get rid of this lactic acid is called an '<u>oxygen debt</u>'. It has to be '<u>repaid</u>' once you've stopped exercising.

> '<u>Oxygen debt</u>' is the amount of oxygen you need to consume while <u>recovering</u> from exercise <u>above</u> the normal amount needed at <u>rest</u>.

5) That's why you carry on breathing more <u>heavily</u> for a while after you've finished vigorous exercise.

...and <u>Long-Term</u> Effects

Exercising <u>regularly</u> also has <u>long-term effects</u> on your respiratory system.

Arrrrh, it be hard work getting a bigger chest cavity.

1) The muscles around your chest cavity get <u>stronger</u> — so they can make your <u>chest cavity larger</u>.

2) With a larger chest cavity, you can breathe in <u>more air</u> — so your <u>vital capacity increases</u>.

3) The larger your lung capacity, the <u>more oxygen</u> you can get <u>into</u> your lungs and <u>enter</u> your blood stream per breath.

4) This means you have <u>better oxygen supply</u> to the body, which means you should be able to <u>exercise</u> for <u>longer</u>.

Smoking <u>Clogs Up the Alveoli</u>

1) <u>Smoking</u> has a really <u>bad</u> effect on your respiratory system. It can lead to lots of different <u>lung diseases</u> — like <u>cancer</u>, <u>bronchitis</u> and <u>emphysema</u>.

2) Cigarette smoke contains <u>tar</u>, which <u>clogs up</u> the <u>alveoli</u> and makes it <u>harder</u> for gas exchange to take place. Eventually the alveoli will <u>collapse</u> and <u>stop working</u>.

3) Even if the tar is removed and the alveoli are repaired, they'll <u>never be as efficient</u> as they were.

4) Cigarette smoke also contains the addictive drug and poison <u>nicotine</u>. Nicotine causes the <u>blood vessels</u> in the lungs to <u>tighten</u>, which slows the blood flow in the lungs making the <u>gas exchange</u> in the alveoli <u>less efficient</u>.

<u>Breathe in for 5 — hold for 5 — breathe out for 5...</u>

Breathe in for 5, hold for 5, breathe out for 5. Breathe in for 5, hold for 5, breathe out for 5.
Breathe in for 5, hold for 5, breathe out for 5. Breathe in for 5, hold for 5, breathe out for 5.
Breathe in for 5, hold for 5, breathe out for 5. Well, that'll have wasted about a minute and a half.

Revision Summary — Section Six

So, did reading about the cardiovascular and respiratory systems make your heart go boom–tickety boom boom and your breathing heavy? No? Just me then. Well, whilst I go and take a few moments to calm myself, you have the small task of completing a few little questions on this section. Once they're out of the way you can move on to the last section, hurrah. Well, as long as you can answer all the questions on this section. If not, you'd better go back until you know your HDL from your LDL.

1) What parts of the body make up the cardiovascular system?

2) What is the main function of the cardiovascular system?

3) Define 'stroke volume'.

4) How do you calculate cardiac output?

5) What is the definition of blood pressure?

6) What is systolic pressure?

7) What is diastolic pressure?

8) Give two short-term effects of exercise on your cardiovascular system.

9) Give two long-term effects of exercise on your cardiovascular system.

10) Why is rest important after exercise?

11) Give two effects that a diet high in salt and saturated fat can have on your cardiovascular system.

12) Why is LDL cholesterol considered 'bad'?

13) What do high-density lipoproteins do?

14) What effects do alcohol and smoking have on blood pressure?

15) Describe the anatomy of the lung.

16) Where in the lungs does gas exchange take place?

17) Describe how oxygen and carbon dioxide are exchanged in the lungs.

18) What is vital capacity?

19) Give two short-term effects of exercise on the respiratory system.

20) Define 'oxygen debt'.

21) Give two long-term effects of exercise on the respiratory system.

22) What are two effects of cigarette smoke on the lungs?

The Skeletal System

The <u>skeleton</u> gives the body its <u>shape</u> and has loads of jobs to do. It's made up of various kinds of <u>bones</u>, all meeting at joints that can <u>move</u> in different ways. It's all pretty clever stuff.

The Skeleton has Different Functions

The skeleton does a <u>lot more</u> than you might think. Its <u>three</u> main functions are:

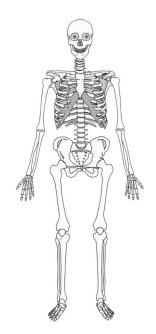

① MOVEMENT:

- There are loads of <u>joints</u>.
- <u>Muscles</u>, attached by <u>tendons</u>, can move various bones.

② SUPPORT:

- The skeleton is a <u>rigid frame</u> for the rest of the body.
- The skeleton <u>supports</u> the <u>soft tissues</u>.
- Without the skeleton, we'd <u>collapse</u> like jelly.

③ PROTECTION:

- Bones are very <u>tough</u>.
- They <u>protect delicate organs</u> — like the <u>brain</u>, <u>heart</u> and <u>lungs</u>.

Your body needs <u>calcium</u> from your diet to <u>build</u> and <u>strengthen</u> bones (see p29). You also need <u>vitamin D</u> to be able to absorb calcium.

Connective Tissues Join Muscle and Bones

There are <u>three types</u> of <u>connective tissue</u> you need to know about.

CARTILAGE — forms <u>cushions</u> <u>between bones</u> to stop them rubbing.

LIGAMENTS — like very strong <u>string</u> that <u>holds</u> <u>bones together</u>.

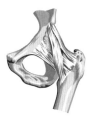

TENDONS — attach <u>muscles</u> <u>to bones</u> (or to other muscles).

There are Five Kinds of Joint Movement

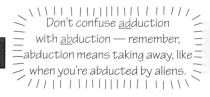

Don't confuse <u>adduction</u> with <u>abduction</u> — remember, abduction means taking away, like when you're abducted by aliens.

Joints are any points where two or more bones <u>meet</u>.

There are <u>five</u> different kinds of movement the joints can allow.

EXTENSION	**FLEXION**	**ADDUCTION**	**ABDUCTION**	**ROTATION**
			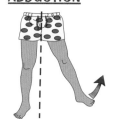	
<u>Opening</u> a joint.	<u>Closing</u> a joint.	Moving <u>towards</u> an imaginary <u>centre line</u>.	Moving <u>away</u> from an imaginary <u>centre line</u>.	<u>Turning</u> a limb <u>clockwise</u> or <u>anticlockwise</u>.

No bones about it — it's a humerus little page...

The skeleton's dead important — we'd all be wobbling about like blancmanges without it. It sounds like a cunning ploy to make you eat yogurt, but getting enough <u>calcium</u> and <u>vitamin D</u> is really important for healthy bones. Make sure you know the different joint movements, there's more joint fun up ahead...

The Skeletal System

These joints are <u>clever</u> old things — they let bits of your body move in certain directions. You need to know two important <u>types</u> of joints, as well as the wonders <u>exercise</u> can do to keep your bones healthy.

There are Two Types of Movable Joint you Need to Know

Your shoulder can move in more directions than your knee or elbow. That's because it's a <u>different</u> kind of <u>joint</u>. Here are the <u>two</u> kinds you need to know:

BALL AND SOCKET — like the <u>shoulder</u>.

The joint can move in <u>all directions</u>, and it can <u>rotate</u> as well.

So this allows <u>flexion</u>, <u>extension</u>, <u>adduction</u>, <u>abduction</u> and <u>rotation</u>.

HINGE — like the <u>knee</u> or <u>elbow</u>.

The joint can go <u>backwards and forwards</u>, but not side-to-side.

This allows <u>flexion</u> and <u>extension</u>.

Exercise Keeps your Bones and Joints Healthy

<u>Exercising</u> regularly has great <u>long-term benefits</u> for both your joints and bones:

Exercise can <u>increase</u> your <u>bone density</u>.

1) The <u>denser</u> your bones, the <u>stronger</u> they are.
2) <u>Exercise</u> usually puts <u>stress</u> or forces through bones, and will cause the body to strengthen those bones.
3) The stronger your bones, the <u>less likely</u> they are to <u>break</u> or <u>fracture</u>.

It's true.

Exercise makes your <u>ligaments</u> and <u>tendons stronger</u>.

Just like muscles, your ligaments and tendons <u>adapt</u> when you exercise. Having stronger ligaments and tendons means you're less likely to <u>injure</u> yourself, e.g. <u>dislocation</u> (see p46).

Weight-Bearing Exercise can Help Prevent Osteoporosis

As you get <u>older</u>, your body gets <u>slower</u> at <u>repairing</u> and <u>strengthening</u> your bones.

<u>Osteoporosis</u> is a disease where your <u>bone density</u> is so <u>low</u> that your bones become <u>fragile</u> and <u>fracture easily</u>. You can help <u>prevent</u> osteoporosis by regularly doing <u>weight bearing exercise</u>.

I'm not sure we've got this quite right...

1) <u>Weight-bearing</u> exercises are where your legs and feet <u>support</u> your <u>whole body weight</u>. E.g. <u>walking</u>, <u>running</u>, <u>tennis</u> and <u>aerobics</u>.
2) These exercises place a <u>larger force</u> on your bones than exercises such as swimming where part of your weight is supported.
3) The <u>larger</u> the force (well... without breaking your bones), the better your body becomes at strengthening bone.

All this talk about joints is making me hungry...

It seems a bit funny at first — to stop your bones becoming weak and easily breakable, make sure you put a large force through them. But it makes sense when you stop and think about it. Remember the best exercises to strengthen your bones are <u>weight-bearing exercises</u>. Next up, the muscular system...

The Muscular System

There's lots to know about the <u>muscular system</u>. You need to know the <u>names</u> of the bigger, or more important muscles, as well as how they work. Here's everything you need...

Antagonistic Muscles <u>Work in Pairs</u>

Muscles can only do one thing — <u>pull</u>. To make a joint move in two directions, you need <u>two muscles</u> that can pull in <u>opposite directions</u>.

1) <u>Antagonistic</u> muscles are <u>pairs of muscles</u> that work <u>against</u> each other.
2) One muscle <u>contracts</u> (shortens) while the other one <u>relaxes</u> (lengthens) and <u>vice versa</u>.
3) The muscle that's doing the work (contracting) is the <u>prime mover</u>, or <u>agonist</u>.
4) The muscle that's relaxing is the <u>antagonist</u>.
5) Each muscle is attached to <u>two</u> bones.
6) Only <u>one</u> of the bones connected at the joint actually moves.

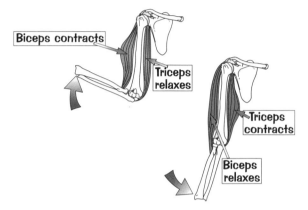

Different Activities <u>Work Different Muscle Groups</u>

You need to know what the <u>big important muscles</u> are called. You also need to know which <u>activities</u> and <u>movements</u> are particularly good for each <u>muscle</u>. Luckily it's all in this lovely diagram — learn it well.

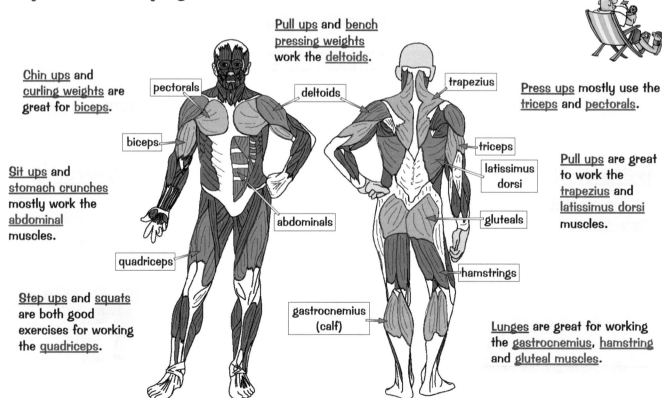

<u>Chin ups</u> and <u>curling weights</u> are great for <u>biceps</u>.

<u>Sit ups</u> and <u>stomach crunches</u> mostly work the <u>abdominal</u> muscles.

<u>Step ups</u> and <u>squats</u> are both good exercises for working the <u>quadriceps</u>.

<u>Pull ups</u> and <u>bench pressing weights</u> work the <u>deltoids</u>.

<u>Press ups</u> mostly use the <u>triceps</u> and <u>pectorals</u>.

<u>Pull ups</u> are great to work the <u>trapezius</u> and <u>latissimus dorsi</u> muscles.

<u>Lunges</u> are great for working the <u>gastrocnemius</u>, <u>hamstring</u> and <u>gluteal muscles</u>.

<u>Is that a bacon rope I see? No, it's a hamstring...</u>

So, muscles work in pairs — one <u>contracts</u>, while the other has a nice little <u>rest</u>. I'm afraid you really do need to <u>know</u> the names of these muscles — it really can help to try and point at each one on your own body — but maybe not in public. Keep going 'til you can name them all without looking back at this page.

The Muscular System

Just like the other body systems, you need to know the <u>long-term</u> and <u>short-term</u> effects of <u>exercise</u> on the muscular system for the exam. You also need to know how you can <u>speed up</u> your <u>recovery</u> from exercise.

Exercise Strengthens Your Muscles

Short-Term Effects

1) Whatever type of exercise you do, your <u>muscles will contract</u>.
   There are two types of <u>contraction</u> that a muscle can undergo — <u>isometric</u> and <u>isotonic</u>.

ISOMETRIC CONTRACTION — tension in the muscle is increased but the <u>length</u> <u>stays the same</u>, so nothing moves.
Like if you pull on a rope attached to a wall.

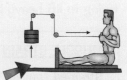

ISOTONIC CONTRACTION — the muscle <u>changes</u> <u>length</u> and so something moves.
Like if you pull on some weights that are free to move.

2) Whenever you exercise, your muscles work harder than usual, and so need <u>more energy</u>. That means your body has to <u>increase</u> the <u>oxygen supply</u> to the muscles to give them the energy they need.

3) If your body can't keep up with the muscles' demand for oxygen, the muscles will release energy without oxygen and produce <u>lactic acid</u> (see p22).

4) If you continue to use your muscles for a <u>long period</u> and they're not getting enough oxygen, they start to feel <u>tired</u> and <u>heavy</u>. This is known as <u>muscle fatigue</u>.

Long-Term Effects

1) Doing regular exercise and strength training will eventually make your muscles <u>thicker</u> and your <u>muscle girth</u> larger (see p33).

2) This thickening of muscles is called <u>hypertrophy</u>. It happens to all muscles when they're exercised, including your heart (see p38).

3) The thicker a muscle is, the <u>more strongly</u> it can <u>contract</u> — so regular exercise increases your <u>muscular strength</u>.

Boring trophy

Number 1 Hypertrophy

Your Muscles Need to Rest and Recover after Exercise

1) After an exercise session, your muscles need time to <u>adapt</u> and <u>recover</u>.

2) If you don't rest for long enough, you could risk <u>injuring</u> yourself (see next page).

3) There are good and bad ways of <u>speeding up</u> the time it takes your muscles to <u>recover</u>...

DIET
Your muscles are made up of <u>proteins</u>. By eating a high protein diet, you can <u>speed up</u> the rate at which your body can <u>build</u> and <u>repair</u> muscle — <u>shortening</u> your <u>rest</u> and <u>recovery time</u>.

DRUGS
<u>Steroids</u> stimulate the body to produce muscle proteins at a faster rate. This also speeds up the time it takes to build and repair muscles.

Some athletes <u>illegally</u> use steroids so they can train harder and <u>improve their performance</u> (see p34).

Mmmm... proteinatious

You know the drill by now — make sure you learn the <u>short</u> and <u>long-term</u> effects of exercise on the body systems, as well as how you can <u>speed up</u> muscle recovery. Steroids have really <u>nasty side effects</u> like paranoia, delusions, hair loss, infertility... Scary — but some people still think the risks are worth it.

Injuries and Treatment

Now for the gruesome bit — injuries. You'll need know the different types of injury, and whether they're caused by a sudden or continuous stress on the body. First up — muscles and joints...

Some Injuries are Caused by Inactivity

1) If you never use your muscles, they'll eventually waste away, getting smaller and weaker. This is known as muscle atrophy.

2) If your muscles are in this state, you're far more likely to injure or strain them e.g. during strenuous activity, or by trying to lift heavy loads.

MUSCLE STRAIN

Strained (pulled) muscles and tendons are tears in the tissue — they're caused by sudden overstretching.

Muscle Tear

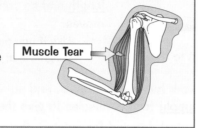

Pulled hamstrings and calf muscles are common injuries in loads of sports like football and cricket.

Joint Injuries can be Caused by Overuse...

Continuous stress on part of the body over a long period of time can cause all sorts of problems:

1) Tennis players can develop tennis elbow — painful inflammation of tendons in the elbow due to overuse of certain arm muscles.

2) Golfers get a similar injury called, wait for it... golfer's elbow.

3) Long-distance runners can develop a nasty bone injury in the leg called shin splints (see next page).

4) You're more at risk of this type of injury if you train too hard or don't rest enough between training sessions.

...or Sudden Stress

1) Sprains are joint injuries where the ligament has been stretched or torn, usually because of violent twisting.

2) Joints can get dislocated as well.
   The bone is pulled out of its normal position — again, it's twisting that usually does it.

3) Cartilage can also be damaged.
   E.g. the cartilage of the knee can be torn by a violent impact or twisting motion.

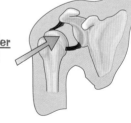

Dislocated shoulder
Humerus pulled out of joint.

This type of injury is common in sports like football.

You deserve more than atrophy for learning all this...

Ouch... that page sounds painful in more than one way. Make sure you can recall every injury mentioned here, describe what it is, and give examples of where it happens. And remember, sprains are a bit like strains but they happen at the joints. Next up — fracture frolics and a nice serving of RICE...

Injuries and Treatment

That's muscles and joints done, now onto breaking bones. You need to know four different types of <u>fracture</u> (ouch...) and how to treat injuries using <u>RICE</u> — <u>rest</u>, <u>ice</u>, <u>compression</u> and <u>elevation</u>.

Bones can Break in Different Ways

1) A <u>fracture</u> is a <u>break</u> in a bone. They're usually accompanied by <u>bruising</u> and <u>swelling</u>.
2) This is because a fracture also damages the <u>blood vessels</u> in or around the bone.
3) They'll also cause a lot of <u>pain</u> because of the damaged <u>nerves</u> inside the bone.
4) There are <u>four</u> types of fracture you need to know:

In a <u>simple fracture</u> it all happens <u>under</u> the skin. The skin itself is alright.

In a <u>compound fracture</u> the skin is torn and the bone pokes out. Urgghh.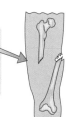

 A '<u>stress fracture</u>' is a small <u>crack</u> in a bone.
It's caused by <u>continuous</u> stress over a <u>long period</u> of time.
All other bone fractures are caused by a sudden <u>stress</u>.

 <u>Greenstick fractures</u> happen in young or <u>soft</u> bone that <u>bends</u> and <u>partly breaks</u>.

Use the RICE Method to Treat Injuries

R   <u>REST</u>   ➡   Stop immediately and <u>rest</u> the injury — if you carry on, you'll make it <u>worse</u>.

I   <u>ICE</u>   ➡   Apply <u>ice</u> to the injury. This makes the blood vessels <u>contract</u> to reduce internal bleeding and swelling.

C   <u>COMPRESSION</u>   ➡   <u>Bandaging</u> the injury will also help reduce swelling. But <u>don't</u> make it so tight that you stop the blood circulating altogether.

E   <u>ELEVATION</u>   ➡   Support the limb at a <u>raised</u> level (i.e. above the heart). The flow of blood reduces because it has to flow against gravity.

1) The <u>RICE method</u> is a good treatment for joint and muscle injuries like <u>sprains</u> or <u>strains</u>. It reduces pain, swelling and bruising.
2) As with everything, a little bit of <u>common sense</u> goes a long way. If the person has hurt their head, neck or spine trying to elevate the injury is <u>not</u> a good idea.
3) If you <u>think</u> someone has an injury you should try and find a <u>first aider</u>, if it looks like a serious <u>injury</u> call an <u>ambulance</u>.

If the RICE treatment doesn't work, try noodles...

RICE is a great technique for treating a lot of injuries. If you think there may be a <u>fracture</u>, you could make the injury worse by moving the person — the best thing is to keep them in the same position and get help. Make sure you learn the different <u>types</u> of fractures and what <u>RICE</u> stands for.

Revision Summary — Section Seven

Well, that's your lot — the final section out of the way. All you have to do now is to make sure you know it all. You never know, some of it could even be useful some day — when someone's got a bone sticking out of their leg, you'll be able to politely inform them they're suffering from a compound fracture and the RICE method of treatment would not be recommended. Seriously though, this can be really useful stuff, not just for the exam. All the more reason to learn it, that's what I say. As always, keep going though these questions 'til you can answer every one without cheating.

1) What are the skeleton's three main functions?

2) Which two nutrients are the most important for bone health?

3) What type of connective tissue joins bones to bones?

4) Are muscles attached to bones by: a) ligaments, b) tendons, c) cartilage, or d) sheep?

5) What is the point of cartilage?

6) Name the five types of movement at a joint.
    (Make sure you can give their proper names as well as describe them.)

7) Name two types of movable joint. Give an example of each type and describe the types of movement they allow.

8) Give two long-term benefits of exercise for your bones and joints.

9) What is osteoporosis? What type of exercise can help prevent getting this disease?

10) Do skeletal muscles work a) alone, b) in pairs, or c) in threes to produce movement?

11) An antagonist relaxes while an agonist does work. **TRUE** or **FALSE**?

12) What are the main muscles in the human body? Either label a diagram, or make sure you can name them on your own body. You should be able to name 11 muscles.

13) Name the main muscle groups being worked in each of these exercises:
    a) sit ups,   b) squats,   c) press ups.

14) What are isotonic and isometric contractions?

15) What is muscle fatigue?

16) What is hypertrophy? Is this a long-term or short-term effect of exercise?

17) Describe how you can change your diet to quicken your rate of muscle recovery.

18) What type of performance-enhancing drug can be taken to speed up muscle recovery?

19) What is muscle atrophy?

20) What is 'tennis elbow'? Is it caused by a sudden or continuous stress on a tennis player's body?

21) Explain exactly what these are: a) strains, b) sprains, and c) dislocations.

22) What's the difference between a simple and a compound fracture?

23) What is a stress fracture? What causes it?

24) Describe a greenstick fracture.

25) What's the RICE method?

Answering Exam Questions

Hurray — you made it to the end of the book. That's everything you need to know for GCSE PE covered. Now there's just the tiny matter (ahem) of the exam left to go. Here's what to expect in your exam and some exam tips to help send you on your way to GCSE PE victory.

In the Exam — Read the Questions and Don't Panic

1) Read every question carefully.

2) The number of marks each question is worth is shown in brackets like this:

> 5 (a)   Identify **one** short-term effect of participation in physical activity on your blood pressure.   (1)
>
> ....

3) The number of marks is normally a good guide to the number of points you need to make in your answer.

4) It also helps you know roughly how long you should spend on each question. You don't want to end up spending half an hour writing an essay for a one mark question.

5) The number of answer lines given in a question can also be a good guide to how much to write.

NOOOOOO...

6) Make sure your answers are clear and easy to read. If the examiner can't read your handwriting, they won't be able to give you any marks.

7) Don't panic — if you get stuck on a question, just move on to the next one. You can come back to it if you have time at the end.

If you do get panicky — stop and take a few deep breaths. It can really help.

Your Exam is made up of Three Types of Question

Multiple Choice — Cross the Right Box

1) The multiple choice questions give you a choice of four possible answers to a question. All you need to do is cross the box next to the correct answer.

2) Sounds easy enough, but you still need to really know your stuff to be able to get the marks.

3) Make sure you only cross one box — if you cross more than one you won't get any marks.

4) Don't worry if you make a mistake and want to change your answer. Just put a horizontal line through the box next to the wrong answer, then cross the box next to your new answer.

5) If you don't know the answer to a question, guess. You don't lose marks for putting a wrong answer — if you guess, you've at least got a chance of getting it right.

Short and Long Answer Questions

1) Short answer questions are usually worth between one and four marks. Long answer questions are normally worth about six marks.

2) Make sure you read the question carefully. If you're asked for two influences, make sure you give two, otherwise you won't get the marks.

3) Remember — the number of marks and the amount of space you've been left are a good guide to how long your answer should be. If you've got two lines to justify something, you don't need to write a book on it.

Ketchup, tea and mustard — a 3 mark question...

Don't Panic — now where's my towel...

So — read the question, look at the number of marks, answer the question and don't panic. Make sure that you sleep and eat well the night before the exam, so you're in tip top condition for the big day.

Answering Exam Questions

It's not just PE those examiners want to test you on, oh no. They've included a few marks for how well you can <u>communicate</u> your answer. It sounds tricky, but if you take care it could mean some easy marks.

When you See a * — Watch Your <u>Spelling</u> and <u>Grammar</u>

1) The longer questions towards the back of the paper have an <u>asterisk</u> (*) next to them.

2) Not only do these questions test your amazing PE know-how — but your <u>written communication skills</u> too (otherwise known as '<u>how well you can write your answer</u>').

3) You can pick up a couple of easy marks just by making sure that you do the things in this fetching blue box.

> 1) Make sure you <u>answer the question</u> being asked — it's dead easy to go off on a tangent. Like my mate Phil always says... have I ever told you about Phil? Well he...
>
> 2) Make sure you're answer is <u>organised</u>. It's a really good idea to have a think what you're going to cover in your answer before you start writing it. That way you can make sure you <u>structure</u> your answer well, and cover all the points you want to.
>
> 3) Write in <u>whole sentences</u> and use correct <u>spelling</u>, <u>grammar</u> and <u>punctuation</u>.
>
> 4) Use the correct <u>terminology</u>.

EXAMPLE

15* The figure shows **three** participants in different physical activities.

Discuss '**muscular strength**' and its relative importance to a participant in **each** of the three activities. (6)

Archer   **Sprinter**   **Boxer**

Good answer

Muscular strength is the force a muscle can exert. It's an important component of fitness in all three activities.

An archer needs muscular strength to be able to pull back the string on a bow to the correct tension to fire the arrow effectively. They also need muscular strength to hold the bow in position to be able to aim.

Sprinters need muscular strength in their legs to be able to push off the ground to accelerate forwards. The greater the force they can exert on the ground, the faster they will be able to run.

In boxing, the stronger your arm muscles are, the greater the force that you can punch with.

Although muscular strength is needed in all three activities, its affect on performance and its importance varies between the activities. Muscular strength is most important in boxing, less so in sprinting, and even less important still in archery. Success in boxing is very dependent on your muscular strength and the force you can punch with. Power is more important to a sprinter than muscular strength alone. Similarly, hand-eye coordination is more important to an archer's aim than muscular strength.

Bad Answer

muscular strength = force muscle can exert.

archer
- hold bow up and aim
- create tension in bow string to fire arrow

Sprinter
-bigger the force they exert on the ground

boxing
- bigger force, harder punch.

order of importance: boxer, sprinter, archer.

There's nothing wrong with the PE in the bad answer, but you'd miss out on some nice easy marks just for not bothering to link your thoughts together properly or put your answer into proper sentences.

For easy marks — communicate well good...

So if you see a *, make sure you write in <u>full sentences</u> and watch your <u>spelling</u> and <u>grammar</u>. Think and <u>organise</u> what you want to say <u>before</u> you start writing, and those marks could be yours for the taking.

Index

Index